SHAKSPERE'S SILENCES

LONDON : HUMPHREY MILFORD

OXFORD UNIVERSITY PRESS

SHAKSPERE'S SILENCES

By ALWIN THALER

CAMBRIDGE, MASSACHUSETTS

HARVARD UNIVERSITY PRESS

1929

PRINTED AT THE HARVARD UNIVERSITY PRESS
CAMBRIDGE, MASSACHUSETTS, U. S. A.

𝕿𝖔 𝖙𝖍𝖊 𝕸𝖊𝖒𝖔𝖗𝖞 𝖔𝖋

MY FATHER AND MY MOTHER

Preface

SHAKSPERE is like religion: theoretically at least new information and fresh interpretation should make him ever more richly and vitally responsive to our changing human needs. Much, of course, depends upon the interpreter. I hope, therefore, that lovers of Shakspere will find these pages not altogether lacking in matter sufficiently new, or a point of view sufficiently unhackneyed, to justify the making of still another book.

In the first part of this volume I have dealt with two ancient and honorable topics — Shakspere's dramatic technique, and the conventional technique of his critics. Happily, as I suggested at the outset, no one need ever expect to say the last word upon these topics. Age cannot wither Shakspere in the library any more than Shakspere on the stage. Critics, however, are far more conventional even than actors, and far more inclined to tread the safe footprints of tradition. Fresh appraisals, of course, may breed new vagaries. Yet some gain should accrue from almost any constructive attempt to brush away a portion of the inevitable dust and cobwebs of custom — to estimate the real worth of received opinions rather than their market price. Such an estimate I have attempted here — partly upon the suggestion of friendly critics who liked certain preliminary studies of mine well enough to encourage me to work through my ideas on these matters and to present the results (with some regard for the interests of the general reader) in the orderly sequence of chapter and verse. It is my hope that scholars who may disagree with my views will find in them sufficient challenge to supplant them with better doctrine of their own.

The second part of the book concerns Milton as well as Shakspere. It has to do with Shakspere's influence, as a poet and dramatist, upon Sir Thomas Browne and Milton, and with Milton's connections with the drama and theatre of Shakspere and his posterity.

I have to thank the Century Company for permission to print the quotation on page 66, and the editors of the *Publications of the Modern Language Association of America* and *Studies in Philology* for allowing me to use as the basis of three of my chapters, three articles — rewritten and considerably augmented for my present purposes — which first appeared in their journals. Two of these chapters, in their earlier stages, owed much to the friendly and painstaking criticism of Professor Carleton Brown. It is a pleasant duty to record my gratitude to him and to other friends — Professors John C. Hodges and Ben C. Clough, and Dr. Wilmon Brewer — who gave me material aid of one sort or another; and to Sir Arthur Quiller-Couch, Professor G. C. Moore Smith, and Professor S. F. Gingerich — who generously volunteered information or suggestions which proved decidedly useful. Those of my readers, finally, who know something of Professor Kittredge, will not be surprised to learn that these obligations are overshadowed by my debt to him. Like many another in this case, I must content myself with an acknowledgment which cannot be an adequate expression of thanks for his wise counsel and unfailing kindness.

ALWIN THALER

University of Tennessee

Contents

I

SHAKSPERE

II

SHAKSPERE AND MILTON

I

SHAKSPERE

Chapter I

SHAKSPERE'S SILENCES

DANTE'S 'silence,'" said Carlyle, "is more eloquent than words." It is significant, I think, that the Apostle of Silence says little or nothing of Shakspere's claims in this kind. Carlyle revered the Florentine prince and saint of poets, but to Shakspere only he bent the knee as undisputed King. Yet in Dante rather than in Shakspere he recognized the divinely "gifted man . . . who sees the essential point and leaves all the rest aside as surplusage." [1] Nor is the reason far to seek. "In real life," wrote Sidney Lanier,

passion is not logical nor voluble, but tends in its highest moments to vent itself in the dumb caress, the pleading look, the inarticulate cry; in Shakspere, on the contrary, *passion is furnished with a tongue adequate to all its wants.* Shakspere's plays always seem to me as if the gods came down and played men and women for our instruction. [2]

The high gods, however, do not always speak with words: one remembers that in the moment of Revelation the very heavens are silent. Is it not also true that the superb power of self-expression possessed by Shakspere's characters, for example, is, in many important instances, the power of silent expression? Everyone, naturally, thinks of Shakspere first and last as the supreme maker of words and thoughts divinely uttered. He is — to quote Carlyle once more — the "articulate voice" of England — and of all mankind. In consequence, perhaps, the fact with which I shall

1. "The Hero as Poet" (*Heroes and Hero-Worship*).
2. *Shakspere and his Forerunners*, I, 300–301.

deal here has had but little notice.[1] At its simplest it is this — that Shakspere, too, had in him what Carlyle would have termed great depths of silence; that, like all true artists, he knew the pity and the power of silent griefs, of unheard melodies.

Take for example but one aspect of a subject which will require closer attention later — the relative artistry of Shakspere's delineation of the silent or reticent type of humanity as against that of the fluently vocal (not to say voluble): the *not* "unexpressive she" — or he. Who would deny that the charming outspokenness of a Rosalind sticks in the memory of most of us more clearly and perhaps more pleasantly than the "gracious silence" whose name was Virgilia, wife to Coriolanus? How many critics have lavished praise upon the sentimental yet infinitely moving fluency of Richard II, and how few upon the masterly conciseness of Bolingbroke! Indeed, most readers will be inclined to agree at first thought that even the tremendously significant reticences of Cordelia and of the queenly Hermione are all but crowded out of view or hearing, like negative shadows in glowing light, by the happily irrepressible chatter of a Beatrice, or the impassioned lyric utterance of a Juliet. I have no desire to exploit these impressions for purposes of vague aesthetic criticism. The facts beneath them bear a significant relationship to the proper understanding of Shakspere's dramatic technique, in a fairly narrow sense of the term. This relationship I propose to examine.

I ought to add at once that I have reference to "silences" of all sorts: to relative as well as absolute silences; to occasional or half-silences, reticences or inhibitions which seem a part of the intrinsic being of Shakspere's characters; to others, more or less silent implications or condensations which served him in the structural

1. Mr. E. E. Kellett's interesting paper (published while this book was in press) on "Dramatic Silences" in general, glances at it more or less effectively. (See *Contemporary Review*, October, 1927.)

management of his plots; and even to notable omissions or disappearances of characters or motives which must be regarded as
peculiarly his own (since he himself was the conscious architect
and master of his dramatic organisms) because they grew out of
his eclectic treatment of his sources.

Still another aspect of the subject, however, I must necessarily
dismiss from this discussion. Sidney Lanier's editor found among
the poet's "rough notes" for "projected papers," some which
refer to "'Shakspere's silences': tobacco and religion, Virginia and
America." [1] These are tempting subjects for speculation — though
I, for one, can see no justification for including *religion* among
them, since Shakspere's religion, Mr. Shaw [2] to the contrary notwithstanding, left its eloquent mark, spoken as well as silent, upon
his every page. As for Shakspere and tobacco, "it must," according to Lanier,[3]

certainly be regarded one of the most curious silences that one whose eye
never missed anything in his time has omitted to make any record of
what we may perhaps fairly call the most novel sight of his age — the
sight of people everywhere swallowing the smoke of a drug and puffing it
out again from mouth and nostril.

But this silence and the others alluded to by Lanier, whatever
their cause, have little or no bearing upon Shakspere's technique
in the matter of characterization or plot. My primary concern is
with those that have.

It goes without saying that these silences, relative or absolute
— the rather appalling mass already referred to — have not been
quietly passed over by the critics and commentators. I venture to
add my voice to the somewhat noisy chorus because I believe that
no one has yet dealt adequately — that is to say, comprehensively

1. *Shakspere and his Forerunners*, I, ix.
2. See Preface, *Back to Methuselah*, p. xcv.
3. II, 193 ff.

— with the technique of silence in Shakspere. "A curious essay," says Dowden,[1] "might be written upon the silences of some of the characters of Shakespeare." This, and more than this, had been my conviction long before I found that Dowden held it also. Hence the present attempt to deal not only with the silences of the characters but also with those in the plots. If it be objected that this is one subject upon which temerity itself might allow Shakspere to speak for himself, I must repeat that many besides him *have* spoken — less than truth, because they do not begin to tell anything like the whole of it. For criticism on this point has not put two and two together. It has given us more or less illuminating but almost always separate, detached, and unrelated notes, — for example, upon certain puzzling silences of Hamlet, upon the silent disappearance of the fool in *Lear*, or upon Isabella's silent acceptance of the Duke in *Measure for Measure*. But it has not troubled itself to determine whether there may be, beneath these phenomena, a unifying principle, a more or less conscious technique. Yet I need scarcely urge that it is futile to attempt to deal with individual difficulties of interpretation without looking at an artist's practice and methods in the large. Each play must, of course, stand or fall on its own merits; but as a measure of mere common sense it is imperative to put parallel difficulties together, lest we dismiss as poetic errors of haste or omission what may be cumulative indications of a purposive technique. Criticism, however, has naturally been so preoccupied with what Shakspere's characters *say* that it has had little time to answer the question whether he really knew what he was about in the many curious things which he *perhaps* implies or which his characters perhaps deny or assert but at any rate do *not* definitely say — in their many teasing silences or disappearances. Most of the writers who have dealt with these prob-

1. *Shakespeare's Complete Works*, with Introduction and studies by Swinburne and Dowden, Oxford, 1924, I, 72–73 (see below, p. 17, n. 2).

lems have too readily disposed of them as puzzles or imperfections, the by-products of Shakspere's fine carelessness in details, the inevitable loose ends of his astonishingly profuse and all but prodigal creative activity. Something of this is suggested not only by critics of the older school (by Ulrici,[1] for example) but also by one of the most challenging of contemporary critics. I must quote at some length from Professor Bradley, not only because, in recognizing the validity of the problem before us, he constitutes an honorable exception to the rule, but also because what he says indicates to my mind the necessity of carrying further than he was able to do in the work he had in hand, the attempt at a solution.

After remarking upon the unevenness of Shakspere's artistry, and more especially upon his "slackness" or "negligence" as to "parts of his scheme that were necessary but not interesting to him," Bradley[2] writes as follows upon certain difficulties of interpretation which arise now and again from the inactivity, the silences, or the disappearances of more or less essential persons or motives of the plays:

In those parts of his plays which show him neither in his most intense nor in his negligent mood, we are often unable to decide whether something that seems inconsistent, indistinct, feeble, exaggerated, is really so, or whether it was definitely meant to be as it is, and has an intention which we ought to be able to divine; whether, for example, we have before us some abnormal movement of mind, only surprising to us because we understand so very much less of human nature than Shakespeare did, or whether he wanted to get his work done and made a slip, or in using an old play adopted hastily something that would not square with his own conception, or even refused to trouble himself with minutiae which we notice only because we study him, but which nobody ever notices in a stage performance. We know well enough what Shakespeare is doing when at the end of *Measure for Measure* he marries Isabella to the Duke — and a scandalous proceeding it is; but who can ever feel sure

1. *Shakespeare's Dramatic Art*, I, 339–340.
2. *Shakespearean Tragedy*, pp. 76–78.

that the doubts which vex him as to some not unimportant points in *Hamlet* are due to his own want of eyesight or to Shakespeare's want of care?

This passage states admirably the first principle of the present study — that it is the business of criticism to seek to understand, by all available means, whatever significance or purpose there may be behind Shakspere's troublesome silences of character or plot; to do at least this much before labeling them "careless," "inconsistent," or "scandalous." And this last adjective — which is not mine but Professor Bradley's — suggests a caution, perhaps I might say a principle, scarcely less important than the first. To wit: though it is our duty to seek to understand the meaning of these silences, we must recognize that in reasoning *ex silentio* it is hazardous to present one's conclusions as though they were incontrovertible facts. They cannot be more — and none of those suggested here are intended to be more — than possible or, at best, plausible explanations. At the end of *Measure for Measure* the austere Isabella, who had begun by seeking to enter a convent, accepts, literally in silence, the Duke's offer of marriage. I have ventured to set forth in the next chapter of this book my reasons for believing that this is not a scandalous proceeding but one pretty much in psychological accord with her character and that of the Duke, a definite and not altogether ill-considered part of Shakspere's plan and purpose in the play. Here and now I must turn to the problem of Shakspere's technique of silence in characterization. In so doing, however, I shall have to consider incidentally the meaning, in terms of characterization, of the ending of *Measure for Measure* and of other comedies in which the final silence, according to most critics, implies a strange or forced consent.

To attack our problem fairly, it will be useful to bear in mind an antecedent question. This question, baldly stated, is bound to sound like a bit of sheer impertinence; but it *is* a question to be asked, for the implications of the answer seem to have escaped many of the critics. The question is this: do Shakspere's own obvious pronouncements, that is to say, the plain words oft-repeated by many of his characters, or his clearly intentional disposition or inhibition of action in the plays, give us any warrant, *a priori*, for assuming that he was blind to the virtue of silence as a measure of dramatic economy, not to say a fundamental principle of art?

Fools and chatterboxes may answer yes — with Launcelot Gobbo, or Gratiano the talker, to whom

> Silence is only commendable
> In a neat's tongue dri'd and a maid not vendible.

Hamlet and the clown in *Twelfth Night* and Jessica's Lorenzo know better. "How every fool can play upon *the word*," [1] says Lorenzo; "I think the best grace of wit will shortly turn into silence, and discourse grow commendable in none only but parrots," — a sentiment more or less shared and illustrated also by the melancholy Antonio and the eloquent and well-graced Portia, who is certainly never more eloquent than in those "fair, speechless messages," those half-revelations of her music ("Tell me where is fancy bred . . . It is engend'red in the eyes") which play so large a part in furthering the action of *The Merchant of Venice*. I have purposely chosen an obvious illustration from one of the comedies because in the comedies especially Shakspere is most often charged with culpable negligence, with "a hasty and even contemptuous indifference" [2] to those principles of good art which the same critics recognize and honor with an enthusiasm only this side idolatry in the tragedies. As an *a priori* proposition it has

1. Compare Hamlet's "Words, words, words!" and *Twelfth Night*, III, i, 28–29: "Words are grown so false, I am loath to prove reason with them."
2. Bradley, p. 76.

always seemed inconceivable to me that one and the same great craftsman — granting that like all mortals he cannot always be at his best, not always equal in inspiration or care — could forget or wilfully ignore his instinct for good workmanship simply on turning from one favorite kind of artistic labor to another. I am of the opinion that the technique of Shakspere's silences is pretty much one and the same in the comedies, histories, and tragedies, but I must let the closer demonstration wait upon another answer or two to the simple question with which I began. These answers are as easy to find in the comedies and histories as in the tragedies; they are as plainly at hand in *The Taming of the Shrew*, *The Merry Wives*, and *Cymbeline*, as in *Henry IV*, or *Macbeth*, *Lear*, *Hamlet*, and *Coriolanus*.

Katherine the shrew, for example, is not one of those persons who never speak out; yet this very Katherine, even before she is tamed, knows how to speak in silence. "'T is bargained," says Petruchio to her father and the other suitors,

> 'T is bargained twixt us twain being alone,
> That she shall still be curst in company;
> I tell you 't is incredible to believe
> How much she loves me. O, the kindest Kate!
> She hung about my neck . . . and won me to her love.

Her father "knows not what to say." Katherine does, and says it: not a word — not even a curst word authorized for company — but silence which implies consent.[1] Nor is the fact that Shakspere knew what he was about in contrasting golden speech with golden silence less evident as between the laconic monosyllables of that Silence with the capital S, the honorable Justice Silence, sober, and the lusty bacchanalian melodies of the same Justice Silence

1. See *Taming*, II, i, 306 ff. Katherine's later assertion (III, ii, 8–9) that she was "forc'd to give her hand oppos'd against her heart," does not carry conviction. It is merely an effort to cover her chagrin at Petruchio's first step in the taming — his late arrival for the wedding.

praising God for the merry year, astonishing Falstaff himself, and shouting "Samingo!" into the sweet of the night when he is gloriously drunk; or as between the voiceless misery of Master Slender of the *Merry Wives* while in the presence of Anne Page, and his sure touch upon the magic strings — "O sweet Anne Page!" — when she is out of sight and hearing. Posthumus, husband of Imogen, is a man of another stamp, but he too sometimes knows what to do or say, and when. In his repentance just before the end he apostrophizes the "good gods" in flowing periods, but he has no words with which to unpack his heart to Imogen:

> O Imogen!
> I'll speak to thee in silence.[1]

We shall do well to remember him and Queen Hermione's faithful Paulina (who reminds us that

> the silence often of pure innocence
> Persuades when speaking fails [2]),

on returning, later, to the endings of the comedies. For the burden of proving that the silences thereof are uncalculated and uncalculable rests upon those who think that the artist who achieved the tragedies went out of his way to forget all he ever knew in order to finish his comedies with as much scandalous bungling as possible. But we have not yet done with our prior question.

Ready answers can hardly escape anyone who has looked at the plays. Mr. Justice Silence, for example, has his tragic counterpart in the wife of Coriolanus, who had tears only to greet her lord home from the wars:

> My gracious silence, hail!
> Wouldst thou have laugh'd had I come coffin'd home
> That weep'st to see me triumph? [3]

1. *Cymbeline*, V, iv, 9–29. 2. *Winter's Tale*, II, ii, 41 ff.
3. *Coriolanus*, II, i, 192 ff.

Nor can Coriolanus himself find any more words than Virgilia in the greatest moment of the play, when he surrenders his pride and hate to love and Rome. At this point [1] Coriolanus speaks to his mother, wife, and child, in eloquent silence — not unlike Cordelia's when Lear demands that she heave her heart into her mouth. I shall have occasion, shortly, to notice at closer range the persistently studied contrast, in the comedies as well as in the tragedies, between fluent outspokenness and innate reticence. For the moment, one or two additional illustrations must suffice to complete our *a priori* case. Thus, one recalls that Richard II for the most part merely *talks* of

> The unseen grief
> That swells with silence in the tortur'd soul,[2]

but that Lady Macbeth, in the sleep-walking scene, really *expresses* it, in broken whispers which are the sighs of a soul unbosoming itself, at last, of long-repressed agonies.[3] And these broken whispers transcend mere words as utterly as Falstaff transcends Parolles, as Cordelia's faltering "No cause, no cause . . ." or Hamlet's "The rest is silence" put to shame the weepy wordiness of a Jane Shore or a George Barnwell. Or, to glance again at the other side, let us recall that even so shallow a youngster as Claudio in *Much Ado* was aware of the fact that silence "may be the perfectest herald of joy." [4] That it may also be the perfectest herald of constant love,[5] of sorrow and pain, or mirth and mischief,

1.   "You shall bear
    A better witness back than words" (V, iii, 203).

2. IV, i, 296–297; or, as Malcolm, son of Duncan, has it, "the grief that does not speak," which "whispers the o'erfraught heart and bids it break" (*Macbeth*, IV, iii, 209 ff.).

3. Cf. Bradley, p. 375.   4. *Much Ado*, II, i, 317.

5. As Proteus of *The Two Gentlemen*, unprincipled though he is, has sense enough to recognize:

> Julia farewell! — What, gone without a word?
> Ay, so love should do; it cannot speak;
> For truth hath better deeds than words to grace it (II, ii, 16 ff.).

Shakspere surely knew at least as well as anybody who can read his plays.

Yet some of his critics, early and late, have altogether failed to see this. Silence to them means simply want of art. In what follows I shall have to give various instances of the curious products of this critical blindness. One case in point, indeed, is immediately in order — John Dennis's remarks concerning the silence, just referred to, of Coriolanus. "For want of . . . Art," writes Dennis,[1] Shakspere

has made his Incidents less moving, less surprizing, and less wonderful. He has been so far from seeking those fine Occasions to move with which an Action furnish'd according to Art would have furnish'd him, that he seems rather to have industriously avoided them. He makes *Coriolanus*, upon his Sentence of Banishment, take his leave of his Wife and his Mother out of sight of the Audience,[2] and so has purposely, as it were, avoided a great occasion to move.

The word "purposely" is to Dennis's credit. He seems to have understood at least that Shakspere was not merely blundering by way of careless omission. For the rest Dennis himself surely blundered egregiously. Shakspere, unlike Dennis, knew that great occasions move different persons in differing ways. Romeo at Juliet's tomb, and Hamlet at the grave of Ophelia, speak out. Coriolanus is not a Romeo nor yet a Hamlet, but Coriolanus at the grave of all his hopes speaks for himself, in terms of silence, as truly and with as much finality as do Romeo and Hamlet. In his silence, Shakspere, perhaps, also speaks. To John Dennis and all his tribe he says, if I read him aright, something like this: Here are two persons, Coriolanus and Virgilia, a Roman and his wife. They stand

1. *An Essay on the Genius and Writings of Shakespear* (1712), Letter 1, p. 5 (cf. Nichol Smith, *Eighteenth Century Essays on Shakespeare*, p. 26).

2. Dennis must have reference here to the final *self*-banishment of Coriolanus, that is to say, to the moment referred to above (p. 12, n. 1), for his family and friends appear upon the stage to bid him farewell on the occasion of his first banishment. (See *Coriolanus*, IV, i and V, iii.)

for a type of humanity endowed with extraordinary reserve, strength, tragic potentiality — for, unlike others endowed with great but different gifts, these two can *not* unpack their hearts with words. Their silence runs deeper than your plummet will ever sound.

Suppose it be granted that upon a *prima facie* view Shakspere seems not to have been unaware of the uses of silence as a working principle of dramatic economy, — to what extent may the prevalent condemnation of the silent endings of certain of the comedies be accounted for on the ground that the critics have misconstrued his purpose or found fault with his psychology simply because it is not identical with their own? Or, to put it more definitely, how many really significant cases in point cannot be thus accounted for? Again, since other "inconsistencies" in the characters and plots of the comedies and tragedies alike, grow out of silences, omissions, or disappearances *in mediis rebus*, how many of these are not to be accounted for on similar grounds? We shall find that there are some; that not even Shakspere, for all his magnificent sweep and power, could find time and space to say the last word for all the men and women and dramatic motives flashed upon the scene by his creative fiat; that his workmanship is *not* altogether impeccable; indeed, that one or two of his silences may justify the complaint that he was not always above sacrificing truth or psychological probability to momentary theatrical effect.[1] But I think it will appear that there are astonishingly few such cases.

A great many silences which are peculiarly Shakspere's own, because, as already indicated, they result from his eclectic treatment of his sources, are of fundamental importance in his manage-

1. See below, pp. 55 ff.

ment of character and plot. Everyone knows that he added many a vital character and course of action to the old plays and stories upon which he worked, and that he made great numbers of significant changes in the material he retained. No one, however, so far as I know, has ever attempted a comprehensive study of the whys and wherefores of his — perhaps equally significant — omissions. Nor can I, though I think such a study might be decidedly useful, attempt it within the limits of this essay. Yet it will not do to pass over the subject entirely. That Shakspere in shaping his sources to his hand omits indecencies, irrelevancies, and ineptitudes without number is one of those matters of common knowledge which everyone takes for granted; but the specific bearing of such external silences upon those within the plays is not always clear. Take, for example, the various and sundry silences or omissions in the histories — such, for instance, as Shakspere's failure to utilize Magna Charta in *King John*, or the Duke of Gloucester, an important historical figure, in *Richard II*. Obviously, the significance of such silences cannot be estimated without determining how much or how many of them are simply carried over from the sources. These silent omissions, however, are of interest primarily to the student of Shakspere's political ideas. Others are of more immediate concern to the student of his dramatic technique. Thus, the fact that we *hear*, from Claudius and Polonius, much talk of Hamlet's "dangerous lunacies" and "broad pranks," whereas we really *see* very little of them in the play,[1] is of decided interest from our point of view — because it shows Shakspere at work, condensing the story as Saxo Grammaticus has it, eliminating some of the grotesqueness thereof, but not its implications in the final reckoning.

The desirability of keeping an eye upon Shakspere's sources will be apparent as we turn to the curious silences of important char-

1. At least not until long after they are spoken of (cf. III, iii, 7; III, iv, 2).

acters in those dénouements of the comedies which have been most
severely and unanimously condemned as contradictory, or merely
conventional, but in any case as not in character. Since I shall
discuss in the following chapter the dénouements of the comedies
in general, I need here consider only those which have proved
troublesome because they literally end in silence. They happen to
be broadly representative of the whole range of Shakspere's work
in comedy,—of the earliest plays, the "dark" comedies, and the
dramatic romances,—for my cases in point are *The Two Gentlemen of Verona*, *Measure for Measure*, and *The Winter's Tale*. The
endings of these plays are precisely the ones that have most seriously disturbed the critics. It should therefore clarify the issue to
note at once that in all three cases the silences which cause the
trouble may fairly be said to be Shakspere's own as well as Silvia's,
Isabella's, and Hermione's, for the ending in each case is distinctly different from that of the sources so far as we know them.
In other words, the corresponding characters in the sources have
no part in these silences. Whatever else may be said, then, Shakspere was not merely copying carelessly someone else's improbabili-
ties; he seems to have invented a fresh ending in each case, and
presumably he thought about it.

The ending of *The Two Gentlemen* has usually been thought less
scandalous than merely ineffective, but various critics early and
late regard it [1] as utterly impossible. Shakspere, they think, could
not have written it; the players must have done it. The fact is that
it is in keeping with the general tone of the play and with Shakspere's practice elsewhere. The difficulty centres about Silvia's
silence concerning the queer ups and downs of the last scene. The

---

1. Or parts of it, especially the couplet (V, iv, 82–83):

> And, that my love may appear plain and free,
> All that was mine in Silvia I give thee.

(For full references and discussion concerning the ending of this play and the next two, see
below, p. 17, n. 2, and Chapter II.)

faithful Valentine, temporarily a benevolent captain of outlaws, is
moved by a quixotic impulse to show that he has really forgiven
his false but repentant friend, Proteus. He shows it by offering on
the spot to resign his Silvia to Proteus — the very Silvia who has
innocently caused the breach between these bosom friends and
also Proteus's treachery to his Julia. But Julia, in disguise, happens to be present to hear this fine proposal. She has hitherto had
to remain nervously in the background, but in the emergency she
first swoons and then, naturally enough, speaks up and fights for
her own. Like the two Helenas,[1] and Hero, and Juliet, she is not
squeamish about the earlier fickleness of her lover, being well content to win back her Proteus, such as he is. Silvia thereupon
silently takes back her romantic captain of outlaws, whose common sense, presumably, comes back by degrees. Her silence, I
think, is not necessarily either tragic or stupid, though most critics
have thought it one or the other.[2] It may be a breathless silence,
for she has but just made her escape from the outlaws and from
Proteus; or it may be merely a sensible silence on general principles. In the circumstances Julia has the right of way, and what
she says meets the situation adequately for Silvia. That young

1. Of *A Midsummer-Night's Dream* and *All's Well*.
2. Dowden, for example, has the following comment upon this point: "The lines in
which the faithful Valentine seems to surrender his rights in Silvia to the penitent Proteus
. . . have been a stumbling-block to many critics. Shall we say that Shakespeare was here
sacrificing truth and nature to a convention of the time? Shall we suppose that the words
were spoken so boldly because Valentine had heard the declaration of Silvia's fidelity to
himself and her detestation of his false friend? Or shall we accept the interpretation of the
words proposed by Dr. Batteson — 'All such love as I have yielded to Silvia, I now extend
to thee'? If the last be the true meaning of the speech, it did not occur to Julia . . . who
instantly swoons, and whatever way we interpret the speech of Valentine, it seems strange
and undramatic that Silvia herself at this moment should utter no word. But a curious
essay might be written upon the silences of some of the characters of Shakespeare." Sir
Arthur Quiller-Couch, to whom I owe the reference (for which see above, p. 6, n. i) to this
passage, agrees with Dowden that the couplet and the situation in question are alike impossible (see his edition, with J. D. Wilson, of *The Two Gentlemen*, Cambridge, 1921; and,
for discussion of his explanation of the difficulties involved, below, "Epilogue," pp. 257 ff.).

lady knows, of old, her Valentine and his fine emotional extrava-
gance on the subject of love and friendship.[1] Valentine, of course,
is slightly ridiculous, but then he is merely the youthful hero of a
youthful play which is nowhere profound in characterization and
which exploits to the full the familiar casuistry of the friendship
theme. Of Silvia, finally, we know very little anyhow ("Who is
Silvia? What is she?") except that she is inclined to be sensible
and not talkative. Perhaps she realizes — for the song tells us that
she is wise as she is fair — that she will have plenty of opportunity
to talk to Sir Valentine later!

Isabella, in *Measure for Measure*, is a character of a very different sort. She is drawn at full length. We know her history, and it
is not to be denied that she is too good for the Duke; though it is
also well to recall that not a few wives on the stage and off are
rather too good for their husbands. In any case I cannot see that
her silent acceptance of the Duke is an altogether scandalous performance on her part or on Shakspere's. That she does accept him
is, I think, all but certain, though at least one scholar [2] thinks it
"perhaps significant that she does not explicitly" do so. If Shakspere had meant us to believe that she would reject the proposal, he
would surely have made her speak out. For one thing at least is
certain as regards Shakspere's silences. They do not violate cardinal principles of Elizabethan stagecraft: Shakspere does not maintain silence upon essential points which require plain speech to be
understood by the audience. And no Elizabethan audience could
possibly have imagined that a royal or ducal offer of marriage
could be silently rejected. Superficially, the immediate cause of
Isabella's silence is perhaps not altogether unlike that of Silvia, for
this proposal comes with something like the effect of stunning surprise at the end of a scene of prolonged strain. And Isabella, far

1. See II, iv, 1–115, 157–185, and below, pp. 76 ff.
2. Neilson, *Shakespeare*, Cambridge ed., p. 326.

more than Silvia, has depth and reserve. The Duke knows this. His proposal is put in guarded, or at least in general, terms; and it calls for no immediate reply. The reasonablenesss of its ultimate acceptance is, of course, another question. The answer depends upon our attitude toward the Duke. Shakspere, I believe, had a more humane understanding of this Duke's good and bad points than the critics. They emphasize his shiftiness and timidity. But, as Shakspere drew him, he is not altogether contemptible at his worst, and not without a Hamlet-like appeal at his best, though he is never more than a weaker, much-diluted Hamlet. His leniency or weakness is a major cause of the evil which makes his Vienna infinitely more rotten than Hamlet's Denmark, but this weakness is merely the negative side of a nature given to keen self-analysis and to the profound disillusionment which goes with it. With it goes also a habit of ironical but not uncharitable reflection upon our common human frailty, and a concomitant sense of the futility of external action against sores that fester within. He is certainly not great enough to be tragic; yet I think he is not too small to deserve a tremendous stroke of luck at the end. Even his detractors (*in* the play) [1] do not deny that he is "a scholar, a statesman, and a soldier"; and his people — including Isabella, who thinks of him during his supposed absence as "the good Duke" who will give her justice — love him in spite of his "crotchets." [2] Nor should it be forgotten that he finds Isabella while he is about the king's business — however furtive and dangerous the method — of probing the evil with which he has to deal, perhaps in order to clear the ground for action. At all events, he has watched Isabella and must know that she will be able to give him the faith and strength he needs to face the future, to make action something more than a vague possibility. She, for her part, has looked forward to his return. She has already, unknowingly, stood by his

1. See III, ii, 155.   2. III, ii, 158; III, i, 197 ff.

side and borne the brunt of a determined fight against evil in the world outside of convent walls. To accept him is to accept a great and effective power for good, which, as experience has taught her, her world needs as much, perhaps, as the prayers of even the most enskied and sainted votary.

Two counts, one general and one specific, weigh most heavily in the critical indictment against the ending of *The Winter's Tale*. The first of these may be dismissed rapidly, if only because its implications run beyond our immediate inquiry. It is the general charge against the dramatic romances: that such madness of heart, such sinners as Posthumus and Leontes, are beyond forgiveness; that the forgiveness they win is conventional, theatrical, "unconvincing." The defense is simple. The forgiveness is not lightly won. And, whether we like it or not, Shakspere in his maturest plays says again and again that long agony mellows and humanizes all sinners — the forgivers and the forgiven; that time and suffering may atone even for madness of heart; that serene mercy is better than vengeance.[1] As for the specific charge against the ending of *The Winter's Tale*, I quote Professor Brander Matthews:

Frankly unfeminine is [Hermione's] forgiveness of her husband without one word of reproach, although his atrocious conduct has caused the death of her only son, the supposed death also of her only daughter, and her own seclusion for sixteen years.[2]

The answer, once more, is simple enough, though it cannot be conclusive, since every man has a right to his own ideas as to what qualities make a woman frankly feminine or unfeminine. It is still possible, for example, to cherish the old-fashioned notion that the decay of reticence in men and maidens is a comparatively

1. "The rarer action is in virtue than in vengeance" (*Tempest*, V, i, 27–28; cf. Chapter II, pp. 93–94).
2. *Shakespeare as a Playwright*, p. 338.

modern phenomenon — Professor Erskine to the contrary notwithstanding. Shakspere, at all events, probably did not think of reticence, poise, dignity, as unfeminine qualities, for he gave them also in greater or lesser degree and in varying combinations to Lady Macbeth, Cordelia, Virgilia, Hero, Isabella, and Imogen. His test and definition of what is feminine is not circumscribed by the bubbling vivacities, charming as these are, of Beatrice and Rosalind. "Do you not know I am a woman?" says Rosalind: "when I think I must speak." [1] True, — but if this be the only qualification then we must count among Shakspere's frankly feminine personages so masculine a fellow as old Menenius, friend of Coriolanus, for "What I think I utter" [2] is his self-announced principle. Beatrice and Rosalind and Juliet [3] all illustrate with much charm or pathos the workableness of this principle, but so do Benedick,[4] Orlando, and Romeo. The point, as Shakspere would seem to have it, is that quiet reticence or abundant expressiveness is not necessarily a prerogative of age any more than of youth, not necessarily peculiar to one sex any more than to the other. Either quality may be dramatically right in man or woman of any age, according to the individual and the circumstances. And Queen Hermione's silence, far from being unfeminine, is surely a credit to

1. *As You Like It*, III, ii, 263 ff. Yet one has only to glance at her next line to recall that she does not always speak out at once. Duke Frederick, indeed, accuses her of artful silences:

> Her very silence and her patience
> Speak to the people (I, iii, 80 ff.).

2. *Coriolanus*, II, i, 58.

3. And Portia (wife to Brutus) whose expression on the subject, it must be admitted, supports Professor Matthews's view:

> O constancy, be strong upon my side;
> Set a huge mountain 'tween my heart and tongue:
> I have a man's mind but a woman's tongue.
> How hard it is for woman to keep counsel! (*Julius Caesar*, II, iv, 6–9.)

Portia, however, is but one of Shakspere's women, and not his highest achievement in the portrayal of the sex.

4. "What his heart thinks, his tongue speaks," says Don Pedro, between jest and earnest (*Much Ado*, III, ii, 14).

her womanliness, her humanity, and to the artistry of Shakspere.[1] Leontes has long "performed a saint-like sorrow." Hermione, never effusive, always queenly, has been schooled in sixteen years of silence. If there is anything hard to believe in all this, it is the fact that Hermione waits, and makes Leontes wait, so many long years. In the end her silent forgiveness speaks more eloquently than any conceivable words. Perhaps it would be to go too far to say that not her silence but the suggested reproaches from her to Leontes, would be, in the presence of Polixenes, all but unfeminine. Each man has a right to his own opinion, but, in my judgment, given Hermione true to herself, reproaches in the circumstances are all but unthinkable.

Thus far we have examined various aspects of the technique of silence in characterization which seem on the whole to be conscious, purposive, calculated—or at least not uncalculable. Before turning to other aspects of our subject it will be useful to recapitulate: to indicate something of the general provenience, range, and variety of this technique as illustrated by the materials already drawn upon or by cognate matter which immediately follows. Clearly there is in Shakspere, to begin with, something more than a general awareness of the possible significance of silence as against speech, or of their comparative merits for purposes of self-expression. The generalizations of Gratiano and Lorenzo on the subject speak for themselves, but the thing goes deeper. In the comedies as well as in the tragedies the technique of silence would seem to be an active principle of characterization. Shakspere reveals his *dramatis personae* primarily by what they say, but to no negligible extent by their silences. Virgilia's gracious silence is notable, among other reasons, because it has no foil, and needs none. Her silence wells from the deep.

1. Not a few critics so regard it. See, for example, citations from Dowden, Mrs. Jameson, and others, in Furness, Variorum.

> Passions are likened best to floods and streams:
> The shallow murmur, but the deep are dumb.

The tragedies at large, however, suggest clearly enough that this is not the whole truth. There is in them a distinctly recognizable tendency to study the clash — or at any rate the effect of the juxtaposition — of silent reserve and fluent self-assertiveness, the contrast between major and minor keys, between Lear and Cordelia. Shakspere reminds us constantly that the C Major of life is not the only key, even though it be the fundamental. Even through the splendid diapason, through all the impassioned harmonies and the grand discords of *Antony and Cleopatra*, one hears the thin minor of Octavius. Hamlet's silences — of which more anon — are significant chiefly in the light of his own utterances, but the contrast to which I allude is more or less in evidence as between the friends and foes that surround him, between Gertrude and Ophelia,[1] Laertes and Horatio. Fluency or reticence in them is, to be sure, a more or less superficial sign of the obvious contrast between maturity and immaturity, shallowness and depth. Similar signs, however, mark more deeply seated differences as between the tragically fluent Richard II and the silently competent Bolingbroke, between the Brutus who dreams, and the Cassius who thinks, too much. The point, of course, may be pressed too far, but I think its incidence may be seen also in *Macbeth*. Macbeth and Lady Macbeth constitute no obvious contrast as between magic speech and tragic silence, but the study of their spiritual disintegration in terms of contrasting silences that envelope and isolate them one from another is one of the triumphs of the play. Macbeth himself, of course, begins and ends with a marvelous gift of imaginative conception and utterance. Even at first Lady

---

1. Lowell speaks of "the piteous 'no more but so' in which Ophelia compresses the heart-break whose compression was to make her mad" ("Shakespeare Once More," *Among My Books*, I, 182–183). Ophelia, however, is not constitutionally loquacious.

Macbeth's valorous tongue sounds no overtones such as his; and thereafter by degrees, her voice loses its timbre, only to sound tragically like itself again, for a moment, in the broken whispers of the sleep-walking scene. But Macbeth's voice, too, grows hoarse at last. He can still, trumpet-tongued, call the alarum for battle, but his words no longer wing upon the sightless couriers of the air. After the death of his wife they grow aweary of the sun. In the end, of all their marvelous music, only a martial resonance remains to sound his knell and gut his candle.

The uses of characteristic silence, reticence, and the like in the comedies are perhaps more varied than in the tragedies, but less complex. They serve often to create essentially simple humorous effects — momentary as in the instance, above mentioned, of Katherine the Shrew's silent acceptance of Petruchio's public report of his successful wooing; somewhat larger in effect in Master Slender's unsuccessful wooing of the Merry Wife's daughter; and broader still when Justice Silence's mellifluous voice soars into the leafy heights of Shallow's orchard. As in the tragedies, there are many instances of contrasts between quiet persons and the other sort. Thus, Gratiano refuses "to be reputed wise . . . only . . . for saying nothing," a position of which the sad Antonio, though he does not play Sir Oracle, disapproves in theory and practice.[1] The charming reserve of Viola, again, is set off against the outspokenness of Olivia and the sentimental effusiveness of Orsino. Nor can one help recalling the nice balance of effect as between the irrepressible Beatrice and her demure cousin, the gentle Hero; or Benedick's excellent stomach for words and Claudio's adolescent speechlessness while Don Pedro goes a-wooing for him. But in not a few of the comedies silence speaks for itself rather than for contrast. Sweet Anne Page has no Beatrice to set her off, and Isabella

1. He is characteristically "dumb" at the last, upon hearing of the safe return of his vessels (*Merchant*, V, i, 279; cf. I, i, 113).

and Hermione stand by themselves. So also does Imogen, who, never tongue-tied, knows, as Posthumus does, that there are times when few words are best, and who, in the end, has scarcely more thought or breath to reproach her husband than Hermione herself.[1] And so these silences or near-silences — the silences of Cordelia and Lady Macbeth, Hermione and Virgilia, Bolingbroke and Hippolyta, Portia and Justice Silence — ring the changes of character. They contrast and individualize the persons of the plays; they signify heartbreak and madness and heart-easing mirth. Demure silence and austere silence, the silences of pride and the silences of stupidity, some mawkish and some perverse, some radiant, exquisite, uproarious — they run the gamut from tears to laughter.

Our recapitulation, however, has run slightly ahead of our exposition. No one needs to be reminded that the technique of silence cannot claim the sole credit, or even the chief credit, for all these effects in characterization. But even so far as silence has an important part in them, it is now one kind of silence and now another. The one most easily recognized is that which runs true to form always — that which is the consistent grace of Virgilia, the pitiable weakness and the uplifting strength of Cordelia. For Cordelia's instinctive reticence, proud and hard at first, softened later and penetrated by the grace of infinite pity, is essentially consistent [2] and true to itself. Her pride as well as her love is more ponderous than her tongue in the beginning. For a moment, before Lear is found and before he finds himself, indignation and pity break through the low voice he loved so well, and speak:

> Alack, 'tis he . . . Was this a face
> To be oppos'd against the warring winds? . . .

1. Cf. Chapter II, p. 91, n. 3.
2. For, though she can speak fluently to France and (in another key) to her sisters, her instinctive tendency, first and last, is to be most reticent when she is most deeply moved.

But in the end, when love only is left, Cordelia has kisses and tears and broken sobs, but no more words.[1]

The silence which falls upon Lady Macbeth is somewhat different in kind. It springs not from the depth but from the tumult of the soul; it is consistent artistically, but it is the product of change and occasion rather than the expression of a fundamental or dominant trait of character. Such silences — the silences, *on certain occasions*, of Hamlet or Imogen, Portia or Hippolyta — do not always spring from the bottommost depths, but they are no less expressive so far as they go. If they do not tell the whole story, they often, as a few illustrations must suffice to indicate, tell much in little. In this connection the silences of Hippolyta, Queen of the Amazons, are particularly instructive, for they are on the border-line between the silences which define and those which reveal a part of the whole.

In the opening scene of *A Midsummer-Night's Dream* Hippolyta says not a word while Egeus and the several lovers plead the pros and cons of their case. When Theseus, who has noticed her silence, ends the long proceedings, he turns to her half hopefully, half inquiringly —

Come, my Hippolyta! What cheer, my love?

But even then she remains silent. Not so Bishop Warburton. "Had a modern poet had the teaching of her," says he, "we should have found her the busiest among them. . . . But Shakspere knew better what he was about, and observed decorum." [2] The critical principle here would seem to be that ladies should be seen but not heard — but Shakspere, as we have noted, did not fancy such unfair discrimination between the sexes. He observed something more than decorum; namely, consistency of characterization. The

1. Cf. Bradley, pp. 315 ff.
2. *A Midsummer-Night's Dream*, I, i, 131; Furness, Variorum, p. 16.

"bouncing Amazon" is easily bored, from first to last, by other people's concerns. She never suffers from an overplus of imagination. Theseus and the rest, as the play goes on, know how to cherish the delightful absurdities of Pyramus and Thisbe; but Hippolyta is insufferably bored, and breaks her silence only to damn the proceedings as "the silliest stuff that ever I heard." In reply to the significant rejoinder of Theseus — that the best in this kind are but shadows — she admits placidly that she hasn't the imagination to amend shadows. One does not envy Theseus his approaching bliss, but one must be fair to the Amazon.[1] After all, she has certain kindly instincts and momentary sympathies. She had asked that the tragical mirth be dispensed with because she does not love "to see wretchedness o'ercharged," and she is touched by the lovers' marvelous "story of the night told over" as by something "of great constancy" and "howsoever, strange and admirable." Indeed, when she is in her own proper element, when she recalls the joys of the chase — "the musical discord, the sweet thunder" of the hounds of Sparta — she can be moved from silence to something like poetry. (The same is true, but infinitely more so, of Enobarbus, friend to Antony. When there is something worth talking about — when, for example, he remembers Cleopatra enthroned upon her barge — he speaks like one inspired. He is *not* "a soldier only"; he does not enjoy playing "your considerate stone"; but he is not a mere chatterbox. During the rollicking scene between Cleopatra's attendants and the soothsayer he maintains an amused and quizzical silence punctuated only by his demand for "wine enough" and his prophecy that *his* fortune will be to go drunk to bed.)[2]

1. My friend, Professor Robert P. Utter, to whom I am indebted for valuable hints in this connection, describes her — a little unkindly, I think — as "a mindless, soulless athlete" (*University of California Chronicle*, January, 1928, p. 67).

2. Professor G. G. Sedgewick kindly reminds me of this passage (cf. *Antony and Cleopatra*, I, ii, 11–82; II, ii, 108–112).

The silences of Portia — Bassanio's Portia — are as resourceful and exquisite as her speech. Such as they are, they illustrate admirably the expressiveness of occasional silence. One of them, to be sure, differs from the rest. Its purpose is merely to enable Shakspere to wind up his plot [1] without answering unnecessary questions [2] which someone might have asked him. In the last scene Portia brings Antonio a letter which tells him that some of his precious argosies have come safely into port after all — but she forestalls questions:

> You shall not know by what strange accident
> I chanced on this letter.

For the rest, however, Portia's silences,[3] as already indicated, speak for herself. Bound by her father's will to abide by the verdict of the caskets, she manages to send her chosen lover fair speechless messages, and when these, remembered, have brought him back to Belmont, she keeps faith, but lets music sound to give him his cue to choose not by the view. These are more pleasant silences than those involved in two or three other cases with which I shall conclude these illustrations.

Two characters in *Romeo and Juliet*, Lady Capulet and that soul of garrulity, the Nurse, are significantly silent on at least two occasions. It will be remembered that Lady Capulet, cold though she is, is not a Roman matron — not altogether averse to saying her say: to old Capulet, for instance, on the subject of his youthful gallantries, or to the Prince after Tybalt is slain, when she is the first to cry out for revenge —

> As thou art true,
> For blood of ours shed blood of Montague.

1. On silence in the plots, see below, pp. 48 ff.
2. In this connection, however, cf. Chapter II, p. 80.
3. Cf. Dowden, *Transcripts and Studies*, p. 369.

When her husband, upon Juliet's submission, suddenly proposes
to move the wedding forward by one day, she objects, — "We
shall be short in our provision," but she really speaks on but one
occasion, and then (not altogether unlike Iago at the end of his
string) by *refusing* to speak. It is the occasion of Juliet's last
plea to her parents:

> Is there no pity sitting in the clouds?
> O sweet my mother, cast me not away!
> Delay this marriage for a month, a week. . . .

To which Lady Capulet replies,

> Talk not to me, for I'll not speak a word.
> Do as thou wilt, for I have done with thee.[1]

(As regards Iago—honest, fluent Iago—it is worth while to recall
the last sure touch by which Shakspere reminds us that there is
iron as well as venom in the blood of his demi-devil. Witness Iago's
last words,[2]

> Demand me nothing; what you know, you know.
> From this time forth I never will speak word.

With which he grits his teeth, and keeps them shut for many a
long minute while threats of torture, and perhaps the torture of
Othello's last word or two, and yet more threats, ring in his
ears.)

Juliet's Nurse, when she wishes, can speak as much to the
point [3] as anybody. Obviously there is more or less method in her
breathlessness. She keeps Juliet on tenterhooks because she has
the gossip's unfailing instinct for dramatic suspense. I think she
remains silent on one all but fatal occasion because she loves to
keep a secret, or to stage-manage its revelation, even more than
she loves to hear herself talk. When Juliet has fought her way

1. IV, iv, 11; III, i, 154 ff.; v, 198 ff.   2. *Othello*, V, ii, 303–304.
3. I, v, 144 ff.; II, v, 70 ff.

through the agony that comes to her with the news of Tybalt's death, she sends the Nurse to Romeo with her ring — in token of her steadfast troth. The Nurse takes it, and when Romeo frantically asks her what Juliet has said—whether she thinks him a confirmed murderer, whether she considers their love "cancelled" because he has slain her kinsman — the Nurse answers that Juliet "says nothing" but equally "on . . . Tybalt calls, and then on Romeo cries." Of the ring, which belies this report, our Nurse says nothing. She keeps the situation in hand — literally so, for when Romeo offers to stab himself because his hope in Juliet is gone, she snatches the dagger away.[1] But even then she says nothing of the ring until after Friar Lawrence has finished the long harangue in which he suggests a way out. Possibly she forgets the ring momentarily in her enjoyment of the Friar's rhetoric,

> O Lord! I could have stay'd here all the night
> To hear good counsel.   O what learning is!

Yet one recalls that she did not forget the purport of her several messages to Juliet while withholding them until (what she considered) the proper moment. If she did not forget in this instance, and if she thought about the matter at all, it is pretty certain that the postponing of Romeo's "comfort" would have seemed to her a small price to pay for her own edification. In any case, one may guess that she would have held on to the ring like grim death for any length of time rather than offend her sense of climax.[2]

Let us consider, finally, the meaning and effect of another "occasional" silence which strikes deeper than most of those thus far mentioned. It has to do with the ending of *Hamlet*, and it is worth considering if only to reënforce a point which has seldom been sufficiently emphasized — that this tragedy is not merely the

1. The case remains substantially the same whether the Nurse or (as some editors have it) the Friar, seizes the dagger.
2. See *Romeo and Juliet*, III, ii, 142–143; iii, 80–162.

tragedy of the Prince of Denmark.[1] Hamlet's mother for the most part speaks freely and like a queen [2] whatsoever is in her mind. Yet on one vital occasion Queen Gertrude promises and maintains silence — and that silence, like Lady Macbeth's, becomes final: at once the symbol and the immediate cause of her tragedy. Hamlet bids her hide the "dear concernings" he has unfolded to her. She promises. She has "no life to breathe" what he has said. Nor does she break her promise. King Claudius urges her to confide to him what has happened ("'T is fit we understand") but she tells him only a small part of her thoughts and fears — that Hamlet is "mad as the sea and wind," but not that, mad though he be, he knows what has gone before and is armed against the King's dark purposes. And this is the beginning of the end for this imperial couple. Thereafter they nurse in silence the "sick soul" of their several sins. Externally they stand together, as of old, for a while longer, and together they are more than a match for Laertes and the fickle mob. But a barrier of silence has grown up between them. Gertrude is more than ever conjunctive to the life and soul of Claudius, but he cannot tell her of his private instructions to his agents. In the end he must mix, alone, the poisons by which he unwittingly gives death to his wife. He is forced to suppress into a futile outcry — "Gertrude, do not drink!" — the agony that grips him as she lifts the cup; but he himself really drains its dregs even before Hamlet makes an end, for he hears his wife breathe forth her last word of love not for him but for his mortal enemy: "O my dear Hamlet, — the drink, the drink!"

1. It is, writes Professor Kittredge, "not the tragedy of any individual," but "the tragedy of a group, of the whole royal family" (*Shakspere*, p. 36; cf. subsequent discussion, pp. 36–38). Professor Bradley, however, states the case as follows: "The plot is single; Hamlet and the King are the 'mighty opposites'; and Ophelia, the only other person in whom we are obliged to take a vivid interest, has already disappeared. It is therefore natural and right that the deaths of Laertes and the Queen should affect us comparatively little" (p. 256).

2. It being understood that not every queen is an Hermione.

Let us turn to another aspect of what I have ventured to term the technique of silence in characterization, that is, to the more or less silent *disappearances*[1] of certain characters at various stages of the action. I am prepared to admit at once that some of the lesser disappearances contribute little or nothing to this technique — or to any other good technique — except in so far as the removal of surplusage is good technique. Indeed, a few of the characters that disappear might well have been dispensed with altogether. Yet it is well to remember that most of the many scores of "mute" characters in the plays (such, for instance, as Violenta, neighbor of the old Florentine widow in *All's Well*[2]) are really not personages of the play at all, but merely a part of the stage setting. So far they obviously have their uses. We shall see later[3] that certain others, such as Lafeu's daughter Maudlin, in *All's Well*, and the "other Hero" in *Much Ado*, likewise have no essential being, since they are mere shadow-shapes made to serve momentary needs of the plot. But there remain still other characters who properly disappear early in the game and who might better have been left out altogether. One of them is the "brave son" of the Duke of Milan, apparently the one person really lost in the shipwreck of *The Tempest*, for he is not heard from after Ferdinand mentions him in the second act;[4] and Claudio's uncle in *Much Ado*, who is mentioned in the opening scene of that play, but who thereafter does not pay his awkward young nephew the least bit of attention, is another. One naturally expects something of these two. Since Shakspere does not use them, he might well have elim-

1. Mr. W. J. Lawrence's recent study of "The Practice of Doubling and its Influence on Early Dramaturgy" (*Pre-Restoration Stage Studies*, 1927, pp. 43 ff.), is an important contribution to this subject. I regret that it appeared too late for me to make full use of it.

2. III, v.

3. Below, pp. 56 ff.

4. II, i, 43; cf. Coleridge, "Notes on *The Tempest*," *Works* (N. Y., 1871) IV, 77 n., and Schücking, *Character Problems in Shakespeare's Plays*, p. 114.

inated them altogether.[1] This holds true, more or less, also for
Antonio's son, who is once called upon to provide music in *Much
Ado*, only to be so utterly forgotten, thereafter, by all concerned,
that Leonato, his uncle and Hero's father, speaks of Hero as sole
heir to Antonio as well as himself.[2] In these cases the technique of
silence perhaps did not go far enough. But there are not many
such cases, and such as there are do not make any particular
trouble — unless one looks for it.

That there are those who will look for trouble, perhaps because
they love to lose themselves in a mystery, is undeniable. Witness
the fantastic theory of certain commentators [3] that the ghost who
responds to Macbeth's courageously reiterated dinner-table challenge

> to our dear friend Banquo . . .
> Would he were here! (III, iv, 90–91)

is that of the gracious Duncan (who sleeps well)! Almost equally
far-fetched — in view of the fact that the first principle of Elizabethan as of all dramaturgy is to put essential things clearly, so
that the audience will not need to guess — is the notion which
would identify the "third murderer" of Banquo [4] with Macbeth
or with Ross or with anybody but himself, — namely, the trusted

1. Obviously, however, their presence or absence matters not at all in the acting.

2. Cf. I, ii, 2; V, ii, 300. Editors suggest that Leonato intentionally misstates the case,
but this seems very unlikely. A brother's son of the governor of Messina could not easily
have been hidden from visiting royalty even if there had been any motive for hiding him,
and no such motive appears. It may be held also that Jacques, second brother of Orlando, might have been left out of *As You Like It*. Orlando mentions him in the opening
scene, and he brings word of Duke Frederick's conversion in the end — which, to be sure,
anybody else might have done. Lodge, in the source, made more of him; still, except for
the possible confusion (in the minds of school children — but cf. Variorum *Much Ado*, p.
xix) between him and the other Jacques, he certainly does no harm, and his two appearances round out, pleasantly enough, the story of the three brothers.

3. Cf. Furness, Variorum, p. 176, textual variants on III, iv, 93, "Enter Duncan's
Ghost."

4. III, iii, 2; Furness, Variorum, p. 160; cf. E. K. Chambers and E. A. Allen in Arden,
Macbeth, pp. 117–118, notes on III, iii, and III, iv, 17.

henchman of Macbeth who brings his last instructions, "the perfect spy o' the time." Commentators who suffer from a curious sort of far-sightedness, who can see full-length characters only, may be expected to be troubled by a technique which, besides holding the mirror up to nature at full length, affords brief but significant glimpses also of shadows that pass in the night. Such difficulties, however, are chargeable to the defective vision of the commentators; not to Shakspere. For the rest, even though a few of the persons of the plays might have been dispensed with altogether, the most serious charge that can be brought against Shakspere in this connection is that he did not concern himself unduly about unessentials.

It is perfectly evident, from other cases, that he purposely dismissed many of his minor characters as soon as they had served their turn — the less said the better being the thoroughly artistic principle involved. Thus, Marcellus and Bernardo, though they share a dangerous secret with Hamlet and Horatio, disappear from the play promptly after they have been sworn to secrecy. Of course no one misses them, any more than one misses Sir Eglamour, who literally (and somewhat unceremoniously, it must be confessed, for so valiant a gentleman) runs out of the play when he runs out of the romantic forest of *The Two Gentlemen*.[1] These, and others like them, simply make way for their betters, to enable Shakspere to give us in full measure, as it were, a Juliet for a Rosaline. Still others, such as the King of France, Cordelia's husband, are purposely kept out of view for the good and sufficient reason that their presence is dramatically undesirable, — in this case, obviously, to avoid the awkwardness of stressing the appearance of the pelican daughters as the champions of England against the foreigner.[2] On somewhat the same principle we are given all but too brief a glimpse of King Henry V's pleasantest conquest —

1. IV, iii, 13; V, iii, 7.   2. *Lear*, V, i, 25.

Katherine, Princess of France; though here as in all the histories it must be remembered that many characters are inevitably crowded off the stage by the logic, or at least by the sequence, of events. It is worth noting, however, that Shakspere, when he has room enough, does not hesitate to bring back to the stage persons who interested him, even though their work is about over. Thus the other lively Kate, Hotspur's wife, reappears sadly changed, but effectively so, in the light of events, in the second part of *Henry IV*.[1]

The early disappearance of Rosaline, Romeo's first "love," suggests another word on the general principle of dramatic economy involved. *Romeo and Juliet* was an early play, but it is almost as rich in indications of a ruthless if not altogether unerring instinct for artistic economy as it is in the impassioned music of a lyric love as young and sweet and lavish as youth itself. The fate of Rosaline, and, in another sense, that of Mercutio, is among the chief of these indications. Of Rosaline's beauty, her wit, and her obstinate devotion to a life of cold chastity, so much is heard early in the play from Romeo and others that one is scarcely aware of her actual absence from the stage. At a first glance it seems not improbable that Shakspere may once have thought of putting her side by side with Juliet at the Capulets' feast. We know that she is one of the "fresh female buds" that grace this feast, and the possibility of some such confrontation is twice hinted at—once by old Capulet to Paris, and once when Benvolio urges Romeo to compare Rosaline with "all the admired beauties of Verona" at the same feast.[2] But, if Shakspere ever did think of such a confrontation, he probably did not think of it long. Romeo refuses to dance. He plays the candle-holder and looks on; but, so far as we know, he does not see Rosaline — at least not until after he sees

1. Cf. *I Henry IV*, III, ii, 241 ff. and *II Henry IV*, II, iii.
2. I, ii, 29; 72, 87 ff.

Juliet. And thereafter he can see no one else. Shakspere lets him waste never a word — not even when he reports his new passion to the anxious friar[1] — in vain comparisons as between Rosaline and Juliet. Of course Shakspere's purpose (for *he* withdraws Rosaline, and, for once, keeps even Romeo silent) is to push Romeo's fickleness into the background; but the main point is that there *is* no comparison. Rosaline is ruthlessly annihilated, not for Juliet's sake but to prove with the simplest finality that a callow amorist has become a true lover. In the retrospect the artistry thrown into this shadow drawing of a Rosaline becomes the more apparent. She must vanish because she no longer exists for Romeo — and lo, she departs as gracefully as only a shadow can, for she never has shown her face and never spoken a word on the stage.[2]

Mercutio is anything but a shadow. He speaks many a winged word. But he is forced to take his quietus as ruthlessly as Rosaline herself as soon as his work is done. It does not follow, as various critics[3] have suggested, that he had to be killed lest he kill Shakspere or, at least, Romeo. Shakspere might have reprieved him as he seems to have reprieved Benvolio, who is "deceased too," ac-

1. Whose remarks (II, iii, 44) suggest that the Rosaline affair might have become more than a youthful infatuation.

2. Some time after I had completed this essay, my friend, Professor B. C. Clough, called to my attention Mr. St. John Ervine's pleasant speculation on "The Mystery of Romeo's Rosaline" (*The London Observer*, December 12, 1926). Mr. Ervine recalls that he had "on several occasions" seen Rosaline introduced into the ball-room scene "in the Capulets' house, where Romeo first sees Juliet," but he dismisses this Rosaline as "a theatrical invention made in the muddy mind of an unimaginative stage-manager." Then Mr. Ervine proceeds to draw a spirited portrait of a Rosaline of his own fancy: a "roguey-poguey" young person, "whose eyes were deep with laughter . . . none of your dowdy intellectuals . . . knew about poets . . . but not schoolmarmy. She could frivol, God bless her! She had eyes like Ethel Barrymore . . . and the lovableness of Ellen Terry." In the end Mr. Ervine all but confesses to falling in love with his own Rosaline, and, though he doubtless understands as well as anyone Shakspere's reason for keeping *his* Rosaline in the background, expresses the wish that Shakspere "had been more informative" about the young lady, and the conviction that "he should have let us have a look at her."

3. *Romeo and Juliet*, III, i, 92; Furness, Variorum, p. 159.

cording to the first quarto, but saved, as Steevens [1] puts it, from "unnecessary slaughter" (that is, allowed to disappear) in the second and better quarto. Shakspere gave Mercutio essential life, and [2] he may well have thought him too vital a figure to be relegated to mere obscurity. In any case it is sheer blindness not to see how poignant an effect Shakspere attains by making Mercutio drain the cup a round or two before. The lightning of the ancient hate strikes down as its first victim the gayest, happiest spirit in all this company of friends and foes; and thereafter the end is not far to seek.

So dies Mercutio, and so dies the fair Ophelia. Lesser figures — less important, less pathetic, or less dignified — are justly allowed to disappear into the shadows. Orlando carries the venerable burden of old Adam into the forest of Arden, but thereafter Adam is heard and seen no more. He fades into the background, where he belongs — for Arden is something crowded with young lovers and sentimental philosophers, old and young. Adam has lived his philosophy, and spoken it too, at intervals, [3] for fourscore years, and he is not another Lear. Lodge makes him captain of the Duke's guard; Shakspere gives him peace.

He gives peace, too, and quiet after the tempest, to Lear's fool. Professor Bradley [4] complains that we are left "in ignorance" as to the fate of the fool — that is to say, he objects to the fact that immediately after the storm the fool is allowed (according to his last words in the play) "'to go to bed at noon' as though he felt he had taken his death," without further or more explicit comment upon Shakspere's part. But to have made too much of the fool's death — if, indeed, he does die — would have been to ignore essen-

1. *Romeo and Juliet*, V, iii, 210; Furness, Variorum, p. 291.
2. Irrespective of the question (on which see Verplanck's note, Furness, Variorum, III, i, 92, p. 159, and Neilson, *Shakespeare*, Cambridge ed., p. 834) as to whether or not he followed the earlier dramatist in killing him at last.
3. *As You Like It*, II, iii, 47 ff.   4. Pages 314–315.

tial human as well as dramatic distinctions. Some critics [1] still doubt that Lear's last words, "and my poor fool is hanged," are meant for Cordelia. There is no arguing about such a point, but I think it scarcely too much to say that Lear's fool has no more right to these words than Touchstone has to the tears which Jacques weeps for his "poor . . . fools" [2] of the forest. The end must belong to Cordelia. The fool disappears long before, because he has done his work. He has outjested his master's heartstruck injuries in the storm, but he has been a bitter fool withal, a pestilent gall to Lear. Cordelia brings true healing, and so the fool, his occupation gone, disappears. So far as we know, he is faithful to the end — even though his last speech may be, after all, merely a jest to cap Lear's immediately preceding "We'll go to supper i' the morning." [3] In any case, Shakspere probably remembered that he had on his hands not a second Mercutio but a much-loved fool slightly touched in the brain. Perhaps he purposely allowed the fool to drop quietly out of sight because he also remembered that there was another person of the play who *must* go to bed at noon — Cordelia, a daughter and a queen. [4]

I shall have little more to say concerning the disappearances of characters. Certain terminal "disappearances," to be sure, remain to tempt curious inquiry — but who can answer the questions they

1. Alfred Noyes, for example (cf. *Some Aspects of Modern Poetry*, p. 211).
2. *As You Like It*, II, i, 22–40.
3. *Lear*, III, vi, 90–92.
4. Professor Tolman (*Falstaff and Other Shakespearean Topics*, pp. 93–94) mentions approvingly another explanation of the fool's disappearance — a conjecture (ascribed to Professor Brandl) to the effect that the parts of Cordelia and the fool may originally have been played by the same boy actor. If this was the case, who can say whether it was the cause rather than the effect of Shakspere's conception of the fool's part in the play? At all events, whatever the practical circumstances of the theatre may or may not have contributed to the fool's disappearance (on which point see below, pp. 257 ff.), it is *dramatically* right. (Compare, however, W. J. Lawrence's view on this point. Mr. Lawrence, I find, rejects the idea of the doubling in this case. — *Pre-Restoration Stage Studies*, pp. 72–73, 66.)

raise? We know what became of Falstaff, though even Shakspere could not tell us in less than three plays. But what becomes of Shylock [1] — Shylock turned Christian — and of the rogue Autolycus turned honest, and of Caliban? [2] What song the sirens sang? These puzzling questions, too, are not beyond all conjecture; but for us, they are questions not to be asked. On the whole, we may be grateful to Shakspere for his questions no less than for his answers. Meanwhile, to complete our examination of the technique of silence in characterization it is necessary to consider three or four moot points as to the meaning, in terms of character, of certain difficult silences in *Hamlet*, *Macbeth*, *King Lear*, and *Othello*.

Most of the problems connected therewith have not long since been subjected to the acute analysis of Professor Bradley, the consistent challenge of whose work is never more in evidence than when it forces partial dissent. Especially illuminating is his analysis of one highly complicated question, the meaning of Hamlet's silence on the subject of his love for Ophelia — an analysis which attempts no final judgment and is therefore perhaps the more compelling. Dowden [3] has stated clearly the difficulties in the way of any interpretation based merely upon the spoken words and the deeds of the principals themselves:

One silent interview, one distracted or ironical letter, one scene of invective and reproach, and some few ambiguous or indecent speeches . . . not one word of trust and confidence spoken on either side. . . . This is the account in brief of all the communications between Hamlet and Ophelia with which we are made directly acquainted.

1. Mr. St. John Ervine's answer to this question (his play, *The Lady of Belmont*, 1924) does not, I think, dispose of it.
2. "I'll be wise hereafter," he promises Prospero, "and seek for grace." But if he remains in Prospero's service,— with Prospero settled far from the magic island: in *Milan*, without his book and staff,— then what becomes of Prospero — unless Caliban really suffers a sea-change! (Cf. *The Tempest*, V, i, 294–295, 310; I, ii, 358–365.)
3. *Transcripts and Studies*, p. 371.

Yet the popular view has always been that "Hamlet's love for
Ophelia never changed " — that everything which seems to be at
variance with his outburst at Ophelia's grave is mere acting, sometimes painful but always tender at heart, and always consciously
intended to make Ophelia understand the inevitable, — that all is
over between them. Bradley [1] distrusts this view and finds himself
unable to resist the conclusion that Hamlet's love does change,
that at times it is all but displaced by resentment and suspicion.
In proof he calls attention to the fact that Hamlet does not directly
allude to Ophelia in a single one of his soliloquies or in his most
intimate revelations to Horatio; and that not even in his harshest
moments — in the Play scene and when he suggests the nunnery
— does he give Ophelia or the audience an unmistakable sign to
indicate that his affection remains unchanged. Yet Bradley
admits that it is never possible to determine "how much of Hamlet's harshness is intended to be real," and he frankly discounts
the force of his other contentions. He recalls that Hamlet does in
one soliloquy mention "the pangs of despised love"; that, in
general, the love story seems to be purposely subordinated; that,
therefore, Shakspere may purposely have refrained from stressing
it in the soliloquies, which, as they stand, carry a sufficient burden
of general reflection and poignant self-analysis. Finally, and perhaps most important of all, Bradley admits that "scarcely any
readers or spectators of *Hamlet* notice" his "silence" concerning
Ophelia. This is so, I believe, because it is what one expects: because these silences are true to the man. No one thinks aloud more
fluently than Hamlet — upon psychological or philosophical gen-
eralities; no one can "reason" more keenly with false friends or
discourse more methodical madness to open enemies. But no one
has less patience than he with the triple emptiness of "words,"
with mouthing rant in general; or more instinctive reluctance to

1. Pages 153 ff.

enlarge upon the ultimate intimacies that one treasures in one's heart of hearts. He has no fewer words of love for Ophelia in his soliloquies than he has for her ear when he suddenly appears in her chamber and remains silent there because his heart and mind both are too full for such futile words as Ophelia could fathom or he, under the circumstances, could utter.[1] And he apologizes to Horatio — whose own reticences make him something of an enigma, and whom Hamlet certainly values the more because he does not wear his heart upon his sleeve — for his one outspoken word of friendship: "something too much of this." In short, except by way of oblique reference in his generalizations upon the frailty of woman, in his almost impersonal recollections of his cherished devotion to his father, and in the concomitant reminders of his loathing for Claudius, he really speaks his dearest loves and hates but twice, and then only in moments of tremendous strain and in outbursts of irrepressible emotion: to his mother, and to Ophelia in her grave. If, then, his love for Ophelia did not remain untouched by momentary suspicion and resentment, it would seem that the signs thereof must be read in the Nunnery scene and in his remarks while the Mousetrap is acting, rather than in his silences.

All this proves at least that it is inadvisable to draw very positive inferences *ex silentio*. Bradley recognizes this in dealing with the complexities of *Hamlet*, but it seems to me that he is somewhat less circumspect in another case. He interprets the silence of Banquo concerning his suspicions of Macbeth as out-and-out guilt on Banquo's part. This interpretation he bases, essentially, upon two speeches of Banquo. The first of these is the one immediately after the murder of Duncan:

1. This is equally true whether his disordered attire is due "to intention or preoccupation" (see Bradley, p. 155, and cf. Arden, *Hamlet*, p. 170, note on II, i, 85).

Fears and scruples shake us;
In the great hand of God I stand, and thence
Against the undivulg'd pretence I fight
Of treasonous malice.   (II, iii, 135 ff.)

"His solemn language here," writes Bradley,[1] "reminds us of his grave words about 'the instruments of darkness' and of his later prayer to the 'merciful powers.' He is . . . full of indignation, and determined to play the part of a brave and honest man. But he plays no such part. When next we see him . . . we find that he has yielded to evil. The Witches and his own ambition have conquered him. He alone . . . knew of the prophecies, but he has said nothing of them. He has acquiesced . . . in Macbeth's accession . . . in effect 'cloven to' Macbeth's 'consent.'" A second speech of Banquo's, Bradley adds, "tells us why."

Thou hast it now, king, Cawdor, Glamis, all
As the weird women promised, and, I fear,
Thou play'dst most foully for 't: yet it was said
It should not stand in thy posterity,
But that myself should be the root and father
Of many kings.   If there come truth from them —
As upon thee, Macbeth, their speeches shine —
Why, by the verities on thee made good,
May they not be my oracles as well,
And set me up in hope? (III, i, 1 ff.)

Banquo, in a word, has "kept his secret" and becomes Macbeth's "chief adviser . . . in order to make good *his* part of the predictions after Macbeth's own precedent."

This is a consistent interpretation, and in a sense it elevates the character of Banquo to more tragic proportions than those may see in him who regard him as an innocent victim. "His punishment," says Bradley, "comes quickly." Yet it need hardly be said that in these tragedies disaster more or less unmerited, rather than

1. Pages 384 ff.

punishment, falls not infrequently upon persons of no lesser stature than Banquo's. One thinks, for example, of Romeo and Kent and Macduff. At all events, it seems to me by no means certain that Banquo's silence is the silence of guilt. To interpret it so requires the definite assumption that he seriously suspected Macbeth's purposes *before* the murder of Duncan, and this assumption is scarcely warranted. At the outset Macbeth and Banquo are friends and comrades who trust and believe in one another. Banquo, certainly at first, is frank, plain-spoken, and transparently honest.[1] He is half inclined to laugh off the witches and their prophecies:

> The earth hath bubbles, as the water has
> And these are of them.

When Macbeth has become Thane of Cawdor, he asks Banquo, "Do you not hope your children shall be kings?" Banquo thereupon exorcises the instruments of darkness, with the half-jocular frankness characteristic of him,[2] for himself no less than for Macbeth:

> That trusted home
> Might yet enkindle you unto the crown, —

which is probably exactly what he would *not* have said had he had secret fears of Macbeth. In other words, he is inclined to dismiss these questionable "hopes" of either party as palpable absurdities. Before the murder of Duncan he has bad dreams and presentiments, and these lead him to say again, for his own benefit and that of the audience, that he keeps *his* "bosom franchised and allegiance clear." But this gives us no warrant to assume that he distrusted Macbeth any more than he distrusted himself. If Shakspere had wanted his audience to understand that Banquo

---

1. Compare Coleridge's remark concerning the "*unpossessedness*" of Banquo's mind ("Notes and Lectures upon Shakespeare," *Works* [N. Y., 1871], IV, 167).

2. As of the historical Banquo, according to Holinshed.

did have definite fears in Macbeth, he would presumably have made the point clear — in accordance with those first principles of Elizabethan dramatic art recently referred to — in Banquo's soliloquy, as he does later when Macbeth tells the audience that his fears in Banquo stick deep. To read back into the time before the murder, or even *immediately after* the murder, the suspicions which have had time to take definite shape in Banquo's mind during the considerable interval between the murder and Macbeth's return in the full panoply of his new dignities, is to convict Banquo *ex post facto*. Macbeth fears his royalty of nature and credits him with the soldierly wisdom that guides valor to act in safety. But there is little subtlety in Banquo. What ready means were at his command, immediately after the murder, to expose the "undivulged pretence of treasonous malice" which he was prepared to fight? Duncan's sons by their flight had given color to the charge against them; Ross, Macduff, and presumably the people at large, are inclined to believe them guilty. In the emergency accentuated by their absence Banquo need have yielded to no dishonorable impulse in giving his allegiance to the man who must have seemed to him the strongest and best, in fact the only available candidate for the royal office. That, on second thoughts, he puts two and two together and comes to the conclusion that Macbeth probably played foul, does not prove him to have been selfishly guilty at the outset. Does not his silence convict him, at worst, only of incompetence in dealing with an exceedingly complex situation? [1]

Another curious "silence" in *Macbeth* deserves mention here, even though Bradley considers it "immaterial." He puts it thus: "Whether Macbeth had children or (as seems usually to be supposed) had none, is quite immaterial. But it is material that, if he had none, he looked forward to having one; for otherwise there

---

1. For basic suggestions underlying this view I am indebted to Professor Kittredge.

would be no point in the following words in his soliloquy about
Banquo:

> Then prophet-like
> They hail'd him father to a line of kings;
> Upon my head they placed a fruitless crown,
> And put a barren sceptre in my gripe,
> Thence to be wrench'd with an unlineal hand,
> No son of mine succeeding. If 't be so,
> For Banquo's issue have I filed my mind . . .
> Rather than so, come, fate, into the list
> And champion me to the utterance! (III, i, 59 ff.)

Obviously he contemplates a son of his succeeding, if only he can
get rid of Banquo and Fleance. . . Nothing else matters. Lady
Macbeth's child (I, vii, 54) may be alive or may be dead. . . *It
may be that Macbeth had many children or that he had none.* We
cannot say, and *it does not concern the play.*" [1] Two considerations
seem to me to make against this disposition of the case. In the
first place, if Macbeth had a child or many children, that fact or
even that possibility is, I think, not immaterial. It would seriously
concern the play. That Macbeth at one time "contemplated a son
of his succeeding" is, of course, undeniable, as is the fact that his
undaunted wife might have borne him the men children he wanted.
But the fact that, by the time we reach the middle of the play, far
from having any children, he has only the fear, inspired by the
witches' prophecy, that he never will have any, and the knowledge
that Banquo *has*, is a part of his tragedy, and not the least part of
his bitter fears in Banquo. He challenges fate to meet him, champion to champion, in a duel to the death, less in hope than in the
first stages of desperation. This duel can give him no assurance of
an heir, but it may dispose of Banquo and his issue. For, to pass to
our second consideration, it is inconceivable that Macbeth in his
soliloquy about Banquo and Banquo's children could have failed

---

1. Pages 488 ff. (my italics).

to mention his own, or at least his hopes, had he had any. No
Elizabethan playwright would have failed to take the audience
into his confidence on so vital a point as this — least of all the
dramatist who gave life to young Martius, man child of Coriolanus, to Lady Macbeth's child, and to young Macduff. We know
that Lady Macbeth's child has lived. It is not altogether dead so
far as the play is concerned, for it has taught Lady Macbeth that
it is sweet to be a mother. Macbeth's children taught him nothing
of parental love because he never had any. It is his fate to fall into
the sear, the yellow leaf, in tragic isolation. His wife is lost to him
considerably before the end, and among the consolations of old
age which he must not look to have there is not even the hope or
memory of the love of a child. Shakspere says so not only in
silence but in Macduff's reply to Malcolm after the report of the
murder of Macduff's children,

> *Malcolm.*   Be comforted:
> Let's make us medicines of our great revenge
> To cure this deadly grief.
>
> *Macduff.*   *He has no children.*   All my pretty ones?
> Did you say all? O hell-kite! All?   (IV, iii, 213 ff.)

For the one who has no children is the "hell-kite" of the next line
— the author of Macduff's griefs and the only possible subject of
his thought in this moment of agony — as surely as Lear's "poor
fool" is Cordelia. That the unfledged youngling, "the boy Malcolm," [1] has no children, goes without saying.[2] Shakspere, in such
moments as these, makes his persons *speak*. No flat juxtaposition,
no unmeaning distance in time or space, circumscribes or wings
their words, but immediate, essential love or hate.[3]

---

1. V, iii, 3.   2. For the contrary view, cf. Bradley, pp. 489–492.

3. On the same principle, the "very forward March-chick" upon whom Don John
vents his spite in *Much Ado* (I, iii, 52–71) is "the most exquisite Claudio," the "young
start-up" whom he hates because Claudio had "all the glory" of his overthrow, and whom
he longs to "cross . . . any way." It cannot be right to refer the phrase to Hero, as some
editors (cf. Arden, *Much Ado*, p. 86) do.

Perhaps something like the converse of this principle will serve to explain a case of silence or inhibition in *King Lear* which I mention last because it encroaches upon the final part of our inquiry, — the technique of silence in plot structure. I refer to Edmund's failure to speak, in time, the words which might have stayed the fate of Cordelia. Edmund, towards the end, in acknowledging his crimes to Edgar, speaks darkly of the "more, much more" that time will bring out. He is so far moved by Edgar's report of Gloucester's death as to say that "it shall perchance do good"; but, though he had ordered the captain to dispatch his victims "instantly," he does not make known this last piece of villainy until after the bodies of Goneril and Regan are brought in, when it is too late. This silence or delay, and the consequent disaster, Bradley considers "not . . . satisfactorily motived," for, though "from a wider point of view one may . . . reject with horror the wish for a happy ending, this wider point of view . . . is not strictly dramatic or tragic." [1] But Bradley, in effect, answers his own objections. Perhaps Edmund hesitated in the first place lest his confession embarrass Regan or Goneril, and perhaps he delays finally because "he is sunk in dreamy reflections on his past" ("Yet Edmund was beloved"). In any case, he is a dying man; he listens to Edgar, but he speaks few words of any sort after he receives his mortal hurt. And it may be questioned whether his delay — the delay of a dying man who has behind him a life-long habit of putting himself first, and no experience in the luxury of yielding quickly to unselfish impulses — is inconsistent or undramatic even from a narrow point of view. Yet it would, of course, be folly to deny that Shakspere must have been aware of the usefulness of Edmund's silence from the point of view of plot, in the management of the catastrophe.

1. Pages 253, 302–303.

To the silences which primarily serve Shakspere's plots not a few of his characters make useful contributions. I shall give further illustrations of their services in this kind — after glancing at certain rather more simple if not more fundamental aspects of the technique of silence in the management of plot. Some of these are so simple and self-evident that they have had little systematic notice, and might be thought to require none, were it not for the fact that their cumulative effect and usefulness is anything but negligible. Take, for example, what might be termed the use of silent action for the sake of dramatic compression.

Every intelligent reader of Shakspere is aware of the fact that there are in the plays many scenes between scenes and between acts — scenes that Shakspere did not write, but which cannot safely be ignored,[1] since the off-stage action is sometimes as important as that on the boards. I do not believe, however, that anyone has ever attempted to estimate the relative or cumulative importance of this element as a part of Shakspere's working technique. And yet it is scarcely possible to realize, until one comes to look at the matter closely, how considerably these scenes that Shakspere did not write expedite and diversify the action of the plays, how much they contribute to their setting and atmosphere, and how decidedly they aid in the characterization.

One illustration must suffice for the moment. At the end of Hamlet's scene with his mother (IV, i, 199) he remarks casually, "I must to England; you know that?" The Queen admits that she knew, though she had forgotten. Hamlet, however, has not forgotten, when, a little later, he hears, with a well-managed pretense of the utmost astonishment ("For England!"), the King's announcement that "everything is bent" for the journey. Not a word is said by anyone in the play to indicate how Hamlet got his information. He got it, of course, between scenes — possibly

1. The foregoing discussion of Banquo's guilt, for instance, turns largely on this point.

from friends of whom we hear little, though we know that Horatio is not the only one who loves him; [1] more probably by keeping his own ears open. His words mean that besides playing mad pranks and "hesitating" he has watched every move of his fell opposite with the fierce relish of one who longs to hoist the enginer with his own petard, and with the craft which brings success in this dangerous game. It may be worth while to add that in this one play there are at least a dozen unwritten scenes [2] which, like the one at the bottom of Hamlet's fore-knowledge of the English expedition, further the action. And this reckoning does not include scenes such as that of Ophelia's death, or Hamlet's affair with the pirates, which, though not *staged*, are described at full length.

It is necessary to draw this distinction in order to define our terms as well as may be for what follows. Carefully elaborated descriptive scenes such as these and others like them (the scene on Cleopatra's barge, for instance, and Macbeth's early victory over Macdonwald as described by his "sergeant," or Touchstone at his dial as seen and reported by Jacques) can hardly be numbered among the scenes that Shakspere did not write. Touchstone and

---

1. According to King Claudius, "he's loved" also by "the distracted multitude" (IV, iii, 4).

2. Besides the one mentioned in the text, (2) the unwritten scene in which the Queen learns of the plan to send Hamlet to England (before III, iv); (3) the scene in which Hamlet informs Horatio of "the circumstance *Which I have told thee*" (not on the stage) "of my father's death" (before III, ii, 81); (4) the scene (before III, ii?) in which Hamlet gives the players his "dozen or sixteen lines" for insertion in "The Murder of Gonzago"; (5) the scene, perhaps between the King and Queen, after the springing of the Mousetrap, in which Claudius appears "marvelous distempered" (before III, ii, 312); (6) an early scene between King Claudius and his council, which advised and consented to the marriage of Gertrude and Claudius ("Nor have we herein barred Your better wisdoms, which have freely gone With this affair along" — before I, ii, 14); (7) a later council of war, after the death of Polonius ("we'll call up our wisest friends," — after IV, i, 38); (8) Rosencrantz and Guildenstern "go to 't" (V, ii, 56); (9) and (10) two early appearances of the Ghost to the officers of the watch (before I, i, 25); (11) earlier attempts of the officers to convince Horatio ("Let us once again assail your ears") that they have really seen the Ghost (before I, i, 31); (12) various scenes, before the marriage of Gertrude and Claudius (*i. e.*, before I, iii, 91), in which Hamlet devoted his "private time" to the wooing of Ophelia.

Jacques, however, as Christopher Morley has most pleasantly noted,[1] have "often met"[2] in the forest, though, except through the one delightful report by Jacques,[3] we do not once actually see them by themselves on the stage. In other words, we may fairly count among the scenes which Shakspere did not write a good many others which differ from the scene in *Hamlet* to which I have called attention. That scene is not the only one of its kind [4] which Shakspere boldly asks the audience to take for granted without saying a word about it. There are others at which he barely hints in passing, some that are touched off with a deft phrase or two, and still others that go a little further but, even so, are *suggested* rather than presented.[5] All these are scenes that Shakspere did not write.

Two questions may occur to the reader at this point. Are the instances of "silent action" noted in *Hamlet* really representative and significant — that is to say, do they exemplify a conscious and persistent element of Shakspere's plot management? If so, for what recognizable purposes is it employed?

I referred a moment ago to certain of Shakspere's full-length descriptive scenes. No one doubts for a moment that these are consciously employed to give variety to the action; nor can there be any question but that some of them, while adding lyric grace or pictorial splendor to the setting, serve to compress the action. In *Antony and Cleopatra*, for example, the description of Cleopatra's barge is far more compact than the acted scene on Pompey's galley; yet both scenes are, in the largest sense, essential to the action. Again, everyone recognizes that Shakspere, like every good dram-

1. "So This is Arden. *As You Like It*. Act IV, Scene 2 1/2," *The Literary Review, New York Evening Post*, May 12, 1923.
2. *As You Like It*, V, iv, 42.
3. "I met a fool i' the forest" (II, vii, 12) — for which, to be sure, Touchstone makes more or less graceful acknowledgment in III, iii, 75: "God 'ild you for your last company."
4. For other examples thereof see below, pp. 53–54.
5. Illustrations are given in the pages immediately following.

atist, consciously and consistently attains dramatic compression
in the scenes which he did write by beginning the spoken dialogue
at the end of conversations which open before the scene does — as,
for example, in the scene which presents the Merry Wives [1] ex-
plaining to their husbands, very briefly, what they have done to
Falstaff. Nor, it will be remembered, do they waste time in ex-
plaining what they propose to do for Falstaff thereafter. In short,
it is perfectly evident, generally speaking, that Shakspere knows
the tricks of his trade. Besides, the very abundance and variety of
his materials must have forced him to think of ways and means of
compressing them. Since he certainly used consciously the devices
just referred to, it is scarcely possible to doubt that he knew what
he was about in those unwritten scenes of his which compress so
much important matter into little room.

They serve him, first of all, in exposition. Scenes upon scenes,
some anterior to the action, some coincident with its opening, some
long delayed (like that suggested in the belated supplement to
Othello's account of his wooing — Desdemona's recollection that
Michael Cassio came a-wooing with him) [2] but all essential to the
audience's understanding of its conditions, flash into view for the
briefest moment. A word, an implication, a passing memory, a
jest or a smile to recall old hopes or awaken young desire — and
these scenes are over with, to make way for the current business of
the play. The Ghost in Hamlet, we learn, has appeared twice
before we see him; Hamlet, bereaved, has given gifts and spoken
love in music vows — before his mother remarries; Celia and
Rosalind have been childhood friends; Viola has heard her father
name the noble Duke, Orsino; Signior Benedick and his dear Lady
Disdain have crossed swords (or poniards) in many a drawn battle
of wits before they renew their pleasant combat; Bassanio has

1. IV, iv, 1 ff.
2. I, iii, 127; III, iii, 70 ff. (cf. Bradley, pp. 432 ff.).

made an earlier voyage in search of his golden fleece; Coriolanus has heaped unforgotten scorn upon the plebeians; and Lear, in public or private council, has made known his darker purpose to Gloucester (and, perhaps, indirectly to Goneril and Regan) if not to Kent and Cordelia.

It may be urged, as Professor Bradley does, that some of these scenes are so brief as to be "dramatically faulty."[1] But if, for example, one wonders why no one seems to have told Cordelia what the others seem to know, one does so only long enough to conclude that she would have taken no other action than she did if she had known twice over. The important point, after all, is to recognize the principle that these scenes, brief as they are, define and include all[2] significant initial facts as Shakspere meant his audience to understand them — and that on the whole they do this admirably.

The unwritten scenes, however, are not used for expository purposes only. We have already observed that not only descriptive scenes, such as that of Cleopatra's barge, but also such unwritten scenes as those between Touchstone and Jacques make

1. Though "these tragedies are, in essentials, perfectly dramatic" (pp. 248, 251).
2. In spite of the fact that perverse critical ingenuity has been expended, for example, upon the effort to prove that some scenes, as it were, antedate the exposition: that Macbeth must have sworn to murder Duncan *before the opening* of the play, because he had not explicitly done so in any *written* scene within the play up to the time when Lady Macbeth charges him with cowardice for seeking to evade his oath:

> I have given suck, and know
> How tender 't is to love the babe that milks me;
> I would, while it was smiling in my face,
> Have pluck'd my nipple from his boneless gums
> And dash'd the brains out, *had I so sworn as you
> Have done* to this (II, i, 54 ff.).

But the opening of the play, as Bradley notes (pp. 482 ff.) shows that the idea of murder is new to Macbeth. Nothing *can* antedate the exposition. *If* Macbeth really did swear to "do . . . this" he must have done it between scenes within the play, just as he must have told Lady Macbeth, between scenes, of the air-drawn dagger which, he said, led him to Duncan (III, iv, 62 ff.) and just as Orlando must have sworn between scenes on a less tragic occasion ("But why did [Orlando] swear he would come this morning, and comes not?" — *As You Like It*, III, iv, 20) — for he, like Macbeth, does not so swear in any written scene.

rich contributions to the internal setting and atmosphere of the plays. Still others give invaluable aid in the forwarding of the action. These may be said to fall into two classes, according to their nature and purposes. Both are used, frequently, to indicate the passing of historical or ideal time, though they are all the while actually saving dramatic time. But the first serves especially to give such emphasis as may be required to secondary personages, situations, or moods; to do this — by virtue of silence or quasi-silence — unobtrusively; to keep them in their proper places, yet save them from being lost to view in the crowding of major motives and events. Thus, a brief phrase, a glance afar, or an afterthought or two, reveal many things: Sir Toby Belch woos and wins the redoubtable Maria (or *vice versa*) almost before we know it, besides acquiring a marriage portion at the expense of Sir Andrew Aguecheek;[1] Claudio and Don Pedro, benighted and "afar off" from Hero's chamber-window (and still further off-*stage*) are induced to swallow Don John's monstrous fabrication against Hero's good name;[2] the warring factions at the court of the dying King Edward IV make their sham-peace, and the shallow Lady Anne is first married and then murdered, between scenes, by Richard III, the murderer of all her kin;[3] Romeo, at Juliet's tomb, recalls for a moment the scene of his terrible journey back to Verona, when his "betossed soul did not attend" his servant's news of the proposed marriage of Juliet and the County Paris;[4] and Rosalind in the forest of Arden casually tells Celia how she ran into the good Duke, her father — but without wasting a word in talk about him, for there is Orlando to talk about![5]

I have already illustrated the function of the remaining class of scenes unwritten but not unplotted. Hamlet's keen watch — off-stage — upon his enemies is kept in one of many unwritten scenes

1. *Twelfth Night*, II, iii, 195 ff.; I, v, 29 ff.; III, ii, 58.
2. *Much Ado*, III, iii, 153.   3. *Richard III*, II, i, 1; IV, iii, 39.
4. *Romeo and Juliet*, V, iii, 76.   5. *As You Like It*, III, iv, 38–42.

which help, silently but effectively, in this play and in others, to drive the *main* action to its conclusion. The scene, off-stage once more, in which Hamlet tells Horatio of "the circumstance" of his father's death, is another case in point.[1] So is the encounter of Brutus with Caesar's ghost at Sardis [2] *before* the meeting at Philippi, and Macbeth's unwritten vow (which only Lady Macbeth has heard) to slay the gracious Duncan [3] — not to mention his unwritten scene [4] (before the main one) with the murderers of Banquo, and his off-stage inquiries, referred to in his letter to Lady Macbeth,[5] as to the source and scope of the witches' knowledge.[6]

The technique of silence proved useful to Shakspere for still other purposes which require no elaborate analysis. He employed it, as one might expect, in manipulating his plots to attain surprise and suspense. I have already referred to the pleasant surprise silently arranged for Antonio and the audience by Portia's last-minute news of the safe arrival of the long-lost argosies.[7] Again, one remembers how effectively the wife of Ægeon is made to sink out of sight in the opening scene of *The Comedy of Errors*, and how well hidden she remains, so that she may make the more startling a reappearance in the person of the Abbess at the end.[8] For the rest, it must suffice to recall that Portia, by her silences, achieves pointed suspense as well as pleasant surprise. Her management of the trial scene certainly proves this. Her eloquent plea for mercy

1. See above, p. 49, n. 2.   2. *Julius Caesar*, V, v, 18.

3. See above, p. 52, n. 2.

4. "This I made good to you in our last conference" (III, i, 79 ff.).

5. "I have learn'd by the perfect'st report, they have more in them than mortal knowledge" (I, v, 2).

6. Unwritten scenes are hinted at also in *All's Well*, V, iii, 199 ff.; *King Lear*, III, iii, 2–6, — I, ii, 193–194, 110–111; and in *Much Ado*, III, ii, 76 (Benedick "breaking with" Leonato concerning Beatrice), and II, iii, 140–145 (a rehearsal for the premeditated jests of the Arbor scene?). Many others, no doubt, might be added to the list.

7. See above, p. 28.

8. The family reunions in *The Winter's Tale* and *Pericles* differ from this one in that they do not surprise the audience.

gives Shylock his chance, while his heartlessness is ample excuse for leading him on — and the audience too — to the end, and for the slightly melodramatic quibble about the *pound* of flesh. For though the quibble can scarcely be said to be essential to the dé-nouement (since Portia knows of laws against those that "seek the *life* of any citizen"),[1] she certainly does make it exceedingly effective for stage purposes. While leading Shylock on to whet his knife, she hides her trump card so carefully to the last as to achieve an all but perfect triumph of breathless suspense and breath-taking relief.

Her silence as to her trick, far from being blameworthy, is thoroughly understandable, and, like her plea for mercy, thoroughly in character. It is not altogether possible to say as much for certain other silences — the last to be mentioned in all this unsilent muster. These are "character silences" once more, but character silences of which some, perhaps, are not quite in character, or which, at all events, contribute more to plot than to characterization.

I have already suggested that Edmund's long-continued silence as to his order against the lives of Lear and Cordelia meets fairly equally the requirements of both character and plot.[2] In other cases the balance is not struck so evenly; but some of these are of slight importance, because the characters involved are themselves insignificant. Thus, as I have observed elsewhere in this book,[3] no one cares (or no one *should*, seriously) about the inconsistencies of some of the figureheads — those dukes and kings who, like Theseus in *A Midsummer-Night's Dream* and the crowned heads of *The Two Gentlemen of Verona* and *The Comedy of Errors*, are, on the whole, not much more than lay figures with only an external relationship to the main action. All three of these make silent concessions to the plots in which they are concerned. They begin

1. *Merchant of Venice*, IV, i, 351.   2. See above, p. 47.
3. Cf. Chapter II, p. 77.

by pronouncing the law and the penalty against disobedient daughters, unsuitable suitors, and straying Syracusans; and they end by forgetting, or at least by silently setting aside, the law or the personal objections which had started most of the complications.

Equally negligible from the point of view of characterization, but equally useful, and more curiously interesting as mannikins who render somewhat important service withal in the plot, are the second Hero (she whom Claudio hails as "another Hero") in *Much Ado*, and fair Maudlin in *All's Well*. Each appears but for a moment; neither speaks a word; but neither can well be spared from the action. The "second" Hero is the unknown cousin of the wronged and presumably dead Hero, in whose place Claudio agrees to marry this second victim.[1] I have said that she does not speak a word, and this is literally true; for as soon as Hero number two does speak, it becomes apparent that she is identical with Hero number one.[2] In this connection the question arises whether one aspect of number two's silence must not have seemed a little strange to Claudio, Don Pedro, and the other noble visitors. Did they not think it queer that this cousin of Hero and Beatrice, this daughter of Antonio, Hero's father's brother, managed to keep so silent that no one ever heard of her in all the court festivities, or even suspected her very existence until well into the fifth act?[3] The answer is that Claudio, who was chiefly concerned, was not in a position to consider such questions too curiously. He is confronted with proof of the wrong he has committed, and is glad to accept unconditionally the queer terms of peace which are to bring him an unknown bride the next day. Neither he nor Don Pedro is very subtle anyhow, or they would not have been taken in by

---

1. *Much Ado*, V, i, 298 ff.   2. *Id.*, V, iv, 60 ff.

3. See above, p. 33, n. 2, concerning Antonio's son. Antonio's children are an elusive pair! Macduff (see above, p. 46) might have had Antonio in mind almost as well as Malcolm, for Antonio really has no children either.

Don John's villainy. The audience, finally, being in the secret and on Hero's side (and pleasantly preoccupied to boot, with Dogberry, Benedick and Beatrice, *et al.*), is not likely to think the worse of any convenient device for putting things to rights. The second Hero, therefore, serves well enough for all purposes: to right the wrongs of her supposed predecessor, to test Claudio's penitence, and to give the signal for general satisfaction, if not rejoicing, at the end.

In *All's Well*, fair Maudlin, Lafeu's daughter, does not actually show herself in person at all, but for the rest her function is very similar to that of the second Hero in *Much Ado*. Bertram, more or less like Claudio, has wickedly lost one wife. Like Claudio again, but with a significant difference to be noted presently, he agrees to take another at the behest of those whom he has wronged. This other, fair Maudlin, like Hero number two, vanishes immediately after she has prepared the way for the return of the first wife (Helena) by prevailing upon the culprit to express, through his acceptance of the new affiance, his penitence for the past. That Maudlin should vanish silently is altogether fitting and proper, but — and herein lies the point of difference to be noted — she is not only silent herself but the cause of curious silence in others, and of curious speech, too. When the King, upon taking Bertram back into favor, asks him whether he knows the lady who has been officially chosen to become his second wife, Bertram replies,

> Admiringly, my liege. *At first*
> *I stuck my choice upon her*, ere my heart
> Durst make too bold a herald of my tongue,
> Where the impression of mine eye infixing,
> Contempt his scornful perspective did lend me,
> Which warp'd the line of every other favour . . .
>   Thence it came
> That she whom all men prais'd and whom myself
> Since I have lost, have lov'd, was in mine eye
> The dust that did offend it. (V, iii, 44 ff.)

It is to be noted that the King in his reply virtually ignores Bertram's attempt to justify his conduct toward Helena by this belated discovery of a favored rival. He says, "Well excused," but refers thereby only to Bertram's recent change of heart toward Helena, for he adds at once,

> That thou didst love her, strikes some scores away
> From the great compt; but *love that comes too late*,
> Like a remorseful pardon slowly carried,
> To the great sender turns a sour offence,
> Crying, "*That's good that's gone.*" (V, iii, 55 ff.)

Clearly the "love that comes too late" and the "good that's gone" refer to Bertram's recent love for Helena, and to nothing else. Of Bertram's early infatuation for Maudlin the King says not a word, neither here nor anywhere else in the play; nor does Lafeu, who rarely hesitates to speak what is in his mind on other subjects. Unlike him, some of the critics do not avoid this particular subject. Hertzberg, for example, accepts Bertram's plea at its face value. Bertram, he thinks, was justified in rejecting Helena, because he "already loved another, the chosen of his heart, with all the fire of youth and all the concentrated force of his thoughts and feeling." [1] Elze, who had his doubts about this, points out that if it were so Bertram should have raised this valid objection early in the game, and that Lafeu would have said something about it. But Elze's own explanation [2] does not explain things satisfactorily. He conjectures (1) that the King might have hinted at a match between Bertram and Maudlin before Helena cured him; (2) that the unsuspecting Lafeu "may have" innocently "brought his daughter along" on one of his early visits to the Countess — also before Helena's claims upon Bertram were established; (3) — apparently

---

1. Translated from a quotation by Elze (cf. n. 2), who refers to Hertzberg's *Shakespeare Uebersetzung*, XI, 353, which is not accessible to me.

2. *Shakespeare Jahrbuch* (1872) VII, 225 ff. (Cf. Dowden, *Shakespeare, His Mind and Art*, p. 91, n.)

in spite of (2) — that Bertram probably had no objection to the second bit of royal match-making because Maudlin "is presumably altogether strange to him." Bertram's belated excuse, in other words, is an out-and-out fabrication. Now Bertram is quite capable of lying, but it does not seem likely that Shakspere gave him this speech merely to fasten another lie upon him. Its purpose seems to be to say a good word for him (he needs a good word or two at this point!) but to say it guardedly, for the whole Maudlin episode is managed as unobtrusively as possible, and things are made to happen so rapidly immediately afterwards that the audience has no time to think of the curious silences of *all* concerned. Helena, of course, knew nothing of the Maudlin affair (if there was any.), nor could it be stressed early in the play without ruining Helena's case dramatically. But there is absolutely nothing to indicate that *anyone* knew of it until Bertram's speech. The King, Lafeu, Bertram, Maudlin herself, the Countess, — some of whom must have known, — all remain obstinately and perversely silent concerning the matter. Perhaps the most charitable guess would be that Bertram saw and liked Maudlin from afar once upon a time before Helena arrived to cure the King, and that later, when he sees what seems like a harmless opportunity to make a virtue of a not altogether unpleasant necessity, he politely exaggerates the case. Perhaps he thereby reëstablishes himself momentarily with the audience, which, not having time to put two and two together, may take him at his word. The chances are, in any case, that fair Maudlin was an afterthought on Shakspere's part, and that he invented her little romance in order to strike something off the score against Bertram for the moment. Perhaps it does so in the rush and bustle of the stage, but the silences here invoked make less satisfactory *reading* than most in Shakspere.

This case resembles the few others still to be mentioned. All are instances of "character silences" and all either accelerate or complicate the action under conditions which require more or less aid of this sort — that is to say, when farce or intrigue is the chief motive force. Under such conditions the niceties of characterization are not the first consideration. Thus, it is not surprising that the character of Falstaff plays second fiddle to the jolly intrigues of the Merry Wives. The old Falstaff, whose winged words and wary hesitancies were delightfully adequate for all occasions but one,[1] merely *peeps* once or twice in *The Merry Wives:* he does not really speak. Once, in the second act, he puts a sensible question to Mistress Quickly, — "But, I pray thee, tell me this: has Ford's wife and Page's wife acquainted each other how they love me?" [2] But he swallows her disclaimers, and, later, those of the two principals,[3] without a murmur from first to last, though he is in the meanwhile so tumbled and ducked and kicked about that he should have spoken many a word even though he had been merely a fat log instead of Falstaff fallen upon evil days. Once only, toward the end, there is a flash of the old Falstaff, — in his comment upon Sir Hugh Evans's heavy-footed fairy-masquerade: "Heavens defend me from that Welsh fairy, lest he transform me to a piece of cheese," [4] — but thereafter he relapses into silent ineptitude, which becomes outspoken but all the more gross and palpable when he stoops to moralize upon his fall.

One or two more or less analogous silences in the sub-plot of *King Lear* may also claim another word, though I cannot see that they raise any serious difficulties. Professor Bradley [5] has given sufficient emphasis to the questions that arise if one looks closely at the beginnings of Edmund's intrigue: how Gloucester managed to avoid asking a pointed question or two about the letter ascribed to Edgar, and why Edgar allowed himself to be silently duped,

1. When he first greets the new "King Hal" (*II Henry IV*, V, v, 43 ff.).
2. *The Merry Wives*, II, ii, 113 ff.   3. III, iii, 96 ff.
4. V, v, 85 ff.   5. Pages 256 ff.

with never a word to his father. Shakspere, after all, answers these objections.

> A credulous father and a brother noble,
> Whose nature is so far from doing harms
> That he suspects none (I, ii, 195 ff.),—

why should these two stop to ask questions? Edmund's intrigue succeeds because his father and his brother could not have thought of any good reason to suspect him — because it is so absurdly but boldly impossible that no one but himself (at least no one else in his credulous family) could have imagined it. Again, it justifies itself — and the antecedent silences[1] — on the stage because it precipitates the action at such a pace that there is little or no time for afterthoughts. For much the same reason, the rapidity of the stage action palliates — though it scarcely furnishes an adequate *off-stage* excuse for — Margaret's silence, in *Much Ado*, concerning her share in the dastardly trick[2] played upon Hero.

The situation is somewhat different as regards my last case in point — Emilia's silence about Desdemona's handkerchief. The difficulty here does not arise from the fact that Emilia steals it, in spite of her fondness for Desdemona and in spite of her knowledge of its immense value to Desdemona. Again, it is not merely a matter of accounting for Emilia's failure to connect Othello's

1. See above, p. 52.
2. That Margaret "was not an accomplice is evident, and yet it is difficult to explain how she could have been induced to help forward the conspiracy without knowing it, and at the same time remain silent when a word from her would have explained the mystery. This is the defect in the plot" (W. A. Wright; cf. Furness, Variorum *Much Ado*, pp. 102–103). Furness observes that this defect is not noticed on the stage, but adds, that "for aught we know" early in the play, Margaret may have been "none too good to enter fully into the plot." Margaret, however, is mischievous rather than base; and Shakspere makes Leonato say plainly that so far as she was at fault it was "against her will" (V, iv, 5). Her greatest fault is her acquaintance with the lewd Borachio (V, i, 342). To do her justice, we should remember, (1) that the conspiracy is uncovered almost before she could have acted; (2) that Borachio, with whom she would naturally have wished to consult before confessing, was under arrest and beyond her reach (or, as Furness puts it, that a confession which might have saved her mistress "would also carry with it the ruin of her lover").

jealousy with the loss of the handkerchief, or her failure to suspect
Iago — for, so far at least as Iago is concerned, she is no more
blind than anybody else in the play. That she did fail to make this
connection appears clearly [1] from her heart-broken outcry at the
end — "O God, O heavenly God!" — when Othello finally brings
up the handkerchief as evidence against Desdemona. The trouble
is that considerably *before* the end, an ambiguous speech of
Emilia's,

> I will be hang'd if some eternal villain,
> Some busy and insinuating rogue,
> Some cogging, cozening slave, *to get some office*,
> Have not devis'd this slander (IV, ii, 130 ff.),

reminds the audience — which cannot be expected to foresee the
end — of the queer circumstances of the original theft, and of the
strangeness of Emilia's continued silence — since her speech
sounds, for the moment, as though she did suspect Iago. And this
ambiguity is repeated before Emilia's final outcry, as already indicated, clears away the confusion. Shortly before this moment
comes she screams out hysterically,

> I think upon 't, — I think I smell 't, — O villainy!
> I thought so then, — I'll kill myself for grief —
> O villainy, villainy! (V, ii, 191 ff.)

Now this "I thought so then" in view of her final outcry can refer
only to her general fear of some undetermined act of villainy, but,
coming as it does on top of the previous ambiguity, may easily be
mistaken for a confirmation of her supposed suspicion of Iago.

The end clears away these difficulties. It makes certain that if
Emilia had known, her loyalty would have spoken out; that she
would have confessed her theft in time, in spite of any remaining
fear of Iago,[2] or loyalty to him, or of any other feeling. Emilia,

1. Cf. notes by Cowden-Clarke, Rolfe, and others, in Furness, Variorum, IV, ii, 154;
V, ii, 185, pp. 266, 312; and Bradley, pp. 240, 439 ff.
2. Cf. in H. C. Hart's edition of the play, note on III, iii, 297, p. 147.

then, stands convicted, at worst, merely of "gross stupidity." [1] It is gross stupidity indeed, for Iago had wooed her "a hundred times" to steal the handkerchief — and Emilia seems to have an adequate allowance of common sense in most other respects. It is to be remembered, however, that she, like everyone else, is so completely taken in by Iago that any amount of stupidity would have seemed more reasonable to her than the possibility of suspecting him of the outrage he had actually committed. Finally, though it may be that Shakspere did not stage the intermediate phases of Emilia's silence as skillfully as he might have done, he made it none the less a tragic fact. She pays, for her theft and her stupidity — and, all things considered, she pays royally.

Shakspere, might, to be sure, have managed the handkerchief episode without the aid of Emilia's silence; and he might, conceivably, have written *Othello* without the handkerchief episode. Indeed, he might perhaps have told his stories and drawn his characters at large without recourse to silence, whether by way of a conscious technique or otherwise.[2] If he had done so he might have saved himself a few infelicities, but he would surely have lost graces beyond number and power beyond measure. For the greatest moments in the plays as they stand are moments of mingled harmony. In their music heard melodies and those unheard blend together. And this music rings through the eternal silence.

1. Cf. Bradley, p. 240.   2. Cf. "Epilogue," below, pp. 257 ff.

Chapter II

SHAKSPERE AND THE UNHAPPY HAPPY ENDING[1]

A HAPPY END—thus runs the burden of a song by one of the "uncertain" authors of *Tottel's Miscellany* — "A happy ende exceadeth all." It is a sentiment, so we are often reminded, by no means unknown to the greatest of the Elizabethans. Indeed, according to the consensus of critical opinion, All's Well That Ends Well would seem to be the false divinity that, from first to last, shaped the ends of all too many of Shakspere's comedies. Thus, Mr. H. C. Hart, in the Arden edition of *Love's Labour's Lost*, states that that play disintegrates (has "broken down") by the time the last scenes get under way; and Sir Arthur Quiller-Couch, speaking, in effect, for a host of others, holds that the ending of *The Two Gentlemen of Verona* "blows all character to the winds." "For stage effect Valentine must surrender his true love to his false friend with a mawkish generosity that deserves nothing so much as kicking."[2] A more or less similar judgment has been pronounced upon some of the great romantic comedies, the problem plays, and the dramatic romances. Armado, in *Love's Labour's Lost* (IV, i, 77), touches upon the essential point. "The catastrophe," says he, "is a nuptial." All the critics would agree that this proposition and its converse are equally incontrovertible. *As You Like It*, for instance, is marred, according to Swinburne,[3] by that "one unlucky smear on one corner of the canvas . . . the be-

---

1. Reprinted, with additions, from *PMLA*, XLII (1927), 736 ff.
2. *Shakespeare's Workmanship*, p. 67.
3. *Shakespeare*, p. 152; cf. Furness, Variorum *As You Like It*, p. 252.

trothal of Oliver to Celia," a "sacrifice" (like the concluding marital
sacrifices in *Much Ado*, *All's Well*, *Measure for Measure*, *Cymbeline*, and other plays) falsely motivated by "the actual or hypothetical necessity of pairing off all the couples" so as "to secure a
nominally happy and undeniably matrimonial ending." "In the
Fifth Act," says Hartley Coleridge, "ladies have no time for discretion" [1] — nor gentlemen either, if we may believe his fellow
critics. By the fifth act, as Quiller-Couch would have it in the outburst already referred to, "there are *no* Gentlemen in Verona"; and
so — allowing only for change of scene, as the case may require,
to Messina, Roussillon, Vienna, Sicily, or Ancient Britain — says
many another commentator. "Kill Claudio," the command of
Beatrice to Benedick,[2] springs out of a fine and humanly altogether
excellent moment of white-hot anger, but Coleridge and Dr. Johnson [3] would do as much in cold blood for Angelo in *Measure for
Measure*. Helena (in *All's Well*), says Lounsbury,[4] is "untrue to
her sex" in pursuing and finally marrying Bertram; and "frankly
unfeminine," according to Professor Brander Matthews' account [5]
of the conclusion of *A Winter's Tale*, is Hermione's forgiveness of
her husband "without one word of reproach." Hartley Coleridge,[6]
finally, urges that "the exhibition of such madness of heart" as
that of Leontes in this play — to which instance Mr. G. C. Macauley [7] adds, by implication, that of Posthumus in *Cymbeline* —
"should be confined to the sternest tragedy," since such sinners
could "surely never again be worthy of a restoration to happiness."
And all this sacrifice of poetic justice and psychological truth, this

1. *As You Like It*, Furness, Variorum, p. 252.
2. *Much Ado*, IV, i, 291.
3. Coleridge, *Literary Remains* (for citations cf. *Measure*, Arden ed., p. xxiii); Johnson's *Shakespeare* (1765), I, 378.
4. *Shakespeare as a Dramatic Artist*, p. 390.
5. *Shakespeare as a Playwright*, p. 338.
6. *Essays and Marginalia* (for citations cf. *Winter's Tale*, First Folio ed., p. 277).
7. *Cambridge History of English Literature*, VI, 124.

"holocaust of higher and better feelings" (to quote Swinburne once more),[1] is exacted by our "theatrical idol," the conventional happy ending: "the . . . liquorish desire to leave the board of fancy with a palatable morsel of cheap sugar on the tongue." In a word, the unhappy happy ending ("nominally happy and undeniably matrimonial") — this really would seem to have been the fatal Cleopatra for which Shakspere lost his sense of humor — not to mention his artistic conscience — and was content to lose it.

Perhaps he did. Before coming to grips with the problem at closer range, it may be well to consider one or two of the antecedent probabilities. Listen for a moment to Malachi of the Long Glen, speaking in Donn Byrne's *Messer Marco Polo:*

> The people aren't as wise as they used to be, brown lad. The end of a story now is a bit of kissing and courting and the kettle boiling to be making tea. But the older ones were wiser, Brian Donn. They knew that the rhythm of life is long and swinging, and that time doesn't stop short as a clock . . . But a story is how destiny is interwoven, the fine and gallant and the tragic points of life . . . Oftentimes the stories that grocer's daughters do not be liking are the stories that are worth while. And the worth-while stories do be lasting . . .
>
> I call to your mind the stories of the great English writer — the plays of the Prince of Denmark and the poor blind king on the cliff and the Scottish chieftain and his terrible wife. The Widow Robinson will not like those stories, and she will be keeping her white coin . . . But those stories will endure forever.[2]

And so they will. These plays, however, are tragedies. Have they not, therefore, very little to do with the case? This much only: in *Hamlet* and *Macbeth* Shakspere profoundly deepened the tragic outcome of the familiar stories he found in his sources. And in the case of *Lear* he actually ignored the traditional outcome of the story as reported by the chroniclers — which is favorable to Lear and Cordelia — and the distinctly happy ending of the practically

1. See above, p. 64, n. 3.
2. Quoted by permission of The Century Company.

contemporary chronicle play of *King Leir*. This familiar fact is of no slight significance. It proves definitely that Shakspere was capable of exercising independent judgment even in the treatment of familiar stories — capable, at least on occasion, of flying in the face of the happy enders and of theatrical convention. There has been a tendency of late, it seems to me, to overemphasize the undoubtedly important fact that Shakspere was strongly influenced by current dramatic conventions, modes, and fashions. The counterbalancing probability, that he knew his own mind and art at least as well as that of his contemporaries, and that in general he used dramatic conventions (for example, the dramatic unities, the conventions of Plautine comedy and of Senecan tragedy) not slavishly but eclectically and critically, bids fair to be forgotten. Thus, Professor W. W. Lawrence, in an admirable study of the mediæval background of *All's Well*, states that "the problem plays . . . were written with the solutions fixed in advance, and fixed by the convictions of the Elizabethan age "[1] — a statement undeniably sound so far as it goes, but — except as qualified thereafter — open to misinterpretation in that it seems for the moment to put aside the dramatist's artistic responsibility for the management of his story and characterization. In so far it plays into the hands of those who suggest or imply that in the dark comedies or in the other comedies Shakspere yielded carelessly, and rather blindly, to the convention of the happy ending. His making over of the old *King Leir* is, in my judgment, but one of several indications that point in the other direction. And, even though it be objected that in this case he could afford to make the change because tragedy may for the moment have been in greater demand than tragicomedy, the fact remains that here he must have found a fresh occasion — when he was at the height of his career and shortly before he started upon the dramatic romances — for thinking

1. *PMLA*, XXXVII, 464.

about the public's appetite for the happy ending, and about the artist's duty to make the ending consonant and harmonious with the whole of the play, that is to say, with characterization. I say the case gave him "a fresh occasion" because, as will appear presently, he had certainly thought of the problem long before — that is to say, before he had finished his first play, *Love's Labour's Lost*. As regards the tragedies, meanwhile, no one questions the principle that the end must be in psychological accord with the means, indeed that it must crown the whole. With respect to the comedies, on the other hand, it is customary to urge in defence of the conventional ending certain excuses which sound plausible enough but do not after all meet the case.

The best excuse for the happy ending is that it satisfies (in Lounsbury's phrase) "that characteristic of human nature which prefers a fortunate ending of any story said or sung to a sad one," [1] a characteristic so obviously and powerfully operative to-day that it requires no illustration.[2] In recognizing this characteristic of human nature the Elizabethans had, of course, ample authority in the theory and practice of the fathers. "Diversity of character, seriousness, tenderness, hope . . . variety of events, changes of fortune, unexpected disaster . . . and a happy ending" are among the recognized elements of comedy set down by Cicero [3] and adopted in the earliest critical writings of the Middle Ages.[4] And these elements were, of course, utilized for better or for worse from first to last — in the *Alcestis* of Euripides, for example, in the Plautine comedy of intrigue and the Terentian comedy of sentiment, in the early Elizabethan academic imitations thereof, and in

1. Pages 308–309.

2. Though one is tempted to recall the late B. L. T.'s indignant protests against movie producers who ruthlessly violate O. Henry's best stories by screening them with stupidly impossible happy endings.

3. *Rhetor ad Herenn.*, Lib. 1 (quoted by Steele in the motto of *The Conscious Lovers*).

4. Chambers, *Medieval Stage*, II, 209, cites the *Catholicon* (1286) of Johannes Januensis: "Comœdia a tristibus incipit sed cum lætis desinit."

the indigenous development of romantic comedy: not without reservations by Peele (who, in *The Old Wives Tale*, pokes fun at the happy ending), but whole-heartedly by Greene, in *James IV* and *Friar Bacon and Friar Bungay* — to mention no earlier instances among the "old plays" in which, as Shakspere himself reminds us,[1] each Jack had his Jill in the end. In one sense, indeed, the dispensing of large morsels of "cheap sugar" at the end of a comedy was perhaps even more distinctly to the taste of the Elizabethans than to that of these aftertimes, strong as the craving for the confection remains, simply because the Elizabethans had sturdier stomachs than we. A stage strewn with corpses at the end of a tragedy, or with potential newlyweds or reconciled elders at the end of a comedy, satisfied the taste of lordlings and groundlings alike, for strong effects.

Human nature craves a happy ending at any cost, and Shakspere's predecessors and contemporaries had given him ample precedent for satisfying the craving. To these two explanations of Shakspere's supposedly unqualified yielding to the convention still another has been added, and this involves a slight enlargement of the field of our inquiry which must be taken into account in this preliminary survey of the conditions. "In many of [Shakspere's] plays," said Dr. Johnson,[2] "the latter part is evidently neglected. When he found himself near the end of his work and in view of his reward, he shortened the labour to snatch the profit." Many later critics [3] have quoted this dictum of Johnson with approval, and even to-day the prevailing critical opinion still holds Shakspere guilty of hasty terminal workmanship, especially in the comedies,[4] where the hasty ending is almost of necessity practically

1. See below, p. 72.   2. *Preface*, 1765.
3. Cf., for example, n. 4 and p. 91, n. 3, below. The only notable exception to the usual view of which I know is that of Hazlitt: "Dr. Johnson is of the opinion that Shakspere was generally inattentive to the winding up of his plots. We might think the contrary true" (on "Cymbeline," in *Characters of Shakespeare's Plays*).
4. Cf. E. P. Kuhl, *PMLA*, XL, 567, n. 1, *ad fin.*

identical with the conventional ending. Professor W. W. Lawrence [1] accounts for the "singular abruptness" which he finds in
the "final unravelling" of many of Shakspere's comic plots partly
on the ground that the poet recognizes the audience's impatience
"when the end of the piece has obviously arrived." "We all
know," Mr. Lawrence observes, "the restlessness in the modern
theater in the last five minutes of the average play." A plausible
suggestion on the face of it — but the question remains whether it
goes to the root of our problem. For one thing (as Professor J. Q.
Adams reminds me) Elizabethan audiences were not in the habit
of rushing off the moment the play was over, for in those days "*the
jig* was called for when the play was done." We know, moreover,
that in the tragedies Shakspere, like other great artists, shaped
many a well-rounded story into a consciously wrought beginning,
middle, and end; that in them his characters live and move and
have their being in artistic and psychological accord with the end
as well as the means of the action. Did he knowingly neglect or
violate this cardinal principle of dramatic art by yielding unqualifiedly to the conventional subterfuge of the artificial happy ending
in the comedies?

I shall review the evidence bearing upon this question by glancing at representative instances of his practice, in chronological
order. In doing so, however, I must premise that I am here concerned with essentials only. That Shakspere throughout his career, in the endings of his plays as well as in their beginnings,
handled details — minor persons and events — with something of
what Barrett Wendell termed "the carelessness of disdainful mastery," I should not for a moment wish to deny. Nor would I question the fact that in certain of the plays — such, for instance, as
A Midsummer-Night's Dream — the problem of characterization,
and hence of an ending in consonance therewith, is not of prime

1. *PMLA*, XXXVII, 468.

importance. In my discussion I shall have occasion to return to Dr. Johnson's charge of hasty terminal workmanship, and to indicate that it is partly based upon his disapproval of Shakspere's refusal to load the end of his plays with outspoken didacticism. For to Dr. Johnson, it will be remembered, Shakspere seemed "to write without any moral purpose . . . His precepts and axioms drop casually from him. . . . At the close [he] dismisses [the moral] without further care." [1] It will appear, I think, that the critics have followed Johnson in complaining of Shakspere's hasty endings without recalling what it was the good doctor missed at the end. Upon Johnson's authority, and on the assumption that Shakspere must have accepted the convention of the happy ending, many a bit of hasty or inverted criticism has been propounded.

Of the early comedies, *Love's Labour's Lost*, *The Two Gentlemen*, and *A Midsummer-Night's Dream* especially demand attention here. We must begin with the beginning — with *Love's Labour's Lost*; but it will be well to bear in mind that these three early plays are alike in that all three primarily exploit a special theme or occasion rather than characterization. *Love's Labour's Lost* writes large the finding that "young blood doth not obey an old decree"; *The Two Gentlemen* dramatizes afresh the favorite Elizabethan theme of the sacred claims of friendship; and *A Midsummer-Night's Dream* is a graceful fairy masque, a dramatic prothalamion. Characterization in these plays being, on the whole, subordinated to other interests, one may expect to find them a happy hunting ground for the critics who want above all "truth to the facts of life" in the final disposition of the characters. Whatever may be said of the three plays on this score, this much is certain: Shakspere's first play most certainly does *not* flicker out into a conventional happy ending. Indeed, it defies the happy enders. The King of Navarre and his three lords, after acknowledging themselves

1. *Preface.*

forsworn and after having all but won over the four ladies, are suddenly estopped from victory. News comes of the death of the
Princess's father, and therewith the men are sent off for a year's
probation; a savage probation in the case of the jolly Biron, who
is sent to

> Visit the speechless sick, and still converse
> With groaning wretches

— his task, "with all the fierce endeavor" of his wit,

> To enforce the pained impotent to smile . . .
> To move wild laughter in the throat of death. . . .

No wonder he complains to the king:

> Our wooing doth end not like an old play:
> Jack hath not Jill. These ladies' courtesy
> Might well have made our play a comedy.

As Professor Baker[1] stated a number of years ago, "no wholly
satisfactory reason" has yet been suggested for this "curious ending," although recently Professor Austin Gray[2] has offered a most
interesting and ingenious explanation for it. The evasion or post-
ponement of the marriage issue, according to Mr. Gray, shadows
forth allegorically the determination of Shakspere's patron, the
Earl of Southampton, to avoid or postpone a marriage with the
granddaughter of his guardian, Lord Burleigh. Tempting and per-
suasive as is Mr. Gray's argument in this connection, I find it difficult to reconcile the main tendency of the play — the appeal to
"affection's men at arms" to eschew artificial vows of celibacy and
to enjoy rationally the delights of youth and beauty—with an interpretation which would make of the play chiefly an allegorical
travesty upon a threatened case of enforced marriage. And if
Biron is Southampton, the savage task assigned to him at the end

---

1. *Shakespeare's Development as a Dramatist*, pp. 107–108.
2. "The Secret of *Love's Labour's Lost*," *PMLA*, XXXIX, 581.

would seem to strike an even more incongruous note [1] than it does otherwise. In any case Shakspere would seem to have been pleasantly conscious of the fact that in his ending he was not following the beaten path. Nor should it be forgotten that even thus early in his career his knowledge of life and of books — witness the ending of Chaucer's *Parlement of Foules*,[2] and of the first book of the *Faerie Queene*, where the Red Cross Knight must return for six years of service after getting himself betrothed to the Lady Una — might have suggested to him that young lovers can sometimes afford to wait a year.[3] Even so, the ending of *Love Labour's Lost* is distinctly Shakspere's own.

It has generally been felt that in *The Two Gentlemen* he achieved a perfect specimen of the unhappy happy ending. To Pope [4] the dénouement of this piece seemed "very odd," and his opinion is about as mildly put as any. That this is the most lame and impotent conclusion of them all, that it constitutes a "violation of the truth of life," "a complete confession of dramatic ineptitude," that it is simply "quite out of nature," "wholly unconvincing," and "absurd," [5] is the all but unanimous verdict of outstanding critics and commentators, all the way from Hanmer, Johnson, and Coleridge to Lounsbury, Baker, Brander Matthews, and Quiller-Couch — at least three of whom thought the ending so bad that Shakspere could not have written it. On the other hand, the ra-

1. Cf. Baker, p. 113: "The very playfulness of the whole treatment of love throughout . . . makes the grave note of service . . . at the end seem incongruous."
2. A likeness noted by Furnivall. Cf. *L.L.L.*, Variorum ed., p. 363.
3. Cf. Hart's view (cited above, p. 64), that this closing development "breaks down" the mainspring of the play. Professor Royster, on the other hand, finds here "the most skilful part of the comedy" because, with the mention of the death of the Princess's father, "the women cease their mocks and the men cast off their masks of insincerity. . . . They become, in the twinkling of an eye, serious men and women" (*L.L.L.*, Tudor ed., p. xvi).
4. See *The Two Gentlemen*, First Folio ed. (Porter and Clarke), and critical works cited in previous notes, for the opinions quoted immediately below.
5. For an interpretation which goes dangerously near the other extreme see First Folio ed. of the play (Porter and Clarke).

tionale of the thing has been effectively set forth once or twice, especially by Professor Sampson in the Tudor edition.[1] My reason for returning to it at some length is that the old misconceptions seem to flourish as vigorously as ever, and that a review of the whole matter will throw some light upon the remainder of our discussion. I need hardly say that I am not engaged here or elsewhere in this study in seeking to whitewash Shakspere. Certainly Neilson [2] is altogether right in pronouncing this ending "unskilful." It is, however, by no means so blind or incomprehensible as it is almost always represented; and much of the criticism lavished upon it is simply beside the point.

Let us recall the difficulties. (1) The fickle Proteus forgets his love for Julia (who follows him disguised as a page), betrays his faithful friend Valentine, and threatens force to win Silvia — in the forest — after Sir Eglamour, her protector, has run away. Sir Eglamour's unceremonious exit is the first hurdle to stop the critics. (2) Valentine, who has captained the outlaws and has seen and heard Proteus's villainy, charges him with treachery — more especially with falsehood to friendship. Proteus is shamed and asks pardon. Valentine, the perfect friend, grants this, and, to heap coals of fire upon the head of the late offender, resigns the lady to him:

> And that my love may appear plain and free
> All that was mine in Silvia I give thee.

(3) Julia, present in disguise, speaks up and reveals herself; whereupon Proteus's wandering affections immediately return to her — Silvia remaining silent the while. (4) The Duke, who had exiled Valentine rather than accept him as a son-in-law, changes his mind without winking an eyelash. Of these several difficulties, the second — the "mawkish generosity" of Valentine in offering to

1. See also W. W. Lawrence, *PMLA*, XXXVII, 468.
2. Cambridge *Shakespeare*, p. 51.

surrender Silvia to Proteus — is, of course, the gravest. It led
Hanmer and Coleridge severally to denounce as corrupt the couplet I have quoted, and with it the whole ending. Against this view
many editors have urged, with Dr. Johnson and Malone,[1] that
"from mere inferiority" — or immaturity — "nothing can be in-
ferred"; and others have seen [2] that to eliminate this passage is to
cut into the vitals of the play. As recently as 1921, however,
Quiller-Couch and J. Dover Wilson, in their (Cambridge) edition
of the play, have once more insisted that this part of the ending
cannot be Shakspere's. Their chief objections correspond to those
enumerated above. They conclude that the couplet in question,
and most of the other "anomalies" noted, are assignable to an unknown adapter, or to the actors. This conclusion can only be described as a total misunderstanding of what Shakspere was about.
His play, as the title indicates, concerns primarily the friendship of
the two gentlemen, who are types of the perfectly faithful and of
the absolutely faithless friend. The piece is Shakspere's most elaborate essay in the friendship theme, a theme everywhere alive and
active in Elizabethan literature.[3] It appears prominently in *Euphues*, in the *Arcadia*, and in other romances early and late; in the
sonnets (notably in Shakspere's sonnet No. 42), and everywhere
in other lyrics; as also in Shakspere's other plays, especially in
The Merchant of Venice (in which Bassanio tells Antonio that "life
itself, *my wife*, and all the world" are not with him "esteemed
above" Antonio's safety), and in *The Winter's Tale* and *Twelfth
Night*. The theme was a commonplace, moreover, in the work of
Shakspere's fellow dramatists. Lyly's treatment of it in *Endy-
mion* [4] is close to that of *The Two Gentlemen*, and one aspect or an-

1. Cf. Johnson's note on *III Henry VI*, in his *Shakespeare*, V, 225; Malone–Boswell,
Shakspeare, IV, 131; Lounsbury, pp. 387–388.

2. See p. 74 and n. 1, above.

3. On this subject cf. Introduction, Tudor ed. of the play, and Minto, *Characteristics
of English Poets*, p. 215.   4. III, iv, 130–180.

other of it is made much of in plays ranging all the way from
Edwards's *Damon and Pythias* to Greene's *Friar Bacon* and Marlowe's *Edward II*.

In *The Two Gentlemen* the keynote is struck at the start.
"Sweet Valentine" and his "loving Proteus," we learn, from their
infancy have conversed and spent their hours together.[1] In the
course of his betrayal Proteus in so many words admits his
"treachery" to his friend and to his code, "the law of friendship,"[2]
though he dismisses it for the moment: "I to myself am dearer
than my friend." Silvia, of course, forcibly reminds him of his
evil-doing — to her he is "subtle, perjured, false, disloyal," a
"counterfeit" to his "true friend."[3] Valentine himself, a youthful sentimentalist who has had much time to feed his fancy while
superintending his comic-opera outlaws in the greenwood,[4] drives
home the point:

> Thou common friend that's without faith or love . . .
> O time . . . accurst,
> 'Mongst all foes that a friend should be the worst.

Proteus thereupon acknowledges his fault, and Valentine, in the
supposed exaltation of the moment, offers the supreme sacrifice to
friendship — a Silvia for a Proteus. It is quixotic, of course, and
very silly; but not nearly so important or tragic as the critics
suggest. Silvia remains silent, not, as is universally supposed, because she is struck to the heart. She is merely breathless after her
struggle and fright.[5] Moreover, she knows her Valentine and his
fine sentimental whimsies [6] — and she will have plenty of time to
talk later! For the moment Julia, who has as much at stake as
anybody, but hasn't had a chance to say a word, very naturally
breaks in and, after a momentary swoon, takes command of the

1. I, i, 1, 11; II, iv, 62.   2. II, vi, 32; III, i, 4.
3. IV, ii, 95; V, iv, 53.   4. See opening of V, iv.
5. V, iv, 58–60.   6. II, iv, 1–115, 157–185.

situation. That Proteus relapses so speedily to his first love, and that Julia is willing to take him back, may seem incredible — unless one chooses to remember that such things do happen in real life. It is fairly evident, at all events, that Shakspere seems not to have taken the fickleness of young blades too seriously — witness the analogous instances of Romeo and Rosaline, and of Demetrius and Helena in *A Midsummer-Night's Dream*. Julia, moreover, is very much in love, and she, at least, knows all sides of her bargain. To the general problem of the restoration to favor of hardened young sinners such as Proteus, Bertram, and their ilk, I shall have to return later.[1]

The remaining anomalies are merely characteristic instances of Shakspere's free and easy workmanship in the early plays. He does not bother to explain why the brave Sir Eglamour ran away. The man had to be got out of the way — and out he goes. Sir Eglamour is of little account anyhow, and might well have been left out altogether. The Duke's convenient change of front is explicable on the same general principle — a principle operative also in the later plays. Obviously there is a vast difference between those of Shakspere's kings (or dukes) who are also human beings with large potentiality for good or evil — such as King Claudius, and Richard II, and, in my judgment, the Duke in *Measure for Measure*[2] — and those who are only nonentities in royal robes, such as the three dukes of the early comedies and Duke Frederick, the usurper of *As You Like It*. His royal highness of *The Two Gentlemen* swallows his objections without a gulp. His brothers in *A Midsummer-Night's Dream* and in *The Comedy of Errors* politely end by setting aside the law of the land — against undutiful daughters and straying Syracusans, respectively — the sanctity of which they had proclaimed from the housetops at the start. Similarly, Duke Frederick in *As You Like It* begins with an act of vio-

1. See below, pp. 83-85.   2. See below, p. 87.

lent usurpation and ends with an equally violent conversion and
renunciation. But these things and personages belong to the non-
essentials of which I spoke at first. It might be argued that they
are merely tyrants, above the law of the land and the law of plau-
sibility. It is more to the point to remember that they are lay
figures: humanly and dramatically speaking they equal not much
more than zero, and zero inverted at the happy end is zero still. As
regards *The Two Gentlemen*, finally, it is only fair to add that its
final disposition of the characters is in keeping with the slightness
of characterization throughout, and that its chorus hymeneal is
merely an unskillful postlude to the coronation march of the faithful friend.

With the later comedies I shall have to deal in more general
terms, but I must first return briefly to *A Midsummer-Night's
Dream* and to the three farcical plays, *A Comedy of Errors*, *The
Taming of the Shrew*, and *The Merry Wives*. *A Midsummer-
Night's Dream* also has an undeniably matrimonial close, but this
is altogether as it should be in a prothalamion. Here if ever, as
Puck reminds us,

<blockquote>
Jack *shall* have Jill,
Nought shall go ill,
</blockquote>

and no questions asked. No one can help seeing that from the
start two-and-a-half of the couples are sufficiently in love for all
practical purposes: and Oberon himself, by charming the eye of
the fickle Demetrius, spares us the trouble of worrying about the
future happiness of that gentleman and his lady. As for the farcical comedies, no one, to my knowledge, objects to their endings on
the score of conventionality. Everyone is agreed that sweet Anne
Page and Petruchio, Falstaff and Katherine, all work out their
own salvation or damnation, as the case may be. Everyone admits, too, that the ending of *The Comedy of Errors* (with the possible reservation already noted) is admirably managed, especially in

view of the fact that the play is early and follows, at this point, a source of indifferent merit. Luciana and the Syracusan Antipholus do, of course, fall in love at first sight — an excellent thing according to the principle so eloquently and frequently set forth by Marlowe and Shakspere, and according to that other favorite Elizabethan maxim,

> Thrice blessed is the wooing
> That is not long a-doing.

Even so, Shakspere is careful to indicate early in the play that Luciana is quite ready to entertain the joys and pains of the blessed state.[1] For the rest, Ægeon and his wife are reunited by a well-motivated and well-merited accident; and Dromio number one remains in undisputed possession of that mountain of mad flesh, his kitchen wench, while his brother, in spite of the happy enders, is left with never a morsel to stay his stomach. And the troubles of the jealous Adriana with her somewhat free and easy husband are quite properly brought to a conclusion in which nothing is concluded.

We now come to the later comedies, the plays, pleasant and unpleasant, which are at once the fine flower and the fruit of Shakspere's work in this kind. To begin with *The Merchant of Venice*, Portia's happiness does not altogether depend upon the blind verdict of the caskets. Of all the candidates available she chooses the one to whom her eyes had given fair messages long before her music reminds him where fancy is bred. Nor are we left in doubt as to her competency to manage Bassanio in the sequel. Bradley [2] felt that in Shylock Shakspere "drew a figure with which the destined pleasant ending would not harmonize," but in this case both the instinctive reaction of children and the seasoned balance of critical opinion run counter to Bradley. Tremendously vital and signifi-

1. *Comedy of Errors*, II, i, 26–42.
2. *Shakespearean Tragedy*, p. 21, quoted by Baker, *op. cit.*, pp. 268–269.

cant as Shylock is, not Shakspere but Sir Henry Irving made him a consistently tragic figure. Shakspere wove the pattern of his play with both dark and gay threads, but the happy and gracious colors of Belmont are made to dominate the dark shades of Venice, at first, and still more at the close. Perhaps Shakspere pulled the strings a bit at the end,[1] when three of Antonio's argosies "richly come to harbor suddenly." But the good that ill winds blow is sometimes slow in coming to harbor, and we might remember that the account of Antonio's losses at first was kept by that careless female bookkeeper, "gossip report," who is *not* always "an honest woman of her word." [2]

The case is somewhat altered in *As You Like It*. Here Shakspere himself may be held accountable for conveying certain early impressions which in one sense justify Swinburne's lament about the end. Possibly Hartley Coleridge is right in suggesting that "Oliver is made too bad in the first scenes." The real difficulty in the unpleasant comedies and the dramatic romances (though criticism as a whole has ignored it) lies not so much in the happy end as in the unhappy beginning. Forgiveness may be earned by the agony of expiation, prolonged through years or concentrated in a single day. But the reader, on turning back the pages, may be distressed to recall how wicked Leontes and Posthumus and Oliver were at the outset. Suppose it be granted, however, that Shakspere, like his mediæval forebears in and out of the drama,[3] somewhat overcharged his early effects. The real point is that Shakspere's audiences had no earlier pages to turn back to. Shakspere counts upon the actor's art not only to startle us into attention at the outset but also to realize — and humanize — the end.

In another sense, however, all this does not seriously matter so far as *As You Like It* is concerned. The mating of Celia and Oliver,

1. As suggested by Quiller-Couch, p. 97.   2. *M. of V.*, III, i, 6–7.

3. The writers of the miracles and moralities, and Chaucer (witness the impossible husband in the Clerk's tale of Griselda).

after all, is not of much more consequence to the play than that of Phebe and Silvius. The couples who have a more essential being — Touchstone and Audrey, Orlando and Rosalind — are delightfully provided for from first to last, in spite of Quiller-Couch's [1] doleful foreboding that Orlando is fated to be loved but nagged all his life through. Again, Duke Frederick's about-face, as we have already seen, is not to be taken too seriously. Dr. Johnson lamented that Shakspere did not pause at this point to drive the moral home:

> By hastening to the end of his work, Shakespeare suppressed the dialogue between the usurper and the hermit and lost an opportunity of exhibiting a moral lesson in which he might have found matter worthy of his highest powers.[2]

Though later critics do not share Johnson's regret over the lost moral opportunities, they continue to deprecate these "hasty endings." Indeed, I am not sure whether the outspoken strictures of Johnson are as serious as the misunderstanding of Shakspere's method which is revealed by the tone of friendly apology assumed in more recent criticism. The implication, again and again, is that Shakspere achieved the magic charm of his play in spite of himself — in spite of the "semi-comic" [3] haste, the "preposterous . . . device," the "gross . . . oversights" [4] of the conclusion. I humbly submit that Shakspere knew what he was about. One or two such dramatic fantasies as *A Midsummer-Night's Dream* and *As You Like It*, which, on the whole, are not subject in beginning, middle, or end, to the ordinary laws of cause and effect,[5] are more precious than whole libraries of critical animadversion or apologetics.

1. Page 109.   2. II, 108.
3. Brander Matthews, p. 161.
4. Furness, Variorum *Much Ado*, pp. xix–xx.
5. Except that Duke Frederick's sudden and complete conversion, being proportionate to his utter wickedness at first, is in accord with what might almost be termed the ordinary phenomena of religious conversion observable in life and literature at large. (See below, p. 93 and n. 1.)

"The celerity of the mating," or, to use Shakspere's own phrase, "the sudden wooing . . . sudden consenting," [1] which he quite consciously chose to adopt as a recurring motif in his comedies, has again given pause to the critics in the case of *Twelfth Night*. Dr. Johnson thought the piece diverting as a whole but wanting in "credibility" and, once more, in "proper instruction" at the last. One wonders — for criticism sometimes makes strange bedfellows — whether the author of *Back to Methuselah* shared Dr. Johnson's scruples. "Shakspere," according to Mr. Shaw's preface, "did not make *Hamlet* out of its final butchery, nor *Twelfth Night* out of its final matrimony" — which may be quite true and yet quite irrelevant, unless Mr. Shaw could demonstrate that Shakspere *marred* either of these great plays by the endings he provided. As regards *Twelfth Night*, it is but fair to add that the critics in general take exception merely to the speed with which the conclusion is effected.[2] Hardly anyone nowadays seriously questions that in their nuptials the sentimental Olivia and the supersentimental Duke fare exceedingly well, nor that Viola and her brother have charm and brains enough to make any four persons reasonably happy. Malvolio, of course (like Shylock, but to a lesser extent), is left high and dry in the end; yet to all but the sentimentalists he remains a broadly comic figure. The fears for Maria which are expressed by Dr. Furness — "however disastrous a marriage to so turbulent a husband [as Sir Toby] may prove" [3] — are certainly not well founded. Sir Toby tells us that Maria "adores" him; [4] we know that he is proud of her,[5] and that she has long set her cap for him.[6] Once married, we may rest assured Sir Toby will not be unreasonably turbulent — lest he find that Maria did not exhaust her bag of tricks upon Malvolio.

1. *As You Like It*, V, ii, 8–9.
2. "All that is improbable in *Twelfth Night* is the celerity of the mating" (Brander Mathews, p. 164).
3. See Variorum *Twelfth Night*, note on I, iii, 51.
4. II, iii, 196.   5. II, iii, 195.   6. I, v, 29–32.

As regards, next, the ending of *Much Ado*, we may at once dismiss the queer notion expressed by the poet Campbell that Benedick's life will be made unhappy by Beatrice's supposed "bad temper." Our only problem is that presented by the Hero–Claudio story. Professor Brander Matthews [1] minimizes this problem by reminding us that we need not take too seriously an affair which is merely "ancillary to Beatrice and Benedick"; nevertheless his suggestion, though obviously in point, does not take account of all the rather complicated elements involved. The Hero–Claudio story falls in line with the problem of the "unpleasant" plays, *All's Well* and *Measure for Measure* — *Troilus and Cressida* being excluded from this discussion because its ending is obviously anything but conventionally happy. One may have misgivings as to the outcome of Hero's marriage as well as that of Helena in *All's Well*, in view of the treatment accorded them (before marriage) by young Claudio and Bertram. These two, being, according to our lights, lewd fellows of the baser sort,— flippant, stupid, brutal, and untrustworthy,— seem as unpromising husbands as Proteus, and Angelo of *Measure for Measure*. But one should not condemn Shakspere for patching up these marriages without pausing to consider the actual conditions under which these plays were presented to the audience and also the different standards by which conduct was judged in Shakspere's age. Some of these matters, of course, have been touched upon by the commentators, but, so far as I am aware, they have nowhere been discussed connectedly and comprehensively. I must content myself here with a brief summary of these considerations:

To hold (with Coleridge) that offenders such as Angelo and Hero's Claudio are morally as guilty as though their evil-doing had actually brought tragic consequences, is to propound ethics in a vacuum. The audience is too busy to do this. It laughs uproari-

1. Page 154.

ously at Dogberry in the one piece, and enjoys playing Haroun al Raschid with the Duke in the other. Knowing that things are sure to come out reasonably well, it is not inclined to pass capital sentence against the chief offenders.

Again, we should not forget that the women of these plays knew their men better than we do, and perhaps knew them to be less impossible than the more obvious passages of the action necessarily suggest. "When Imogen forgives Posthumus, who may dare to refuse his pardon?" asks Campbell,[1] and the question will apply also to Helena, Hero, and the rest. Helena has watched her bright particular star "every hour"[2] of many days, at home, where she had opportunity to learn something of young Bertram's everyday qualities. Similarly, the quiet Hero shows in the arbor scene with Beatrice that she is by no means too blind or stupid to weigh her ultimate chances with her "dear Claudio," although her case is somewhat complicated by her father who, like many a modern parent in fact or fiction,[3] insists upon a marriage primarily to save appearances. If Mariana of the moated grange, finally, craves "no other nor no better man"[4] than Angelo, it is after she has had ample time and opportunity to decide that Angelo is not an altogether impossible risk. Before condemning these "marital sacrifices," even from the modern point of view, as quite irrational, let us not forget that women still marry men to reform them. Moreover, these women possess the advantage, such as it is, of dealing with contrite sinners whose past is known and whose future will be under strict observation.

It may be well to recall the suggestion already made, that Shakspere perhaps somewhat theatrically overstates the case against some of his near-villains early in the game, relying upon the audi-

1. *Dramatic Works of Shakespeare* (cf. *Cymbeline*, First Folio ed., p. 262).
2. *All's Well*, I, i, 97–104.
3. See, for example, Sheila Kaye-Smith's *The George and the Crown*.
4. *Measure*, V, i, 431.

ence to forget, and upon the actor to emphasize the good side later. Nor should Claudio's frivolous readiness to marry "another Hero" or Bertram's easy consent to the match with Lafeu's daughter count too heavily against them. They merely yield, more or less callously, to marriages of convenience, in accordance with the custom of the time and the exigencies of their several situations.

The single standard of morality, of self-control, and gentle conduct simply was not an Elizabethan standard. Proteus, Hero's Claudio, Bertram, and even Angelo, are all young men, and in the case of such, Shakspere and the Elizabethans made large allowances.[1] In *King Lear* Gloucester's frank talk about the "pleasant vices"[2] of his youth bears its own significance. As Luciana in *The Comedy of Errors*[3] reminds her married sister, a young man then was "master of his liberty"; "time" only was his ultimate master. Hence her advice — "Be patient, sister." The corollary is obvious. In the heritage of the Elizabethan young woman from her mediæval grandmothers, patience — Griselda's virtue — constituted no slight portion, though time would, of course, play into the hands of the Elizabethan wife. All this Professor Lawrence[4] has so admirably set forth in his studies of *All's Well* and *Cymbeline* that it requires no further illustration here.

The studies just referred to emphasize the fact that the themes of the "devoted wife" and the "chastity wager" which underlie these plays, together with the substitution device of *Measure for Measure*, are drawn from mediæval stories thoroughly familiar to

1. Johnson's objection to the ending ignores this consideration while stressing, once more, his point that Shakspere's hasty endings do not properly enforce the moral: "Decency required that Bertram's double crime . . . should raise more resentment. . . . His mother might easily forgive him" but "his King should more pertinaciously vindicate his own authority and Helena's merit: of all this Shakespeare could not be ignorant, but Shakespeare wanted to conclude his play" (III, 386).
2. I, i, 10–18; V, iii, 170; cf. Brander Matthews, pp. 308–309.   3. II, i, 7–9.
4. *PMLA*, XXXVII, 421 ff. (for quotations immediately below see pp. 448, 439); XXXV, 391 ff.; see above, pp. 67 and 70.

Elizabethan audiences, which accepted these stories without psychological scruple and without prejudice to the heroine. The ending of the plays, however, Professor Lawrence believes to be more or less irrational — a convention taken over by Shakspere simply because "it was also a convention of story-telling," in which "the cold light of reason is no guide." In short, according to Mr. Lawrence, these endings have something of "the inconsequence of fairy tale." This conclusion I am unable to accept. The fairy tale inconsequence in these plays, as in such a tragedy as *King Lear*, lies not in the end but in the beginning. And if the license of the men and the patience of the women in these plays did not far exceed the standards of the Elizabethan code, then the endings, too, are not altogether irrational. Happiness is a relative condition, which each age must define anew in its own terms. Accordingly, it is possible that the modern reader may make excessive requirements — especially in view of the fact that modern women continue to take large matrimonial risks of their own. Helena and Hero and Mariana, Elizabethans all, who were more or less aware of what they were doing and what they had reason to expect, may have had at least a fighting chance for happiness.

Measure for Measure ends with four prospective weddings — if we include the one in which the irrepressible Lucio is an unwilling principal. We have considered thus far, however, only the marriage of Mariana, and she is a comparatively unimportant character in the play. The critics are right in centering attention upon Isabella, the Duke, and Angelo. What of the pardon granted to Angelo and the marriage of Isabella to the Duke? Johnson, Coleridge, Hazlitt, Andrew Lang, Brander Matthews, and Neilson are but a few of the critics who join, more or less heartily, in condemning these aspects of the ending.[1] I shall have to quote from one or

1. For the other side, cf. Walter Pater, *Appreciations*, cited in *Measure*, First Folio ed., and the Introduction to that edition, neither of which, however, covers the case as here

two of them to put the case fairly. Coleridge, for one, while recognizing the power of the play, condemned its ending as "painful . . . hateful . . . disgusting . . . horrible" and "degrading." Neilson,[1] more guardedly, suggests that Isabella's appearance "as the prospective bride of the Duke . . . may be regarded as a concession to the convention of the happy ending," and this view is more fully and positively presented by Brander Matthews,[2] who puts it thus:

> That Isabella, resolved as she was to enter a nunnery . . . should pair off with the Duke at the end . . . so that the so-called comedy may end with three weddings, leaves her in our memory as a figure sadly diminished from the heroic. The Duke has not wooed her . . . yet she accepts him offhand, practically selling herself for rank, although she had refused to sell herself to save her brother's life. . . . Even the villain Angelo is spared and dismissed to matrimony.

Whether the end Shakspere arranged for these characters is in any sense defensible is to my mind a matter of interpreting them as Shakspere intended. I feel that the critics have not altogether done this, especially in the case of the Duke, who is the central figure of the play. The indictment against him[3] is, in brief, that he is shifty, timid, and inclined to intrigue — and that he "gains a wife who is a million times too good for him." The answer is that, in spite of his faults, he is not so bad as he is painted. *Measure for Measure* was written within a year of *Hamlet*, which it obviously resembles at certain points.[4] The Duke is, to my mind, curiously like Hamlet,— at least the Hamlet of conventional criticism,— for he lacks the Dane's power of straightforward action in emergencies and has absolutely no sense of humor. The Duke would not have known how to handle Hamlet's pirates, and Hamlet (as well as

presented. For comment by the critics named, and others, and for fuller reference, see Introduction, Arden ed., and "Selected Criticism," First Folio ed. of *Measure*.
1. Page 326. 2. Page 229.
3. As outlined by Hart, Introduction, Arden ed.
4. See text immediately below, and p. 90, n. 1.

King Henry V [1]) would have scorned to punish Lucio merely for poking fun at him behind his back. But the Duke, though he "has crotchets in him" and a somewhat theatrically secretive way with him, is, notwithstanding, "a scholar, a statesman, and a soldier." [2] He is, as Isabella tells us early in the play, "the good Duke" who "loves the people" but not the shows of office, and whom the people, including even the rascal Lucio, love in turn.[3] His weakness, of which he is well aware ("'T was my fault," he says, "to give the people scope"), grows out of his Hamlet-like habit of self-analysis and ironical reflection, his love of "the life removed," in which latter respect at least he is no more culpable than the good Duke of *As You Like It*, or Prospero, neither of whom anyone especially blames for his early neglect of his dukedom. Like Hamlet, this Duke is profoundly disillusioned.[4] In his case, as in Hamlet's, untoward circumstance strengthens a native tendency to hold life off at arm's length for ironic observation. He watches Angelo as Hamlet watches King Claudius and Rosencrantz and Guildenstern — shrewdly, ironically, all but too curiously, and yet, in the last analysis, by no means ineffectively. For him, too, the times are out of joint, and though he, unlike Hamlet, has chiefly himself to blame, it must be said for him that he knows human frailty [5] and has the qualifying charity which makes one resent the tyrannous necessity of decisive action against the mere surface of evil. Like Isabella he holds that it is excellent to have a giant's strength but tyrannous to use it like a giant. Unlike Angelo, he would condemn the fault but not the actor of it. But the situation demands action. The Duke suspects Angelo as a "seemer," but knows that Angelo, unlike himself, has no hesitation in facing the complicated problem of doing essential justice. Angelo, therefore, is put in charge. The

1. See *Henry V*, IV, i, 216–235; IV, viii, 53–63.
2. *Measure*, III, ii, 155.   3. III, ii, 158.   4. Cf. III, i, 6–41, etc.
5. "But that frailty hath example for his falling, I should wonder at Angelo" (III, i, 189–191).

Duke carries on a double experiment — to see what decisive action will do to cure social corruption, and how austere hypocrisy, placed in authority, will unmask itself —

> "Hence shall we see
> If power change purpose, what our seemers be." (I, iii, 53–54.)

But he remains behind the scenes to check the evil that threatens, and to this extent he does not shirk his responsibilities. In fact, the results of his experiment are not altogether futile. He sees corruption boil and bubble as he could not have seen it in any other way, and, though he finally lets off most of the rascals, he has secured first-hand knowledge for future reference. But he also finds, in the persons of Escalus, the Provost, and, most of all, in Isabella, that truth and honor and hope still live, even in Vienna. The Duke, in short, if this analysis is sound, is a curious, but not altogether contemptible, fellow. Is Isabella a million times too good for him? Whose wife is not — if she be an Isabella! Her good Duke, at all events, has power, which she can help him use. Has she not hungered for power to fight evil in this world, and will she not now be able to outdo, in this world at least, the service of many votaries? And certainly Isabella is the very person for the Duke. If Hamlet's Ophelia had been such a one, Hamlet would probably not have needed to play the madman for long, and would certainly not have said, "To a nunnery go." Our Duke says the right thing. He lacks faith in men, resolute strength, joy. All these things Isabella can give him. Not till the end does he tell her that he has found her "lovely," but he has watched her under fire and found her true and strong of heart. Long wooings, as we have seen, were not the fashion in Elizabethan times, and a duke's wooing would certainly not be unfashionably long, though it is not strange that Isabella should remain speechless when his dukeship, in the midst of all his other closing revelations, suddenly puts the essential question.

What has just been said as to the Duke goes far to explain the case of Angelo. The Duke himself shares responsibility for Angelo's evil-doing, since he put Angelo in power in spite of, or rather because of, his doubt of the man's integrity. For this reason, and for Mariana's sake, Angelo is allowed to live. To the precisian Angelo, however, — who is as merciless and clear-sighted in his self-judgment as King Claudius in *Hamlet*,[1] — the public shame of his exposure is a punishment scarcely less severe than the death for which he himself asks shortly before the end.[2] "The idea that death spells the height of tragedy," as we have recently been reminded, "has long since proved itself wrong."[3] Conversely, it may be observed, such a happy ending as that achieved by Angelo, if it does not exactly spell the height of everyday comedy, is not without its ironic force.

It is unnecessary to examine in detail the endings of the several dramatic romances. Shakspere's mood and method in these are so much alike that it will suffice to deal briefly with the group as a whole; moreover, the tests already applied to the earlier plays are to some extent valid here also. The faults of workmanship already observed, are, it may be admitted, especially in evidence here — particularly those that grow out of the "carelessness of disdainful mastery." These plays are romances, with the readily recognizable characteristics of the type: an idealized background, crowded action, an occasional melodramatic emphasis upon situation, or a striving for surprise at the expense of characterization — especially of the secondary characters. It is to be expected that these conditions should have their effect upon the endings of the plays.

1. Compare *Measure*, II, iv, 1–17 with *Hamlet*, III, iii, 36–72.
2. V, i, 376–379.
3. See Kathleen Millay's essay, "On a Cowardly Tendency," *Literary Review*, N. Y. *Evening Post*, July 14, 1923.

At the end of *The Winter's Tale*, for example, Paulina and Camillo are married off in summary fashion, but with the reëstablishment of the Queen, Paulina's occupation's gone, and Camillo has long been homesick, which — being interpreted by Leontes [1] — means that he is not disinclined to the match. On the other hand, in *Cymbeline*, it is difficult to escape the feeling that the villain Iachimo is melodramatically conceived and handled, both in his early misdeeds and in his ultimate repentance. Criticism, however, not content with this, has brought a similar indictment against the main personages of the plays — Posthumus and Leontes, for example; and it has challenged as incredible or merely conventional the dramatist's solution of the problems which confronted Imogen, Hermione, and Prospero. This judgment I believe to be mistaken, although I do not question the likelihood that Shakspere was influenced by the prevalent conventions of the type in which he was working, that he knew his Beaumont and Fletcher [2] and what the public wanted, and did not scruple to utilize any or all conventions for his own purposes. In his earlier comedies, however, as we have seen, he did not slavishly accept the convention of the happy ending, but rationalized it by characterization. Did he fail to do so in the dramatic romances?

The chief point [3] against the endings of these plays has been

1. *Winter's Tale*, V, iii, 142.
2. As Professor Thorndike has shown; though it is also well to recall that Shakspere's earlier plays contain not a few of the elements which became especially marked in the dramatic romances: surprise in the ending of *A Comedy of Errors*, forgiveness in *As You Like It* and *Measure*, etc.
3. Barrett Wendell (*Shakespeare*, pp. 358–368, cf. First Folio ed., *Cymbeline*) finds in both *Cymbeline* and *The Tempest* a "deliberately skillful handling of dénouement." Most critics agree so far as *The Tempest* is concerned, and few question the admirable workmanship of the closing (statue) scene of *The Winter's Tale*. In the case of *Cymbeline*, however, Furness and Professor Lawrence (cf. *PMLA*, XXXV, 391 ff.) see another instance of the hasty ending. In fact, "the development of the main plot in the last three acts," according to Mr. Lawrence, gives the impression of "hasty and careless workmanship, as if the dramatist had lost his interest." The critic takes exception, especially, to the last speeches of

strongly put by Creizenach,[1] whose conclusions are in substantial agreement with those of many other critics.[2] Creizenach is astonished to find

how easily in these closing scenes the wrong-doers are pardoned, even when through their criminal devices they have conjured up the greatest dangers . . . The most unbelievable [forgiveness] in this regard is that of the innocent and suffering women who in many pieces are forsaken by their husbands for a mistress . . . or even pursued with attempts to kill. Conclusions about the moral convictions and feelings of the dramatists cannot be drawn from all this; it is obviously a part of the style of the romantic-fantastic drama. . . .

This view has three implications: first, that the conversion of the chief evil-doers is in itself impossible or that it is not made dramatically plausible; second, that the act of forgiveness itself is humanly unbelievable; third, that the ending is purely conventional — not in consonance with characterization nor in any recognizable

Posthumus and Imogen. Their reunion should have been staged and phrased "with appropriate dignity. Instead, all that the scene has to offer is this:

> *Imo.*   Why did you throw your wedded lady from you?
> Think that you are upon a rock, and now
> Throw me again.   [*Embracing him.*]
> *Post.*   Hang there like fruit, my soul,
> Till the tree die.

A mixture of wrestling, horticulture, and banality which could hardly be surpassed." In a footnote Professor Lawrence adds: "Perhaps not everyone will agree. Charles Cowden Clarke thought this reunion 'perfectly divine!'" — *De gustibus non disputandum est!* To me the thing seems not "divine" but sufficiently natural and reasonable, for in such a case actions speak louder than words. It is a moment of high emotional strain. Posthumus had struck the page, not knowing that the page is Imogen. Then comes the final revelation, which Imogen brings to a period by embracing her husband, and daring him, as it were, to cast her off again. O. Henry's story, "The Proof of the Pudding," illustrates the point that some human beings in a state of high emotional strain express themselves with a curious lack of dignified formality. Are not a couple of hyperboles and a mixed figure or two quite pardonable under the circumstances?

     1. *Geschichte des Neueren Dramas*, IV, 306 ff. Cf. next note.

     2. The passage is quoted approvingly by W. W. Lawrence, *PMLA*, XXXVII, 440. Quiller-Couch (p. 200) says somewhat the same thing. Compare text, above, p. 65, and nn. 6 and 7.

accord with the poet's own convictions. We must look briefly at the other side.

It should be noted, in the first place, that the sudden conversion of sinners is not a motif which Shakspere employed for the first time in the dramatic romances. One remembers Oliver in *As You Like It*, to cite no further instances. In his case, as I have already suggested, the will to believe is not so much staggered by his return to decency — he is, after all, the brother of Orlando and the son of good Sir Roland — as by his early misdeeds. And does not the same hold true of Posthumus and Leontes? Shakspere is careful to inform us that Posthumus, besides having won the love of Imogen, is universally beloved as a noble gentleman; and that Leontes has long been a true friend and a good husband. The incredible thing about them — deftly touched off at the beginning, where it can soonest be forgotten — is not their "conversion" but the original lunacy which leads them to their mad villainies. Are they so far removed, after all, from Lear, whose repentance is much more humanly true and believable than his aberration at the outset? "Man's liability to sudden and complete conversion" is, according to William James,[1] "one of his most curious peculiarities." Sudden conversions may be unconvincing dramatically, — as witness the case of Iachimo, — but Posthumus and Leontes are not converted; they simply return to sanity.

"It would be unchristian," says an anonymous commentator,[2] "not to forgive Leontes." At all events, it is entirely human and plausible to do so, and at least as logical as to parole a life-prisoner who has served sixteen years on excellent behavior. For the final forgiveness in Shakspere's dramatic romances is to some considerable extent earned by suffering. Not mere surprise for the audi-

---

1. *Varieties of Religious Experience* (1907), p. 230 (cf. on this point, Arden ed. of *Measure*, p. XXV).

2. *Winter's Tale*, Variorum, pp. 362–363.

ence but agony suffered by the chief offenders motivates the end.
Posthumus and the King of Naples (confederate with Prospero's
usurping brother) do not suffer for sixteen years, but time is not
the only measure of agony. And, to turn to the side of the forgivers, Imogen, Hermione, and Prospero have been mellowed and
humanized by time and suffering. In short, the "unbelievable forgiveness" of these dramatic romances is *not* unbelievable. It is the
serene mercy which grows out of suffering, ripening into wisdom
and charitable judgment. "The rarer action," says Prospero, is
"in virtue than in vengeance." Prospero in the large is not Shakspere, but the whole tendency of the dramatic romances indicates
that this sentiment which he expresses is not merely "a part of the
style of the romantic drama." It is Shakspere's own: one of the
noblest and most definite of the "moral convictions" of his maturity.

It is not necessary in such a study as this to end in Johnsonian
fashion by stressing the moral. I would conclude, instead, by pro-
pounding a question: Granted that the ingenuous public wants a
happy ending at any cost, is it not also true that the blasé critics
(like Cecily in *The Importance of Being Earnest*[1]) have a way of
condemning the thing on general principles — without much concern for the merits of any special case? If so, who is more conventional, Shakspere or his critics?

---

1. Cecily hopes her governess's novel "did not end happily? — I don't like novels that
end happily. They depress me so much."

   Miss Prism. " The good ended happily and the bad unhappily. That is what Fiction means."
   Cecily. " I suppose so. But it seems very unfair." (Act II.)

II

SHAKSPERE AND MILTON

Chapter III

SHAKSPERE AND SIR THOMAS BROWNE

THE field of knowledge hath been so traced, it is hard to spring any thing new." Thus, long ago, and with the delightful candor worthy of a great scholar who was also a man of humor, wrote the beloved physician of Norwich to a learned friend. However hard the assay, Sir Thomas Browne had the courage of his convictions, for the pronouncement I have quoted appeared in the Epistle Dedicatory [1] of his *Garden of Cyrus* — that Quincuncial Lozenge in which, more than anywhere else in all his works, he allowed his curious fancy and his out-of-the-way learning to run riot. The fact remains that, even at the hazard of appearing to woo mere novelty, Browne thought it no vulgar error to try to plant his seed-field, or to graft new truth upon old. It seems worth while, in view of what is to follow here, to recall how strong he was in this faith. Though the "rules," according to his *Observations on Grafting*,[2] "be considerable in the *usual and practised* course of insitions, yet were it but reasonable for searching spirits to urge the operations of nature *by conjoining plants of very different natures* [3] in parts, barks, lateness, and precocities: . . . yellow rose upon sweetbrier . . . broom upon furze . . . bay upon holly . . . peach upon mulberry . . . lilac upon sage." The suggestion which follows seems, once more, admirably adapted to the conditions and purposes of our inquiry: "Nor are we to rest in the frustrated success of some single experiments, but to proceed in attempts in the most unlikely unto iterated and certain conclusions

1. To Sir Nicholas Bacon. See *The Works of Sir Thomas Browne*, ed. Simon Wilkin (hereafter referred to as "W "), London (1889-1894), II, 494.
2. W, III, 347-348.   3. My italics.

... whereby we might determine ... many others of doubtful truths." Since truth — to return to the Epistle Dedicatory of *The Garden of Cyrus* — "may receive addition," Browne thought it praiseworthy "of old things" to "write something new," for he believed that "adventures in knowledge are laudable, and the essays of weaker heads afford oftentimes improveable hints unto better." [1] For several reasons I derive much comfort from these reflections. I neither hope nor fear that the reader will find in this study of the literary relations between Shakspere and Sir Thomas Browne the merits or the defects of another quincuncial lozenge. Its purpose is to set forth certain new facts or interpretations which seem sufficiently important to demand attention even though in the nature of things they are not capable of absolute demonstration, and despite the fact that the main tendency of the views to be presented runs almost diametrically opposite to the generally accepted tenets of orthodox criticism.

Briefly stated, the main point I hope to establish in this essay is that the poet of Stratford exerted upon the sage of Norwich a remarkable attraction and an unmistakable influence. This idea, so far as I have been able to determine, has never been definitely set forth[2] by any of the critical hosts who have said their say upon Shakspere and Browne. Indeed, it will appear that its implications, so far as they have been touched upon at all, have been roundly denied by those presumably most competent to judge. James Russell Lowell, to be sure, describes Sir Thomas Browne as "our most imaginative mind since Shakespeare" — but he does this in the course of a paper[3] which puts strong emphasis upon the contention that the greatest poets, "Dante, Shakespeare, Goethe,

1. *Pseudodoxia Epidemica, Enquiries into Vulgar ... Errors* (hereafter referred to as "*V. E.*") bk. VI, ch. 12; W, II, 203.

2. One or two *oblique* critical remarks upon the point will be noted below (see pp. 116, n. 4 and 118, n. 1).

3. "Shakespeare Once More," *Among My Books*, 2nd series, pp. 152–153, 181.

— left no heirs either to the form or mode of their expression," because "imagination is incommunicable." The present essay in the large (with its companion study on "The Shaksperian Element in Milton") [1] offers an incidental commentary upon Lowell's general contention. By way of poetic justice, meanwhile,—and with the qualifying note that Lowell underrated the imaginative power of Milton, whom he puts beside Sterne and Wordsworth among the geniuses "of the second class,"—it will perhaps not be unfair to make Lowell serve as the devil's advocate. If Browne was indeed our most imaginative mind since Shakspere, is it not likely that the spiritual kinship between them, not to mention their proximity in space and time and literary instinct, would somehow have left its mark upon the work of the later writer of the two?

Browne's biographers and critics, as we shall see, answer "No" or do not answer at all. Shakspere's commentators, on the other hand, seem but half aware even of the more obvious connection between the two writers — that is to say, of the fact that Browne's work significantly *illustrates* Shakspere because it touches upon many aspects of the psychology, demonology, and general science which passed current in the seventeenth century, in Shakspere's England. Coleridge, for example, in his notes on *Hamlet*,[2] printed, side by side with the key passage from the close of the second act:

> *The spirit that I have seen*
> *May be the devil; and the devil hath power*
> *To assume a pleasing shape*; yea, and perhaps
> Out of my weakness and my melancholy,
> *As he is very potent with such spirits*,
> *Abuses me to damn me* (II, ii, 627–632) —

a suggestion to the reader to "*See* Sir Thomas Brown," that is to say, the first line or two of the important passage from the *Religio Medici* [3] which I reproduce at large:

1. See below, Chapter IV.   2. *Works* (N. Y., 1871), IV, 158.
3. (Hereafter referred to as "*R. M.*"), pt. I, section xxxvii; W, II, 380.

I believe . . . that the souls of the faithful, as they leave earth, take possession of heaven; that *those apparitions and ghosts of departed persons are not the wandering souls of men, but the unquiet walks of devils, prompting and suggesting us unto mischief, blood, and villany;* instilling and stealing into our hearts that the blessed spirits are not at rest in their graves, but wander, solicitous of the affairs of the world. But that those phantasms appear often, and do frequent cemeteries, charnel-houses, and churches,[1] it is because those are the dormitories of the dead, where the devil, like an insolent champion, beholds with pride the spoils and trophies of his victory in Adam.

Though Coleridge knew the passage, he — and countless editors and commentators after him — gave it slight weight. Obviously, the passage affords a rational explanation of Hamlet's hesitation, on the ground of the current Elizabethan belief that the ghost might have been not a spirit of health but a goblin damned, a creature of the devil (if not the devil himself) conjured up on purpose to prompt Hamlet "unto mischief." Yet Coleridge, Schlegel, and the balance of critical opinion to this day [2] make Hamlet's tragedy primarily and finally the tragedy of the speculative mind, of "the reflective temperament in excess," [3] of "thought-sickness" and intellectual irresolution.

The reader will find in the Appendix additional references, illustrative of Shakspere, to Browne's utterances upon ghosts, witches, and the devil. I have there collected also representative references to his exhaustive studies of those "fascinating, irresistible popular errors" [4] — many of them survivals of the unnatural natural history of the ancients, popularized afresh by the Euphuists — which Shakspere used over and over again because, like other good poets, he liked them for the poetry that is in them. Our

1. A belief unqualifiedly shared by Sir Kenelm Digby (*Observations on "Religio Medici,"* W, II, 466), James I (*Daemonologie*), and virtually all contemporary writers on witchcraft.
2. Cf. Bradley, *Shakespearean Tragedy,* pp. 104 ff.
3. Sir Sidney Lee, *Life of Shakespeare* (N. Y., 1916), p. 365.
4. Cf. Walter Pater, *Appreciations,* "Sir Thomas Browne."

concern here is not with Browne's general illustrations of Shakspere. We must, instead, seek to determine whether the poetry of
Shakspere — of *Hamlet* and *Macbeth*, for example — left a recognizable mark upon the "form or mode" of Browne's literary
achievement — upon the poetic imaginings, say, of the *Religio
Medici*, the *Hydriotaphia*, and the *Christian Morals*.[1]

The critics unreservedly answer "No." Browne's loving and
copious use of Holy Scripture, of the poets, naturalists, and historians of Greece and Rome, and his acquaintance with certain
dignitaries among the moderns — Boccaccio [2] and "the learned
Italian poet Dante," [3] Machiavelli [4] and Rabelais [5] — is apparent
in all his writings, and no one, I think, questions it.[6] But as regards his contemporaries, the masters of Elizabethan verse and
prose, there appears to be general agreement that he would have
nothing to do with them. Thus, according to one good critic,[7]

he probably read little of the works of his younger contemporaries;
for in his correspondence he scarcely observes upon what made the current literature of his day. Even *Hudibras*, the opinions, the learning, the
humour of which must have been delightful to his taste, appears only to
draw from him an erudite comment upon the antiquity of burlesque
poems. He seems more at home with Hippocrates than with Samuel
Butler. He continued to the last to live apart and aloof amongst his

1. Referred to hereafter as "*C. M.*"; the *Hydriotaphia, Urn Burial*, as "*U. B.*" (The
Christian Morals, highly — and justly — admired by Doctor Johnson, is worthy of a place
beside the better-known works, in spite of the fact that it has had short shrift from modern
critics.)

2. See *R. M., ad fin.*, W, II, 451, n. 8: "a tale of Bocace or Malizpini" — a reading
adopted by other editors.

3. *V. E.*, VII, x — W, II, 236; *C. M.*, II, ii — W, III, 106, n.

4. *C. M.*, II, i — W, III, 109.

5. *V. E.*, VII, xviii — W, II, 279, etc.

6. Saintsbury, curiously enough, asserts that in all the "immense range" of Browne's
subject-matter, "he never touches" upon "pure literature," though he admits that
Browne's "literary knowledge was certainly not small" (*Camb. Hist. of Eng. Lit.*, VII,
272 ff.).

7. Author of the unsigned but solid article on Browne in the *Edinburgh Review* (Oct.,
1836), LXIV, 9.

ancient authors and his quaint but sublime thoughts, a scholar by habit, a philosopher by boast, and a poet by nature.

A query may be in order here. Does a poet who is a scholar by habit and who (like all scholars but especially like the scholars of Browne's time) tends instinctively, in his citations of authority, to draw upon the great names of old, the established reputations, by that token stamp himself as one who lives "apart and aloof" from his contemporaries? As regards contemporary literature in particular, did not the seventeenth century's comparative want of "accepted critical authority applied to literature"[1] inevitably strengthen a natural scholarly tendency to slight the claims of the moderns in the citation of "authorities" — to differentiate between contemporary *letters* and ancient *literature?* At all events, let us observe in passing that Browne in his scientific citations also gave full credit to Aristotle, Hippocrates, Pliny, and the rest, while he scarcely mentioned his contemporaries though he seems to have read them all.[2] Sir Edmund Gosse, in his biography of Browne, touches upon one or two of these considerations, only to neglect them altogether in discussing Browne's immediate literary antecedents. His statement of the case is so pertinent to our inquiry that I must quote once more. Gosse thinks Browne's

case very curious, because we find in him *little sympathy with the current literature of his country*, or the modern vernaculars at all. In his *superb neglect of all contemporary poetry and prose*, in *his scorn of the poets in particular*, he exceeds Jeremy Taylor, whose contempt of modern writing went far. The great English writers from Chaucer down to Milton, from Wycliffe down to Dryden, might never have existed for all the attention they receive from Sir Thomas Browne. Almost the only reference to a living imaginative author which is to be found in the length and breadth of his works is a note written at the time that *Hudibras* was published . . . [and this note] is a mere pellet of sun-dried pedantry without a single word to show that the author had comprehended or read or perhaps even seen Butler's poem.[3]

1. Sir Edmund Gosse, *Life of Sir Thomas Browne* (English Men of Letters), p. 55.
2. *Ibid.*, pp. 77–78, 115.   3. *Ibid.*, pp. 191–192. (My italics.)

By their fruits ye shall know them! If the products of Browne's labors as a man of letters really evince nothing more than a superb neglect of all contemporary prose and poetry in general and a fine scorn of the poets in particular, then I have already wasted many words in attempting to set the stage for the positive demonstration of my own view — that Browne as an imaginative writer was distinctly influenced by Shakspere. It is time, therefore, to call attention to certain facts and implications which Gosse and other critics seem not to have taken into account, and to let the reader judge for himself how far these facts affect the case.

The critics, in the first place, seem not to have observed that there are in Browne's writings many passages [1] which prove indubitably that he was fascinated by the theatre and drama — that, besides *reading* Euripides or Aristophanes,[2] he heartily enjoyed himself in the playhouses of his own London and Norwich, where virtually nothing but the drama of his contemporaries was to be seen. That love of the drama was instinctive with him one might indeed have guessed, if only because he had a certain dramatic objectivity — a habit of setting off one from another (as he says in the *Religio Medici*)[3] that "common and authentick philosophy I learned in the schools, whereby I discourse and satisfy the reason of other men," and that other "more reserved and drawn from experience whereby I content mine own." But one does not need to guess. A glance at the passages which I have brought together below, will indicate that Browne speaks plainly on the subject. It will be granted, I think, that, as in the case of Shakspere himself, Browne's liking for things dramatic manifests itself in his frequent use of metaphors drawn from the stage. For the rest, the reader is invited to ask himself whether certain portions of those passages which I have saved for the last, do not — taken together

1. I have found something like a score, and doubtless there are others.
2. Cf., for instance, *U. B.*, ch. 3, — W, III, 21.   3. II, viii — W, II, 437.

with others to be presented later — afford some preliminary reasons for the belief that Browne, like Milton, felt and remembered, perhaps quite unconsciously, the magic spell of the master of the Elizabethan and Jacobean theatre — that in the turn of phrase, thought, or figure, or in the modulation of the periods, the touch of Shaksperian reminiscence, however slight or evanescent, is none the less unmistakable. Here, then, are some of

BROWNE'S ALLUSIONS TO THE THEATRE AND DRAMA

1. I could lose an arm without a tear, and with few groans, methinks, be quartered into pieces; *yet can I weep most seriously at a play*, and receive with a true passion the counterfeit griefs of those known and professed impostures. (*R. M.*, II, v — W, II, 427.)

2. I . . . know in what *counterfeiting shapes and deceitful visards* [1] times present represent *on the stage* things past. (*R. M.*, I, xxix — W, II, 365.)

3. Enoch and Elias [have] *a late part yet to act upon this stage of earth.* [2] (*U. B.*, ch. 5, — W, III, 47.)

4. Superfluously we seek a *precarious applause* abroad; every good man hath his *plaudit* within himself. (*C. M.*, I, xxxiv — W, III, 106.)

5. The noblest digladiation [3] is in *the theatre of ourselves.* [4] (*C. M.*, I, xxiv — W, III, 99.)

6. [On the Day of Judgment] as in the last scene, *all the actors must enter, to complete and make up the catastrophe of this great piece.* (*R. M.*, I, xlvii — W, II, 393.)

7. Though *the world be histrionical* . . . [5] yet be what thou singly art, and *personate* only thyself . . . To single hearts, *doubling* is discruciating . . . He who counterfeiteth *acts a part, and is, as it were, out*

1. See also *R. M.*, II, xiii: "These *scenical* and accidental differences between us cannot make me forget that common and untoucht part of us both." (W, II, 449.)

2. Cf. Epistle Dedicatory, *U. B.*, "We have enough to do to make up ourselves from present and passed times, and *the whole stage of things* scarce serveth for our instruction." (W, III, 5.)

3. "Fencing-match" — Dr. Johnson.

4. The microcosm. See, *per contra*, *As You Like It*, II, vii, 137: "This *wide and universal theatre.*"

5. See item 8 (*b*) immediately below.

of himself: which if long, proves so irksome that men are glad to pull off their *vizards,* and resume themselves again. (*C. M.,* III, xx — W, III, 136.)

8.   (*a*) *Hamlet to Polonius (concerning the players, and their patrons' reputations)*:

Good my lord, will you see the players well bestow'd? . . . *Let them be well us'd,* for they are the abstracts and brief chronicles of the time; *after your death you were better have a bad epitaph than their ill report while you lived.* (II, ii, 546 ff.)

(*b*) *Jacques. All the world's a stage*
And all the men and women merely players.
They have their exits and their entrances,
And one man in his time plays many parts.
(*As You Like It,* II, vii, 139 ff.)

9.   *Leonato to Don Pedro (concerning the sage and serious Beatrice):*

There's little of the melancholy element in her, my lord. She is never sad but when she sleeps, and not ever sad then; for I have heard my daughter say she hath often *dreamt of unhappiness and wak'd herself with laughing. (Much Ado,* II, i, 357-361.)

Compare:

(*a*) I had rather stand in the shock of a basilisk than in the fury of a merciless pen. It is not mere zeal to learning, or devotion to the muses, that wiser princes patron the arts and *carry an indulgent aspect* unto scholars; but *a desire to have their names eternized . . .* and a fear of the revengeful pen of succeeding ages: *for these are the men that, when they have played their parts and had their exits,* must step out and give the moral of their scenes, and *deliver unto posterity an inventory* of their virtues and vices. (*R. M.* II, iii — W, II, 423.)

(*b*) The *unexpected scenes* of things . . . the *tragical exits* of some eminent persons. (*C. M.,* II, xi — W, III, 117.)

Browne, according to his friend White-foot (*Minutes,* W, I, xxviii) was "always cheerful, but rarely merry." Browne himself writes:

I was born in the planetary hour of Saturn, and I think I have something of that leaden planet in me. I am no way facetious, nor disposed for the mirth and galliardise of company; *yet in one dream I can compose a whole comedy,*[1] behold the action, apprehend the jests, and *laugh myself awake at the conceits thereof.* (*R. M.,* II, xi — W, II, 445.)

1. Hazlitt ("Lectures on the Age of Elizabeth," *Works,* ed. Waller and Glover, V, 334) alludes to this passage — inaccurately and with, for him, a singular lack of humor, or of understanding of Browne's humor and dramatic sense: "He [Browne] tells us that *he often composed a comedy in his sleep.* It would be curious to know the subject or the texture of the plot. It must have been [a colorless morality] or else a misnomer like Dante's *Divine Comedy.*"

10. (*a*) *Macbeth.* I gin *to be aweary of the sun*
And wish the estate o' the world were now undone. (V, iii, 49–50.)

(*b*) *Prospero.*   I must
Bestow upon the eyes of this young couple
Some vanity of mine art . . . These our actors
As I foretold you, were all spirits, and
Are melted into air, into thin air;
And, like the baseless fabric of this vision,
The cloud-capp'd towers, the gorgeous palaces,
The solemn temples, the great globe itself,
Yea, all which it inherit, shall dissolve
And, like this insubstantial pageant faded,
Leave not a rack behind. *We are such stuff*
As dreams are made on, and our little life
Is rounded with a sleep. (*Tempest,* IV, i, 39–41, 148–158.)

As yet . . . hath [not] my pulse beat thirty years, and yet . . . *methinks I have outlived myself,* and *begin to be weary of the sun* . . . I perceive I do anticipate the vices of age; *the world to me is but a dream or mock-show,* and we all therein but pantaloons and anticks . . . (*R. M.,* I, xli — W, II, 386.)

Loves . . . affections . . . are *all dumb-shows and dreams,* without reality, truth, or constancy. (*R.M.,* II, xiv — W, II, 450.)

Let them not therefore complain of immaturity that die about thirty: *they fall but like the whole world, whose solid and well-composed substance must not expect the duration and period of its constitution* . . . the last and general fever may as naturally destroy it before six thousand as me before forty . . . *Our ends are as obscure as our beginnings; the line of our days is drawn by night* . . . by a pencil that is invisible; wherein, though we confess our ignorance, I am sure we do not err if we say, it is the hand of God. (*R.M.,* I, xliii —W, II, 387–388.)

A glance at these remarks — especially those about "doubling" and the entry of all the actors for the catastrophe — shows, first, that Browne writes as one who knew something of theatrical custom in his time. It is to be observed, next, that most of his allusions to the stage appear — as one would, indeed, expect — in the *Religio Medici,* his *L'Allegro* and *Il Penseroso* in one; that is to say, the fine flower of his literary achievement in those full, early years given over to omnivorous reading and to the busy pursuits of a student of medicine — but also of men — in London, Oxford, and abroad. As a boy in London and Winchester between 1605 and 1620 (almost before Shakspere had retired to Stratford), as an

Oxford student in the early twenties of the new century (in those his canicular days when in his warm blood he shook hands with delight: while Shakspere — until the First Folio made its first fresh appeal to the great variety of readers — remained the wonder of those stages upon whose counterfeit griefs and true passions Browne loved to gaze), and for another decade thereafter until his family and his medical practice grew apace, — how, indeed, could he or anyone, given these happy years and circumstances and gifted with the unerring literary instinct of a young Milton or a young Browne, have failed to respond to the spell of the master? And Browne's memory, according to good contemporary evidence,[1] was "capacious and tenacious, insomuch as he remembered all that was remarkable in any book that he had read." My citations from the *Christian Morals*, the last of his works, would indicate, even if no other evidence were available, that Browne retained to the last something of his interest in the stage — at least in so far as it shadows forth the stage of life. Additional evidence, to be presented shortly, of Shaksperian reminiscence in Browne, will convince the reader — if it convinces him at all — that Browne, like Milton, remembered Shakspere from first to last. It is to be noted, meanwhile, that Browne, unlike Milton, is definitely known to have been friendly toward the theatre [2] until late in life. In a letter addressed to his son Edward on April 22, 1661, Sir Thomas,[3] like the staunch though quiet Royalist he was, described with wholehearted approval the Coronation festivities at Norwich — among other things "bonfires, speeches, *and a little play by the strollers* in the market-place, an other by young Cityzens at Timber Hill on a

1. "Some Minutes for the Life of Sir Thomas Browne, by John Whitefoot, M.A.," W, I, xxviii.
2. With which Milton, for obvious reasons, lost sympathy, though he continued to cherish the poetry of Elizabethan drama. (See below, Chapter IV.)
3. Browne was not, in fact, knighted until 1671.

stage, Cromwell hangd and burnt everywhere." [1] A number of years later, when Browne's little grandson Tom was staying at Norwich, the boy seems to have helped his grandfather to renew his youth, for Browne writes that "the players are at the Red Lion hard by and *Tom* goes sometimes to see a play." [2]

Suppose it be granted that Browne himself may sometimes have gone to see a play, and that among the plays he saw or read there may have been some by Shakspere. I think the evidence forthcoming will justify us, presently, in putting the case more strongly and definitely; but it would be futile to proceed without attempting to correct more adequately the current misapprehension — epitomized in Gosse's statement quoted above — as to the basic relationships between Browne and his fellows among the masters of Elizabethan letters. To make the correction, we have only to look closely at Browne's own writings.

Take, for example, the notion that Browne's undeniable devotion to his classical authors led him, *ipso facto*, to visit a superb neglect upon virtually all the moderns. His own words, in his introductory analysis of the general causes of common errors, would seem to belie this charge. "We applaud," he writes, [3]

many things delivered by the ancients, which are in themselves ordinary, and come short of our conceptions. Thus we usually extol . . . the sayings of the wise men of Greece . . . which, notwithstanding [carry] with them nothing above the line, or beyond the extempory sententiosity of common conceits with us.

He then proceeds to state definitely that the magic of the great names of old did not altogether blind him to the claims of the "wise men" of his own time and his *own nation:*

1. "Domestic Correspondence," W, III, 393.
2. Cf. Pater, "Sir Thomas Browne," *Appreciations* (London, 1890), p. 148. I have not been able to see this letter. (W, III, 454, 461, prints various letters, written by Browne in 1679, in which "Litle Tom comes loaded from the fayre," etc.)
3. *V. E.*, I, vi — W, I, 49.

We magnifie the apothegms . . . of . . . Laertius . . . Macrobius, Cicero, Augustus, and the comical wits of those times: in most . . . methinks, exceeded, not only in the replies of wise men, but the . . . urbanities of our times . . . We extol their adages or proverbs . . . paralleled, if not exceeded, by those of more unlearned nations, *and many of our own.*

I must confess, next, that I find it difficult to deal patiently with the strange notion that Browne was in any sense a scorner of poets — that is to say, of true poets — of any age. The simple fact of the matter is that the man had too much of the poet in his own make-up to scorn his brothers. That he took poetry seriously is almost as certain as anything can well be. Let anyone who doubts this look at his brief but sensible letter "Of Ropalic or Gradual Verses," [1] in which he describes himself as "utterly averse from" any poetic technique which "restrains the fancy or fetters the invention" — from "all affectation in poetry." Let him glance, next, at the four or five extant specimens of Browne's own verse — first, perhaps, at the lines ("his dormitive bedward") near the close of the *Religio Medici:*

> The night is come: like to the day
> Depart not thou, great God, away[2]

(verses which, by virtue of their simple but compelling sincerity, are not unworthy of comparison with such, for example, as Herrick's "To His Sweet Saviour"); [3] and, finally, at that curious "Prophecy" in doggerel rhyme,

> When New England shall trouble New Spain,
> When Jamaica shall be lady of the isles and the main,[4]

1. W, III, 221 ff.
2. II, xii — W, II, 446–447; for other verses cf. I, xiii, xxxii, xliv.
3. "Night hath no wings to him that cannot sleep." (Cf. also Herrick's "Bellman": "Along the dark and silent night . . .")
4. "A Prophecy Concerning . . . Several Nations," W, III, 261.

which, if I read it aright, challenges comparison with the "Latter-Day Warnings" [1] —

> When legislators keep the law,
> When banks dispense with bolts and locks —

of another great physician who was also a man of humor and no scorner of poets — our American Thomas Browne, Dr. Oliver Wendell Holmes. Browne, of course, did not publish many of his verses, but who shall say that he did not write more than we know of? At all events, anyone who will read fairly the prose of the *Religio Medici* and the *Urn Burial* can satisfy himself that no scorner of poets could have written these gravely beautiful prose poems. One inevitably recalls in this connection John Milton's proud declaration of the faith: "He who would not be frustrate of his hope to write well hereafter in laudable things, ought himself to be a true poem." Browne loved to lose himself in mysteries, but he could speak his faith as simply and boldly as any man. He paid high tribute to all poetry and all poets, including himself, by describing his life up to the writing of the *Religio Medici* as "a miracle of thirty years, which to relate were *not a history but a piece of poetry*, and would sound to common ears like a fable." [2]

If all this is true, how are we to account for the supposed fact that "almost the only reference to a living imaginative author which is to be found in the length and breadth of [Browne's] work" is his "pellet of sun-dried pedantry" concerning *Hudibras?* In reply, it must be said that this statement of the case does not take account of all the facts. For one thing, Gosse himself [3] believed that the commendatory verses signed "Tho: Browne" which prefaced the posthumous poems of Donne published in 1633, "seem characteristic of the author of the *Religio Medici*," and this as-

1. See the first paper in *The Autocrat of the Breakfast-Table.*
2. *R. M.*, II, xl — W, II, 444.
3. *Op. cit.*, p. 19.

cription appears to be correct.[1] For the rest, my own study of
Browne enables me to add, more or less confidently, the names of
Raleigh, Spenser, Sidney, Marlowe,[2] and Shakspere to the list of
imaginative Elizabethan authors directly or indirectly *alluded* (if
not referred) to, by Browne himself, or called to his attention by
his literary friends. A few notes as to the whys and wherefores of
this list may be in order here.

I find, in the first place, that Browne, in the sixth book of the
Vulgar Errors,[3] mentions "Sir Walter Raleigh" as an authority
upon the redness of the Red Sea — and I would remind anyone
who may be inclined to question the *literary* significance of this
contact between the two men that in Raleigh's writings as in
Browne's the poet is never far to seek even when the explorer, the
geographer, or the historian is ostensibly wielding the pen. Next,
as regards Sidney and Spenser: these two are named, with other
"garden poets," in a letter addressed to Browne by his friend John
Evelyn in January, 1658 — a few months before Browne published his own *Garden of Cyrus*. Browne had already contributed
a chapter, "Of Garlands and Coronarie Plants," [4] to the *Elysium
Britannicum*, one of Evelyn's unfinished literary projects, which
was to have been an exhaustive three-volume work upon Gardens.
With his letter Evelyn sent Browne an abstract [5] of his long chapter "Of the History of Gardens" — "to let you see how farr we
correspond (as by your excellent papers I collect) and to engage
your assistance in supplying my omissions." The last paragraph
of this abstract refers to "Romantique and poeticall gardens out of
Sydney, Spencer . . . Statius, Homer . . . &c." However near or
"farr" the "correspondence" between these two expert literary

1. Cf. H. J. C. Grierson, *Donne's Poetical Works*, I, 372–373; II, 255.
2. Possibly also Greene and Fletcher. (See below, p. 112, n. 1.)
3. VI, ix — W, II, 178.
4. W, III, 203.
5. For the letter and abstract see W, III, 488–492.

gardeners, I think almost everyone will be inclined to grant that Sidney and Spenser could hardly have been among Browne's "omissions," since he was certainly at least as catholic in his tastes and as indefatigable in his reading as Evelyn.

As regards Marlowe we need have no recourse to indirection to find direction out, for Browne in three different places mentions "Tamerlane" and "Bajazet" in terms that virtually establish as a fact the inference that he must have had Marlowe's *Tamburlaine* in mind.[1] And there is reason to believe that he also remembered *Doctor Faustus*.[2]

1. Compare with *Tamburlaine*, IV, ii, 1, Browne's phrase about "Bajazet in the grate" (*C. M.*, II, x — W, III, 116) and his jocular allusion to "Tamerlane ascending his horse from the neck of Bajazet" (*Musaeum Clausum*, W, III, 272 — which also mentions Bajazet's "iron cage") — undoubtedly a hit at Marlowe's heroics, somewhat in the manner of other Elizabethan jibes at the "hollow pampered jades of Asia." In the third passage (*V. E.*, VII, xvi — W, II, 265) Browne "denies," on the authority of the historians Knollis and Alhazen, "that Tamerlane was a Scythian shepherd," as Marlowe, of course, had represented him. *Tamburlaine* held its place on the stage until after 1640 (cf. Tucker Brooke, "The Reputation of Christopher Marlowe," *Transactions Conn. Academy of Arts & Sciences*, XXV, 372). Its popularity was such that no confirmed playgoer or reader, least of all Browne, could have helped knowing it. (Possibly he also knew Marlowe's sources, but at that time of day "vulgar errors" concerning Tamburlaine owed their currency not to Marlowe's sources but to Marlowe's play.)

Another allusion — "Every ear is filled with the story of Friar Bacon, that made a brazen head to speak . . . which [story] is surely too literally received" (*V. E.*, VII, xvii — W, II, 275) — may justify the conjecture that Browne knew also, among other versions of the tale, Greene's *Friar Bacon and Friar Bungay*.

The reader may decide, finally, whether the following parallelism justifies the conjecture that Browne may also have remembered a line from Aspatia's song in Beaumont and Fletcher's *Maid's Tragedy*:

Lay a garland on my hearse . . .　　　[Most men] content with less than their own
Upon my buried body lie　　　　　　depth, have wished *their bones might lie soft*, and
Lightly, gentle earth. (II, i, 72–79.)　the *earth be light upon them.* (*U. B.*, ch. 1 — W, III, 7.)

2. I think Browne echoes it in the following passage:

I have so fixed my contemplations on　　Cf. *Faustus*, III, 80–84:
heaven, that I have almost forgot the idea of　Thinkst thou that I who saw the face of God
hell; and am afraid rather to lose *the joys of*　And tasted the eternal *joys of heaven*,
the one, than endure the misery of the other:　*Am not tormented with ten thousand hells*
to be deprived of them is *a perfect hell*. (*R. M.*,　In being *depriv'd of everlasting bliss?*
I, lii — W, II, 402–403.)

It must be admitted, finally, that Browne does not once actually *name* Shakspere in the length and breadth of his work. How significant the omission may be, the reader must decide for himself. I for one am quite ready to admit — in spite of the casual allusions to writers and plays which I have been able to piece together — that it was not Browne's custom to pay his immediate literary predecessors the tribute of naming them. Nor was he without precedent in this respect. Virgil, as Sir Thomas himself reminds us, "so much beholding unto Homer, hath not his name in all his works." [1] But, though Browne does not actually name Shakspere, I think he does *allude* to him at least once. The allusion is tucked away in the vast bulk of the *Vulgar Errors* — in an unobtrusive corner of the chapter "Of Pigmies." [2] Of the existence of this "dwarfish race" Browne is unable to find any "exact testimony." The "primitive author" of the fables concerning them was Homer, whose account was "more largely set out by Oppian, Juvenal, Mantuan, *and many poets since*, and being only a pleasant figment in the fountain, became a solemn story in the stream, and *current still among us*." Just before the end of the chapter, a note on "the pigmies of Paracelsus" ("By pigmies intending *fairies* and other spirits about the earth") brings the matter closer home; for Browne concludes by remarking that a certain story concerning the pigmies of India [3] is "a relation below *the tale of Oberon*" — that is to say, surely, a fairy-tale less credible (to the serious chronicler of the poetic fictions of vulgar error) than *A Midsummer-Night's Dream* itself. [4]

1. *V. E.*, I, vi — W, I, 44.
2. *Id.*, IV, xi — W, I, 421, 425.
3. Cf. *A Midsummer-Night's Dream*, II, i, 69, 124.
4. I do not mean to suggest that Browne necessarily had in mind only Shakspere's version of the tale. Possibly his remarks about pigmy "archers" may have reference to that goodly archer, "the dwarfe of the fayre, kynge Oberon" in the old romance of *Huon of Burdeaux* (cf. Furness, Variorum *Midsummer-Night's Dream*, p. xxv), and he may also have remembered Spenser's Oberon, not to mention Greene's, Drayton's, and Herrick's.

Having thus surveyed the ground, we may resume our inquiry with better hopes of bringing it "unto iterated and certain conclusions." Must these, after all, be conclusions from which nothing can be concluded? The skeptics who would laugh out of court anything and everything that they can manage to label "parallel-chasing," will say so — but they need to be reminded that all loose generalizations are false, including theirs, and that in the study of imaginative literature anyone whose eyes and ears are open constantly meets with analogies, parallelisms, echoes of thought or language, which sometimes, if in a given instance one unwarily pauses to look or listen more closely, become not the pursued but the pursuers. It is my belief that the cumulative effect of the indications here to be added to those already noted, of verbal or figurative Shaksperian reminiscence in Browne, and of likenesses between the two in thought and *Lebensanschauung*, will establish the soundness of my general hypothesis. But I do not wish to make too large a claim. The relationship between Shakspere and Browne is by no means so close and circumstantial as that, for example, between Shakspere and Milton. Partly, no doubt, because Browne, unlike Milton, wrote very little verse of any kind, and no dramatic verse, the relation is far less roundly demonstrable in Browne's case. Milton once thought of writing a tragedy of his own on the theme of *Macbeth*. He did not do so, but he did transcribe his memories of *Macbeth* into almost all the poems he did write.[1] Browne, on the other hand, had no designs of his own upon the Tale of Oberon, and I have found no clear echoes of *A Midsummer-Night's Dream* [2] in his writings, though I have no doubt

Yet in view of the vastly greater currency and influence of Shakspere's version — its constant, and sometimes notorious, revivals and abridgments during Browne's youth (the 1630's), in Commonwealth times, and after the Restoration — it is safe to look upon a playgoer's mention of the tale of Oberon as an allusion to *A Midsummer-Night's Dream*.

1. See below, pp. 161–162.
2. See, however, the passage quoted below, p. 266, item (14).

whatsoever that he had read or seen the play and many of the other comedies. The evidence, it will appear, suggests that the tragedies impressed themselves most deeply upon Browne's imagination and memory — but I do not wish to overstate the case even for the tragedies. I do not forget Browne's own warning — that there is much in him "not pick'd from the leaves of any author but bred amongst the weeds and tares of [his] own brain" [1] — or his flat denial [2] of indebtedness to Montaigne's *Essays*, after one of the early annotators of the *Religio Medici* had "paralleled many passages" between the two works. In short, I am well aware of the fact that certain likenesses between almost any two authors may be merely, as Browne puts it,[3] the product of "conceits and expressions common unto them with others, and that not by *imitation* but *coincidence and concurrence* [4] of imagination upon harmony of production." But it is desirable to bear in mind also the probabilities on the other side, and here again I shall let Browne speak for me. In his analysis of the causes of vulgar error he gives a prominent place to "the fictions of poets." "Laudable" as he thinks their purposes may be (even though they treat of such "Egyptian notions" as harpies and griffins), they are dangerous in effect, because their poetic beauty tends to make their underlying "errors" stick in the mind, "*settling impressions in our tender memories* which our advanced judgments generally neglect to expunge." [5] After making all reasonable deductions and allowances, I think we shall not be "making cables out of cobwebs" if we recognize in the following illustrations this characteristic reaction of great poetry upon the assimilative functions of the creative imagination: its power of "settling impressions," unexpungeable by space or time, upon the memory of other poets — "makers" in verse or prose.

1. *R. M.*, I, xxxvi — W, II, 377.
2. "Extracts from Common Place Books," W, III, 354.
3. *Ibid.*   4. Italics mine.   5. *V. E.*, I, ix — W, I, 75.

I. Verbal or Figurative Parallels

1. *Richard III.*

Cheer thy heart, and be thou not dismay'd,
God and good angels fight on Richmond's side. (V, iii, 174–175.)

I hold that . . . as the devil is concealed and denied by some, so *God and good angels*[1] are pretended by others. (*R. M.*, I, xxx — W, II, 367.)

2. *King John.*[2]

Within me is a hell . . .[3] (V, vii, 46.)

The heart of man is the place the devils dwell in; I feel sometimes *a hell within myself.* (*R. M.*, I, li — W, II, 402.)

3. *Richard II.*[4]

Bolingbroke. Must I not serve a long apprenticehood
To foreign passages? . . .
Gaunt. All places that the eye of heaven visits
Are to a wise man ports and happy havens . . .
Boling. Where'er I wander, boast of this I can,
Though banish'd, *yet a trueborn Englishman.* (I, iii, 271–309.)

National repugnances do not touch me . . . *All places*, all airs *make unto me one country; I am in England everywhere*, and under any meridian. (*R. M.*, II, i—W, II, 415.)

4. *I Henry IV.*[5]

Yet *such extenuation let me beg*
As, in reproof of *many tales devis'd*,

Be deaf unto the suggestions of talebearers, calumniators, *pickthank* or *malevolent delators*, who, while quiet

---

1. This phrase is not Scriptural. Browne has "God *in* good angels" and "God and good friends" elsewhere ("Common Place Books," W, III, 353; "Letter to Thomas Browne," W, III, 415). Milton also has the phrase. (See below, p. 171.)

2. See also below, p. 118, n. 5.

3. See my note on this passage and Milton's "the hell within him," below, p. 173.

4. "'The world that I regard,' he [Browne] says, in the spirit of the imprisoned Richard II, 'is myself.'" (Leslie Stephen, "Sir Thomas Browne," *Hours in a Library*, 2d series, p. 29.)

5. Compare also the following:

If all the year were playing holiday
To *sport* would be as *tedious* as to work,
But when they seldom come, they wish'd for come,
And *nothing pleaseth but rare accidents.*
(I, ii, 227–230.)

Even in our sensual days, the strength of *delight* is in its *seldomness* or *rarity* [Doctor Johnson here quotes "*Voluptates commendat rarior usus*"] and *sting* in its *satiety.* (*C. M.*, II, i — W, III, 108.)

Which oft the ears of greatness
    needs must hear,
By smiling *pick-thanks*[1] and base
    newsmongers,
I may, for some things true . . .
Find pardon . . . (III, ii, 22–28.)

men sleep, sowing the tares of discord
and division, distract the tranquillity
of charity and all friendly society.
(*C. M.*, I, xx—W, III, 97.)

5. *Julius Caesar.*[2]

O judgment! thou art fled to
    brutish beasts,
And *men have lost their reason.* (III,
    ii, 109–110.)

Men have lost their reason in nothing so
much as their religion. (*U. B.*, ch. 4 —
W, II, 34.)

6. *Hamlet.*[3]

(*a*) To *sleep?* Perchance to *dream!*
    Ay, there's the rub; . . .
    For who would bear the whips
    and scorns of time . . .
    The insolence of office, and the
    spurns

(*b*) That *patient merit* of the unworthy
    takes . . .
    But that the dread of something
    after death,
    The undiscovered country from
    whose bourn

(*c*) No traveller returns, *puzzles* the
    will . . . (III, i, 65–80.)

The smattering I have of the
philosopher's stone . . . hath . . .
instructed my belief how that immortal spirit and incorruptible substance of my soul may lie obscure
and *sleep* awhile. (*R. M.*, I, xxxix— (*a*)
W, II, 383.)

Let thy arrows of revenge fly
short . . . *patient meekness takes in-* (*b*)
juries like pills, not chewing but
swallowing them down. (*C. M.*, III,
xii—W, III, 130.)

(*d*) *There is something* in this *more
    than natural, if philosophy
    could find it out.* (II, ii, 383–
    385.)

There are *more things in heaven
    and earth,* Horatio,
*Than are dreamt of in our philos-
    ophy.* (I, v, 166–167.)

There is in these works of *nature,* (*d*)
which seem to *puzzle reason,* some- (*c*)
thing divine, and hath *more in it*[4]
than the eye of the common spectator (*d*)
doth discover. (*R. M.*, I, xxxix—W,
II, 383).

[On the conversion of dust to lice
(*Exodus*, VIII, 16)]: An act *philosophy can scarce deny to be above the
power of nature.* (*V. E.*, I, x—W, I,
78.)

---

1. Holinshed's word.   2. See also below, pp. 123–124, item (2).
3. See also above, p. 105, item 8 (*a*).
4. See also *V. E.*, II, vi ("Of Mandrakes") — W, I, 199: "Signaturists . . . have
made men suspect *there was more therein than ordinary practice allowed.*"

(e) Give me the cup. Let go!   By
    heaven, I'll have 't! . . .
If thou didst ever hold me in thy
    heart,
Absent thee from felicity a while
And in *this harsh world* draw thy
    breath in pain
To tell my story. (V, ii, 354–360.)

The mischief of diseases . . . the (e)
villainy of poisons . . . the fury of
guns . . . Certainly *there is no happiness within this circle of flesh;* nor
is it in the opticks of these eyes to
behold *felicity.* (*R. M.*, I, xliv—W,
II, 389.)

Court not *felicity* [1] too far. (*C. M.*,
II, x—W, III, 115.)

(f) *In my mind's eye,* Horatio.   (I, ii,
    185.)

Behold thyself by *inward opticks* (f)
. . . the *inward* [2] *eyes* . . . and the
crystalline of thy soul. (*C. M.*, III,
xv—W, III, 133.)

(g)[6] *Fortune?* Oh, most true; *she is a
    strumpet.* (II, ii, 238–240).

Out, out, *thou strumpet fortune.*
(II, ii, 515.)

I cannot justify that contempti- (g)
ble proverb, that "fools only are
fortunate;" [3] or that insolent para-
dox, that "a wise man is out of
the reach of *fortune;*" much less
those *opprobrious epithets of poets,*—
whore,[4] bawd,[5] and *strumpet.* (*R. M.*,
I, xviii—W, II, 345.)

---

1. After completing this essay, I find that Paul Elmer More ("Sir Thomas Browne,"
Shelburne Essays, 6th series, p. 180) quotes a similar passage — "He had no opinion of
reputed Felicities below . . . as well understanding there are not Felicities . . . received
and customary Felicities . . . in this world to satisfy a serious mind" — from Browne's
Letter to a Friend (W, III, 77). More adds, concerning the "thrice-repeated felicities,"
"Echoes of the word come to me from great passages in Spanish and French, and last of all
the plea of dying Hamlet to his friend."

2. Cf. Chaucer's "Thilke yen of his minde." (Man of Law's Tale, l. 552.)

3. *Fortuna favet fatuis.* Cf. *As You Like It*, II, vii, 18–19:

"Good morrow, fool," quoth I. "No sir," quoth he,
"Call me not fool till heaven hath sent me fortune."

4. Cf. *Macbeth*, I, ii, 14–15:

"Fortune . . .
Show'd like a rebel's *whore.*"

5. Cf. *King John*, III, i, 60–61:

France is a *bawd to Fortune* and King John,
That strumpet fortune.

All the poets, of course, say their say concerning fortune; but the epithets to which Browne
alludes are certainly those of the English poets.

6. Compare also: (1) Hamlet's "There is nothing either good or bad but thinking
makes it so" (II, ii, 256–257) with Browne's remark that "contraries, though they destroy

7. *Othello.*[1]

One whose hand, Like the base *Indian*,[2] threw a *pearl* away Richer than all his tribe. (V, ii, 346–348.)	The *pearl* we seek for is not to be found in the *Indian* but in the Empyrean ocean. (*C. M.*, III, xi—W, III, 130.)

8. *King Lear.*[3]

These late *eclipses in the sun and moon* portend no good to us. Though the wisdom of nature can reason it thus and thus, yet nature finds itself scourg'd by the *sequent effects*. (I, ii, 112–115.)	[The devil] doth . . . sometime delude us in the conceits of stars and meteors . . . a rainbow in the night . . . *eclipses of sun or moon* . . . [These], the effects of natural and created causes . . . are always looked on by ignorant spectators as supernatural spectacles, and made the causes or signs of most *succeeding contingencies*. (*V. E.*, I, xi—W, I, 86-87.)
This is the excellent foppery of the world, that, when we are sick in fortune, — often the surfeits of our own behavior, — we make guilty of our disasters the sun, the moon, and the stars, as if we were . . . fools by heavenly compulsion, knaves, thieves, and treachers by spherical predominance. (I, ii, 128–134.)	Burden not the back of Aries, Leo, or Taurus, with thy faults; nor make Saturn, Mars, or Venus, guilty of thy follies. (*C. M.*, III, vii—W, III, 125–126.)

---

one another, are yet the life of one another. Thus virtue (abolish vice) is an idea" (*R. M.*, II, iv—W, II, 426); (2) the following passages:

'T is not alone my inky cloak, good mother, Nor *customary* suits of solemn black . . . Together with all *forms, moods, shows* of grief . . . These . . . are *actions that a man might play;* But I have that within which passeth show, — These but the trappings and the suits of woe. (I, ii, 77–86.)	Covetousness . . . brings *formal sadness, scenical mourning, and no wet eyes at the grave.* (*C. M.*, I, viii — W, III, 91.)

1. Compare also:

The *Cannibals* that each other eat, The *Anthropophagi*. (I, iii, 143–144).	We are what we all abhor, *anthropophagi* and *cannibals*, devourers not only of men but of ourselves. (*R. M.*, I, xxxvii — W, II, 379.)

2. Cf. Furness, Variorum *Othello*, on this line and the disputed reading, "Indian," as against the "Iudian" perversely preferred by some editors. Apparently the *Christian Morals* passage has not hitherto been noted in this connection.

3. Cf. also I, iv, 211–212: "Now art thou an O without a figure" (a line which Milton may have remembered; see below, p. 181, n. 1) with Browne's remark that sins "as they

9. *Macbeth.*

(*a*) See above, p. 106, item 10 (*a*).

(*b*) See above, p. 118, n. 4.

(*c*) Sleep that knits up the ravell'd
sleave of care,
The death of each day's life . . .
(II, ii, 37–38.)

We term *sleep* [1] a *death;* and yet it is
waking that kills us and destroys those
spirits that are the house of life. 'T is
indeed a part of life that best express-
eth death . . . *Sleep* . . . *is that death
by which we may be literally said to die
daily.* (*R. M.*, II, xii—W, II, 446.)

The way to be immortal is *to die
daily.* (*R.M.*, I, xlv—W, II, 390.)

(*d*) Happy *prologues* to the *swelling*
act. (I, iii, 128.)

Swelling beginnings have found un-
comfortable conclusions. (*C. M.*, II, x
—W, III, 117, n. 8.)

(*e*) *1. Murderer.* We are *men,* my
liege.
Macb. Ay, *in the catalogue* ye go
for men,
As hounds and greyhounds, mon-
grels . . . curs . . . are clept
All by the name of dogs; *the
valued file*
Distinguishes the swift, the slow,
the subtle . . .
According to the gift which
bounteous nature
Hath in him clos'd; *whereby he
does receive*
Particular addition, from the bill
That writes them all alike; *and so
of men.* (III, i, 91–101.)

Let us speak like politicians; there
is a nobility without heraldry . . .
whereby one man is ranked with another;
another *filed* before him, *according to
the quality of his desert,* and pre-emi-
nence of his good parts. (*R. M.*, II, i—
W, II, 416.)

---

proceed . . . ever multiply, and, *like figures in arithmetick,* the last stands for more than all
that went before it." (*R. M.*, I, xlii — W, II, 386.)

1. "The brother of death" ("On Dreams," W, III, 342) — with which compare
Cymbeline, II, iii, 31 ("O sleep, thou ape of death"), and Daniel's *Care-Charmer Sleep*
("Sleep . . . Brother to Death").

(f) Will all great Neptune's *ocean wash this blood Clean* from my hand? (II, ii, 60–61.)

Be thou what thou virtuously art, and let not the *ocean*[1] *wash away thy tincture.* (*C. M.*, I, ix—W, III, 91.)

10. *The Merchant of Venice.*

If to do were as easy as *to know what were good to do,* chapels had been churches and poor men's cottages princes' palaces. *It is a good divine that follows his own instructions. I can easier teach twenty what were good to be done, than to be one of the twenty to follow mine own teaching.* (I, ii, 13–18.)

The practice of men holds not an equal pace, yea and often *runs counter to their theory;* we naturally know what is good, but naturally pursue what is evil: *the rhetorick wherewith I persuade another cannot persuade myself.* (*R. M.*, I, lv—W, II, 409.)

It is no mean happiness, therefore, to be seated in the mean. *Superfluity comes sooner by white hairs,* but competency lives longer. (I, ii, 7–10.)

If the nearness of our last necessity brought a nearer conformity unto it, there were a happiness in hoary hairs, and no calamity in half-senses. (*U. B.*, ch. 5—W, III, 41.)

11. *All's Well That Ends Well.*

The web of our life is of a mingled yarn, good and ill together: our *virtues* would be proud if our *faults* whipp'd them not; and our *crimes* would despair if they were not cherish'd by our *virtues.* (IV, iii, 83–87.)

The line of our lives is drawn with white and black vicissitudes, wherein the *extremes* hold seldom *one* complexion. (*C. M.*, II, x—W, III, 116.)

12–15. Concerning *Romeo and Juliet,*[2] *Much Ado About Nothing,*[3] *As You Like It,*[4] and *The Tempest,*[5] see notes as indicated.

---

1. Cf. also *Much Ado,* IV, i, 141–143:

O, she is fallen
Into a pit of ink, that *the wide sea
Hath drops too few to wash her clean again.*

2. See below, pp. 124, 266, item (16).   3. See n. 1.

4. See above, p. 118, n. 3; below, pp. 123, 126, and compare the following passages:

And so, from hour to hour we ripe and ripe,
And then, from hour to hour, we rot and rot,
And thereby hangs a tale. (II, vii, 26–28.)

If we begin to die when we live, and long life be but a prolongation of death, our life is a sad composition; we live with death, and die not in a moment. (*U. B.*, ch. 5 — W, III, 41.)

5. See above, p. 106.

Sir Edmund Gosse [1] significantly observes that Browne, with
his insatiable "instinct for reducing everything in heaven or earth
to the substance of the subject in hand, perpetually *wants* words"
— above all "picturesque" words — and "*seeks* them ardently
. . . far afield and in the most unlikely places." Surely the cumulative indications of the materials just presented justify the conclusion that consciously or unconsciously his memory of Shaksperian
imagery and phraseology helped him in this quest. If so, we have
established a basic relationship which justifies further inquiry into
the difficult question of the relationship between Shakspere's *thinking* and Browne's. That there would seem to be a more or less tan-
gible relationship of this kind my citations suggest incidentally —
as indeed they must, since words and thoughts cannot, in the long
run, be kept apart. Those who first teach our lips language are not
mere language teachers, and he who is wise in words helps, first and
last, to shape the thought as well as the words of those who love
him. As for Shakspere and Browne, no less a dissenter than Lowell
admits that great poets may "influence thought," though he adds
that he thinks "it would be difficult to show how Shakespeare had
done so directly and wilfully." [2] Now the difficulty of estimating
any "direct" (not to say "wilfull") influence of Shakspere upon
Browne, is especially great — as I have already intimated —
because of the pronounced differences between them: because
Browne was a scholar and a scientist, a poet only in the large sense
of the term, a lover of the theatre, but not a dramatist. It seems
certain that in his imaginative as in his scientific writings — to
draw, for the moment, a distinction which breaks down as soon as
one reads consecutively a page or two in the one or the other — he
used to the utmost all available sources not only of words and imagery but of facts and ideas. But it is equally certain that he also
experimented and thought — with the vigor and intuitive bril-

1. *Life of Sir T. Browne*, pp. 193–194.   2. *Among My Books*, 2 Ser., pp. 181–182.

liance of a man of genius — for himself.[1] The probability is, however, that many of his ideas and Shakspere's reflect merely their common Elizabethan and Jacobean heritage. Under the circumstances it would, as a rule, be folly to urge that any one of the notable likenesses between them in thought or general point of view is an absolutely certain or "direct" product of Shakspere's influence. In the aggregate, however, and in view of what has gone before, I believe them to be significant.[2] At worst, the following more or less schematic summary of some of these likenesses should be useful because it illustrates afresh the fact that Shakspere's thought was also the best thought of his immediate aftertimes. It is my belief, however, that these materials in general, and particularly those in the last section, confirm the inferences I have drawn from those already presented, and thereby my general hypothesis that Shakspere's influence upon Browne was substantial and vital.

II. General Likenesses in Thought, Mood, or Point of View

1. *Adversity.*

With the good Duke's "sweet are the uses of adversity"[3] (and Bacon's essay on the subject) compare Browne's admonition:

Quarrel not rashly with adversities not yet understood, and overlook not the mercies often bound up in them: for we consider not sufficiently the good of evils, nor fairly compute the mercies of providence in things afflictive at first hand. (*C. M.*, I, xxix — W, III, 103.)

2. *On the Influence of the Stars.*[4]

Both writers give full weight to the possible "influence of the stars" upon human affairs and character, but both assert the responsibility and the efficacy of the individual will against external instrumentalities:

---

1. Let anyone who doubts this read, without prejudice, a small fragment of the *Pseudodoxia* — say any ten consecutive chapters.

2. Though I do not wish to press too far the claims of any one of the plays as an influence upon Browne's thinking.

3. *As You Like It*, II, i, 12.   4. See also above, p. 119 (8) (*Lear*).

(*a*)   Here
Will I set up my everlasting rest
And shake the yoke of inauspicious
  stars
From this world-wearied flesh.
    (*Romeo and Juliet*, V, iii, 109–
    112.)

      It is the stars,[1]
The stars above us govern our conditions. (*Lear*, IV, iii, 34–35.)

(*b*) This is the excellent foppery of the
world that . . . we are . . . knaves
. . . and treachers by spherical
predominance. (*Lear*, I, ii, 128–
134.)

'T is in ourselves that we are thus
and thus. Our bodies are our
gardens, to the which our wills are
gardeners. (*Othello*, I, iii, 322–324.)

The fault, dear Brutus, is not in our
  stars,
But in ourselves, that we are under-
lings. (*Julius Caesar*, I, ii, 140–
141.)

[Browne discredits the] celestial influence [of the Dog Star] upon the
faculties of men [but does not] reject
or condemn a sober and regulated as-
trology . . . We deny not the influence of the stars, but often suspect the
due application thereof . . . What
power soever they have. upon our
bodies, it is not requisite they should
destroy our reasons . . . and when we
conceive the heaven against us, to refuse the assistance of the earth created
for us . . . There is in wise men a
power beyond the stars. (*V. E.*, IV,
xiii — W, I, 448, 461–462.)

Think not to fasten thy imperfections on the stars . . . Let celestial
aspects admonish and advertise, not
conclude and determine thy ways . . .
Whatever influences . . . there be from
the lights above, it were a piece of wisdom to make one of those wise men
who overrule their stars. (*C. M.*, III,
vii — W, III, 126.)

3. *Silence.*

Anyone who has read thus far along in this book, will agree that
Browne's views on this subject are thoroughly in accord with
Shakspere's:

Think not silence the wisdom of fools;[2] but, if rightly timed, the honour of wise men, who have not the infirmity but the virtue of taciturnity;
and speak not out of the abundance but the well-weighed thoughts of
their hearts. Such silence may be eloquence and speak thy worth above
the power of words . . . Let him have the key of thy heart who has the
lock of his own. (*C. M.*, III, xviii — W, III, 135.)

1. See also Sonnets 14, 15, *etc.*
2. Cf. above, "Shakspere's Silences," pp. 13–14, 24, *etc.*

4. *Avarice.*

This avarice Sticks deeper, grows with more pernicious root Than summer-seeming lust. (*Macbeth*, IV, iii, 84–86.)	To me avarice seems not so much a vice as a deplorable piece of madness . . . There is no delirium if we do but speculate the folly and indisputable dotage of avarice. (*R. M.*, II, xiv — W, II, 448.)

5. *Friendship.*

A famous hyperbole in the *Religio Medici* affords a capital illustration of the continuing vitality of the literary convention [1] of ideal friendship (a theme more real to the Elizabethans than some of the editors of *The Two Gentlemen of Verona*,[2] for example, appear to understand):

I hope I do not break the fifth commandment if I conceive I may love my friend before the nearest of my blood . . . I never yet cast true affection on a woman; but I have loved my friend as I do virtue, my soul, my God. From hence, methinks, I do conceive how God loves man. (II, v — W, II, 430.)

6. *The Vanity of Learning.*[3]

All delights are vain, but that most vain Which, with pain purchas'd, doth inherit pain; As, painfully to pore upon a book To seek the light of truth, while truth the while Doth falsely blind the eyesight of his look. So ere you find where light in darkness lies Your light grows dark by losing of your eyes. (*Love's Labour's Lost*, I, i, 72–79; cf. *Taming of the Shrew*, I, i, 27–41.)	There is yet another conceit that hath sometimes made me shut my books, which tells me it is a vanity to waste our days in the blind pursuit of knowledge . . . which death gives every fool gratis. (*R. M.*, II, viii — W, II, 437–438).

---

1. Browne's biographers, and his own letters, mention many good friends of his, but hardly any *one*, I think, who altogether fits the passage quoted.

2. See above, p. 75.

3. Cf. *Ecclesiastes*, I, 18; XII, 12.

7. *On Satire and Satirists.*

Polonius. What do you read, my lord?

Hamlet. Words, words, words.

Pol. What is the matter, my lord? . . .

Haml. Slanders, sir; for the satirical slave says here that old men have grey beards . . . and that they have a plentiful lack of wit, together with weak hams; all which, sir, though I most powerfully . . . believe, yet I hold it not honesty to have it thus set down. (*Hamlet*, II, ii, 193–204.)

I can . . . behold vice without a satire, content only with an admonition or instructive reprehension; for noble natures and such as are capable of goodness, are railed into vice, that might as easily be admonished into virtue. (*R. M.*, II, iv — W, II, 426.)

Jaques.   I must have liberty
Withal, as large a charter as the wind,
   To blow on whom I please . . .
   Give me leave
   To speak my mind and I will through and through
   Cleanse the foul body of the infected world . . .
Duke. Fie on thee! I can tell what thou wouldst do . . .
   Most mischievous foul sin in chiding sin;
   For *thou thyself hast been a libertine . . .*
   And all the embossed sores and headed evils
   That thou with license of free foot hast caught
   Wouldst thou disgorge into the general world. (*As You Like It*, II, vii, 47–69.)

He that is chaste and continent not to impair his strength . . . will hardly be heroically virtuous. Adjourn not this virtue until that temper when Cato could lend out his wife, and *impotent satyrs write satires upon lust*, but be chaste in thy flaming days. (*C. M.*, I, iii — W, III, 89.)

8. *The Multitude.*

The *blunt monster with uncounted heads,*
The still discordant, wav'ring multitude. (*II Henry IV*, Ind., 18–19.)

If there be any among those common objects of hatred I do contemn and laugh at, it is that great enemy of reason, virtue, and religion, the multitude; that *numerous* piece of *monstros-*

SHAKSPERE AND SIR THOMAS BROWNE   127

The *fool multitude* that choose by
show . . .
. . . the barbarous multitudes.
(*Merchant*, II, ix, 26, 33.)

The distracted multitude
Who like not in their judgment but
their eyes. (*Hamlet*, IV, iii, 4–5.)

You blocks, you stones, you worse
than senseless things . . .

Antony. Now let it work. Mis-
chief thou art afoot,
Take thou what course thou
wilt . . .
Servant. Brutus and Cassius
Are rid like madmen through the
gates of Rome . . .
Ant. Belike they had some notice
of *the people*
How I had moved them. (*Julius
Caesar*, I, i, 40; III, ii, 265–
276.)

Dissentious rogues . . . no surer,
no,
Than is the coal of fire upon the
ice,
Or hailstone in the sun. (*Coriolanus*, I, i, 168–178.)

ity, which, taken asunder, seem men
. . . but, confused together, make but
one great beast, and a *monstrosity* more
prodigious than *Hydra*. It is no breach
of charity to call these *fools*. (*R.M.*, II,
i — W, II, 415.)

The second cause of Common Errors,
the erroneous Disposition of *the people;*
[who] live and die in their absurdities,
passing their dayes in perverted appre-
hensions and conceptions of the world,
derogatory unto God and the wisdom
of the creation . . . *A confusion of
knaves and fools*, and a farraginous concurrence of all conditions, tempers,
sexes and ages. . . . *Unto them a piece
of rhetorick is a sufficient argument of
logick* . . . [their] credulity is illimit-
able. . . . *The multitude . . . are . . .
fools.* (*V.E.*, I, iii, v — W, I, 16–17, 20,
18, 34, 38.)

9. *"The Lamentable Change."*

The lowest and most dejected thing
of fortune
Stands yet in esperance, lives not
in fear:
*The lamentable change is from the
best;*
The worst returns to laughter. (*Lear*,
IV, i, 3–6.)

*Since in the highest felicities there lieth a
capacity for the lowest miseries* [for-
tune][1] *hath this advantage from our
happiness to make us truly miserable:
for to become acutely miserable we are
to be first happy. Affliction smarts
most in the happy state.* (*C.M.*, II,
x — W, III, 116).

10. *On Death and the Circumstance of Mortality.*

No subject was closer to Browne's heart and mind than his
broodings upon "the nearness of our last necessity." Nothing so

1. See above, p. 118, item (*g*).

stirred him to poetry as his meditations upon the dust and decay, the pomp and circumstance, of death. The subject, obviously, had a double hold upon him.[1] As a Christian physician, he never undertook to cure the body of his patient without calling "unto God for his soul"; but, even so, he had often to look upon the face of death and "diseases incurable."[2] His interest in the subject, however, far transcended his professional concern with it. The thought of death stirred him to the depths, — as it always has and always will all men like him, but none more than the great Elizabethans, — because he was a poet at heart, and, by virtue of his finely balanced imaginative and intellectual powers, one of the most subtly and passionately inquiring spirits of his time. The critics, in sooth, think he was too sad. "To Browne," says Walter Pater,[3] "all the grace and beauty" of the world is "of a somewhat mortified kind"; and a French critic remarks that he has "*la tristesse pensive de Shakespeare, sans avoir ses joyeuses vivacités.*"[4] Before proceeding we may, therefore, do well to recall that Browne did know how to laugh on occasion[5] — that he was blessed with an elusive but delicately pervasive sense of humor.[6] But M. Milsand's remark[4] points in the right direction. Between Shakspere's meditations upon death and Browne's — in their common "apprehension of mortality" — there seem to me certain likenesses so challenging as to justify the assertion that some portions of

1. As, indeed, it had upon Shakspere. Shakspere's dramatic objectivity is a primary fact too often put aside by impressionistic or sentimental criticism. But it is also a fact that death came home to him directly and indirectly — through the loss of his only son, for example, and through his (probably) intimate relationships with another good physician, his son-in-law, Dr. Hall.

2. *R. M.*, II, vi, ix — W, II, 432, 441.

3. *Op. cit.*, p. 138.

4. M. J. Milsand, "Thomas Browne, le Médecin philosophe de Norwich," *Revue des Deux Mondes* (April and August, 1858), XIV, 646 ff.; XVI, 632 ff. (see p. 651).

5. See above, p. 105.

6. Cf. *Seventeenth Century Essays*, ed. J. Zeitlin, Introduction, p. xxxix.

Browne's writings upon this theme bear more or less definite marks of Shaksperian influence. In the illustrative matter listed immediately below, it will appear at once that some of the expressions of the two writers (like some of those on other subjects treated above) are merely analogous in a general way. Others are different. Thus, parts of the *Urn Burial*, if I read it aright, reflect intimately the thought and mood of *Hamlet*, — the Hamlet mood in general and the Gravediggers' Scene in particular, — a play which seems also to have stamped itself indelibly upon his verbal and figurative memory.[1] They illustrate the play admirably, but the play, in turn, admirably illustrates them. For in the writing of them, if I am not mistaken, memories of *Hamlet* must have come to mind almost as inevitably as they now do in the reading.

A. General Aspects of the Theme.

1. On death and sleep, see above, p. 120, item 9 (*c*), *Macbeth*.
2. On life as slow decay, see above, p. 121, n. 4.
3. "A lightning before death":

How oft when men are at the point of death Have they been merry! which their keepers call A lightning before death . . . (*Romeo and Juliet*, V, iii, 88–90.)

Men sometimes upon the hour of their departure do speak and reason above themselves. For then the soul begins to be freed from the ligaments of the body, begins to reason like herself, and to discourse in a strain above mortality. (*R. M.*, II, xi — W, II, 446.)[2]

4. Revenge beyond death.

Now might I do it pat, now he is praying . . . Oh, this is hire and salary, not revenge . . . To take him in the purging of his soul When he is fit and season'd for his passage? No! . . .

I am heartily sorry, and wish it were not true, what to the dishonour of Christianity is affirmed of the Italian, who, after he had inveigled his enemy to disclaim his faith for the redemption of his life, did presently poniard him, to prevent repentance and assure his eternal death. (*V. E.*, VII, xix — W, II, 286.)

1. See above, pp. 117–118.
2. Cf. *I. Henry IV*, V, iv, 83: "O, I could prophesy . . ."

When he is drunk asleep . . . or
about some act
That has no relish of salvation
in 't,
Then trip him, that his heels may
kick at heaven,
And that his soul may be as
damn'd and black
As hell, where to it goes. (*Hamlet*,
III, iii, 73–95.)

I cannot believe the story of the
Italian;[1] it is the devil . . . that de-
sire[s] our misery in the world to come.
(*R. M.*, II, vi — W, II, 432.)

B. Immortal Longings.

"Most men," writes Leslie Stephen,[2] "for one reason or another, have at times been 'half in love with easeful death.'" For
one reason or another, few men have so often or so poignantly recorded *this* love-longing as did Shakspere and Browne:

1. Give me my robe, put on my
   crown, I have
   Immortal longings in me.
   (*Antony and Cleopatra*, V, ii,
   283–284.)

O how this earthly temper doth debase
The noble soul in this her humble place!
Whose wingy nature ever doth aspire
To reach that place where first it took
its fire! (*R. M.*, I, xxxii — W, II, 370.)

2. The earth can have but earth,
   which is his due . . .
   My spirit . . . is the better part of
   me. (Sonnet 74.)

These walls of flesh wherein the soul
doth seem to be immured before the
resurrection. (*R. M.*, I, xxxvii — W, II,
378–379.)

3. Within be fed, without be rich no
   more:
   So shalt thou feed on Death, that
   feeds on men,
   And Death once dead, there's no
   more dying then. (Sonnet 146.)

There is nothing strictly immortal, but
immortality. (*U. B.*, ch. 5 — W, III,
46.)

4. Since no man has aught of what
   he leaves, what is't to leave
   betimes? . . .
   Absent thee from felicity a while
   . . . (*Hamlet*, V, ii, 233–235,
   358.)

Were there not another life that I
hope for, all the vanities of this world
should not entreat a moment's breath
from me. (*R. M.*, I, xxxviii — W, II,
381.)

---

1. Nashe has the story in *Jack Wilton*. See also *Hamlet*, Furness, Variorum I, 283,
and Fletcher's *The Pilgrim*, Act II, *ad fin.* — "Let him die thus," *etc.*
2. *Op. cit.*, p. 34.

5. Death, death. O amiable lovely
   death! . . .
   Come, grin on me, and I will think
   thou smil'st,
   And buss thee as thy wife. Misery 's love,
   O, come to me! (*King John*,[1] III,
   iv, 25–36.)

   He hates him
   That would upon the rack of this
   tough world
   Stretch him out longer. *Lear*, V,
   iii, 313–315.)

I, that have examined the parts of
man, and know . . . the thousand
doors that lead to death, do thank my
God that we can die but once. 'T is
not only the mischief ["the grating
torture"] of diseases . . . that make an
end of us: . . . it is in the power of
every hand to destroy us . . .[2] There
is therefore but one comfort left, that
though it be in the power of the weak-
est arm to take away life, it is not in
the strongest to deprive us of death.
(*R. M.*, I, xliv — W, II, 389.)

C. *Mementos of Mortality*.

"All Englishmen," said Taine, "love to write about tombs."[3]
The reason, so far as Shakspere and Browne are concerned, is not
far to seek. The tomb, as they look upon it, does not imprison the
best of that which it contains — nothing more, indeed, than "the
infamy of man's nature." When they have said farewell to the
quintessence of mortal dust, when the last bell has tolled, they do
not forget what a piece of work is a man — how noble an animal,
splendid in ashes and pompous in the grave. No two English
writers have ever combined imaginative and temperamental en-
dowments better adapted than theirs to respond to the challenge
of this theme. The horror of the charnel-house (an evil reality of
their time)[4] gripped their darker imaginings, only to make them
fasten all the more strongly upon the refuge of all the ages — the
faith which holds, among other things, that the human body is the
temple of the living God. They dwell poignantly and impres-
sively, therefore, upon those decent and seemly rites by which we
seek to dispute — or at least to gloze over — its invasion by the

1. See also above, p. 124, item 2 (*a*).
2. For the rest of the passage, see above, p. 118, item 6 (*e*) (*Hamlet*).
3. Cf. Leslie Stephen, *op. cit.*
4. See J. Q. Adams, *A Life of William Shakespeare*, p. 474; cf. below, p. 136.

conquering worm, and to prevent its ultimate desecration by clownish sextons turned graveyard ghouls. I have attempted to arrange the illustrative material — much of which inevitably overlaps — under captions which mark out its chief constituent elements. Here, more than in parts *A* and *B* of this section, possible traces of Shakspere's "direct" influence upon Browne may be read between the lines — if not *in* them. These illustrations, finally, will remind the reader that none of our poets has ever inquired more curiously than did these two into the insoluble contradictions that confront the contemplative mind, dwelling upon the mystery of death, in its effort to balance the gross facts of mortality with the elusive truths of the spirit.

1. The dignity and infamy of man.[1]

What a piece of work is a man! How noble in reason! . . . The beauty of the world! *The paragon of animals!* And yet, to me, what is this quintessence of dust? (*Hamlet*, II, ii, 315–321.)

Man is a noble animal, splendid in ashes, and pompous in the grave, solemnizing nativities and deaths with equal lustre, nor omitting ceremonies of bravery in the infamy of his nature. (*U. B.*, ch. 5 — W, III, 47.)

2. The body, the temple of the Spirit.[2]

Nature crescent does not grow alone
In thews and bulk, but, as *this temple* waxes,
The inward service of the mind and soul
Grows wide withal. (*Hamlet*, I, iii, 11–14.)

Christians have . . . acknowledged their bodies to be the lodging of Christ, and *temples* of the Holy Ghost. (*U. B.*, ch. 4 — W, III, 33.)

3. Burial rites and customs.[3]

(*a*) Dry up your tears, and stick your rosemary

Christians have handsomely glossed the deformity of death by careful con-

---

1. Cf. "The Shaksperian Element in Milton," below, p. 154, item (*c*).
2. Cf. *2 Corinthians*, VI, 16, and *Macbeth*, II, iii, 72–74.
3. Cf. also *Hamlet*, V, i, 256–257, and *Cymbeline*, IV, ii, 215 ff.

On this fair corse; and, as the custom is,
In all her best array bear her to church. (*Romeo and Juliet*, IV, v, 79–81.)

Come away, come away, death,
And in sad cypress let me be laid . . .
My shroud of white, stuck all with yew,
O, prepare it! (*Twelfth Night*, II, iv, 52–57.)

Under yon yew-trees [1] lay thee all along. (*Romeo and Juliet*, V, iii, 3.)

b. Guiderius [*preparing to bury Fidele* (*Imogen*)]
Nay . . . we must lay his head to the east;
My father has a reason for 't.
Arviragus. 'T is true. (*Cymbeline*, IV, ii, 255–256,)

She shall be buried with her face upwards. (*Much Ado*, III, ii, 71.)

(*c*) Here she is allowed her virgin rites,
Her maiden strewments . . .
Sweets to the sweet.[2] (*Hamlet*, V, i, 255–266.)

(*d*) Let us . . . sing [3] him to the ground
As once our Mother. (*Cymbeline*, IV, ii, 235–237.)

sideration of the body, and civil rites which take off brutal terminations. (*U. B.*, ch. 4 — W, III, 33.)

The funeral pyre . . . of . . . cypress . . . yew, and trees perpetually verdant . . . Yew in churchyards . . . an emblem of resurrection. (*U. B.*, ch. 4, — W, III, 35.)

Christians dispute how their bodies should lie in the grave . . . A certain posture were to be admitted: which even Pagan civility observed. The Persians lay north and south; the . . . Phoenicians . . . to the east; the Athenians . . . towards the west, which Christians still retain. (*U. B.*, ch. 3 — W, III, 30.)
That they buried their dead on their backs . . . seems agreeable unto profound sleep, and common posture of dying. (*U. B.* — W, III, 36.)
In strewing their tombs, the Romans affected the rose, the Greeks amaranthus and myrtle . . . Christians have found a more elegant emblem. (*U. B.*, ch. 4 — W, III, 35.)
They made use of musick to excite or quiet the affections of their friends, according to different harmonies. But

---

1. Near the Capulets' tomb.
2. Cf. *Cymbeline*, IV, ii, 218–220; *Twelfth Night*, II, iv, 60–61; *Winter's Tale*, IV, iv, 128–129.
3. Cf. *Much Ado*, V, ii, 294–295; iii, 11.

Flights of angels sing thee to thy rest. (*Hamlet*, V, ii, 371.)

the secret and symbolical hint was the harmonical nature of the soul. (*U. B.*, ch. 4 — W, III, 35.)

(*e*)   O most false love!
Where be the sacred vials thou shouldst fill
With sorrowful water? (*Antony and Cleopatra*, I, iii, 62–64.)

No . . . lacrymatories, or tear bottles attended these rural urns . . . With rich flames, and hired tears, they solemnized their obsequies. (*U. B.*, ch. 3 — W, III, 23.)

(*f*) *Edgar.* Look up, my lord.
Kent. Vex not his ghost; O, let him pass! (*Lear*, V, iii, 312–313.)

Mourning without hope, they had an happy fraud against excessive lamentation, by a common opinion that deep sorrows disturb their ghosts. (*U. B.*, ch. 4 — W, III, 35.)

4. Earthy meditations.

Haml. That skull had a tongue in it, and could sing once . . . *How long will a man lie i' the earth ere he rot?*
1. Clown. I' faith, if he be not rotten before he die . . . he will last you some eight or nine year. *A tanner will last you nine year* . . . his hide is so tann'd with his trade that he will keep out water a great while, and your water is a sore decayer of your whoreson dead body . . .
Haml. . . . Prithee, Horatio, tell me one thing . . . Dost thou think *Alexander* look'd o' this fashion i' the earth . . . And smelt so? . . . Why may not imagination trace the noble dust of Alexander [1] till he find it stopping a bung-hole? (*Hamlet*, V, i, 83–226.)

How the bulk of a man should sink into so few pounds of bones and ashes, may seem strange unto any one who considers not its constitution, and how slender a mass will remain upon an open and urging fire in the carnal composition . . . *Some bones make best skeletons; some bodies quick and speediest ashes. Who would expect a quick flame from hydropical Heraclitus?* . . . Though the funeral pyre of *Patroclus* took up an hundred foot, a piece of an old boat burnt *Pompey*; and if the burthen of Isaac were sufficient for an holocaust, a man may carry his own pyre. (*U. B.*, ch. 3 — W, III, 28–29.)

In the *Hydriotaphia* [2] Browne announced, as follows, his discovery of adipocere,[3] one of his "most prominent services to pure science": [4]

---

1. Or of "Imperial Caesar"?
3. Corpse-fat.

2. *U. B.*, ch. 3 — W, III, 31.
4. Gosse, *op. cit.*, p. 117.

In an hydropical body, ten years buried in the churchyard, we met with a fat concretion, where the nitre of the earth, and the salt and lixivious liquor of the body, had coagulated large lumps of fat into the consistence of the hardest Castile soap, whereof part remaineth with us.

We may, therefore, in hearty agreement, this once, with Sir Edmund Gosse, "fancy Browne's imagination tracing the noble adipocere of Alexander until he found it stopping a hole to keep the wind away." [1]

5. Desecration in grave and charnel-house.

That *skull* . . . How the *knave* jowls it to the ground, as if it were Cain's jaw-bone, that did the first murder! . . . Did these bones cost no more the breeding but to play at loggats with 'em? Mine ache to think on 't . . . Alas, poor Yorick . . . *how abhorred in my imagination it is!* My gorge rises at it . . . Pah! (*Hamlet*, V, i, 83–221.)

Not that I am insensible of the dread and horror [of death]; or, by raking into the bowels of the deceased, continual sight of . . . skeletons, *like* vespilloes, or *grave-makers*, I am become stupid, or have forgot the apprehension of mortality . . . (*R. M.*, I, xxxviii —W, II, 381.)

Antiquity held too light thoughts from objects of mortality . . . some drew provocations of mirth from anatomies, and jugglers showed tricks with skeletons. (*U. B.*, ch. 3 — W, III, 25–26.)

To be knaved [2] *out of our graves*, to have our *skulls* made drinking-bowls, and our bones turned into pipes . . . are tragical *abominations* escaped in burning burials. (*U. B.*, ch. 3 — W, III, 30.)

"It is not less than extraordinary," writes Gosse,[3] "that the one great English author who has expressed a definite terror of having his bones tampered with and his skull exhibited should be the one who has suffered from that shocking outrage" — an outrage per-

1. Gosse, *op. cit.*, pp. 117–118.
2. W has "gnawed," which is said to be the more authentic reading.
3. Page 116.

petrated in 1840 by the sexton of the Church of St. Peter, Man-croft, Norwich, and consummated, after a preliminary sale of the skull to a collector, by its exhibition, to this day, in the *pathological* museum of the Norfolk and Norwich Hospital.[1] The remains of Shakspere, who certainly felt almost exactly as Browne did in this respect,[2] probably escaped a similar fate only because he had the forethought to warn off the ghouls by selecting a proper inscription for his gravestone. Shakspere's vivid memories of the "unusually repulsive" charnel-house at Stratford [3] would seem to be reflected in several plays [4] over and above *Hamlet*. They are curiously matched not only by those utterances of Browne's just noticed but also by his recollections of the "remarkable . . . charnel-house . . . in former times" at Norwich.

The bones [he writes] [5] of such as were buried in Norwich, might be brought into it . . . How these bones were afterwards disposed of we have no account; or whether they had not the like removal with those in the charnel-house of . . . St. Paul's [London — from which, upon the demolition of the chapel] the bones . . . amounting to more than a thousand cart loads, were conveyed into Finsbury Fields, and there laid in a moorish place.

Unfortunately, Browne had no "Good frend for Jesus sake for-beare" inscribed upon his gravestone.

I believe that the materials assembled above, besides confirm-ing the cumulative indications, previously noted, of Browne's verbal and figurative indebtedness to Shakspere, establish beyond

1. Cf. *Hydriotaphia*, ed. W. A. Greenhill, Golden Treasury Series, London, 1911, p. xxv.
2. Cf. the *Hamlet* passage quoted immediately above.
3. See above, p. 131, n. 4.
4. Cf. *Romeo and Juliet*, IV, i, 81–83:

> Shut me nightly in a charnel-house,
> O'er-cover'd quite with dead men's rattling bones,
> With reeky shanks and yellow chapless skulls . . .

See also *Macbeth*, III, iv., 71.
5. "Antiquities of Norwich," W, III, 299–300.

reasonable doubt the probability that Shakspere's world of ideas is intimately reflected in Browne's. On the whole, "intimately" does not mean "directly and willfully" — least of all, with logical exactness. In the nature of things, the impact or influence of the creative imagination *in transitu* cannot be safely estimated except in terms of general probabilities. Any attempt to conclude this study with an exact and final analysis of the evidence offered, could, therefore, produce nothing beyond a fruitless contradiction in terms. The evidence must speak for itself, and the reader has about as good a right to interpret it for himself as I have. Something may be gained, however, by a summary of its general bearings and implications as I see them.

The evidence proves, first, that Browne was an enthusiastic playgoer. From this fact, added to the certainty that he was indefatigable in his general reading and possessed of catholic taste and fine literary instinct, follows the antecedent presumption that Shakspere's work must have been known to him. This is supported by other evidence, which demolishes the mistaken idea that he ignored his Elizabethan predecessors in general and scorned the poets in particular — because it proves that he wrote as one who knew them. The many parallelisms, in word and thought, here noted, justify the conclusion that he knew especially, and remembered most vividly, the greatest of them all.

In degree and kind, however, Browne's Shaksperian memories defy ready classification. Since he did not write dramatic verse, the Shaksperian element in his work is virtually incommensurable with that in Milton. It is safe to say only that there is less of it in Browne, and that qualitatively the difficulties of analysis are greater in proportion to the differences between the three men. Quantitatively, however, Shakspere left no negligible mark upon Browne. He seems to have drawn verbal or figurative reminiscences from something like a third of the plays — to take no account of more general likenesses in thought. As one would expect, the tragedies — especially *Hamlet* and *Macbeth* — made the deepest impression upon him. Above all things else in Shakspere, he remembered the Gravediggers' Scene, but he also recalled most of the outstanding histories and not a few of the comedies.

With fluent and all but literal ease he fitted into the very tissue of his own thought certain Shaksperian phrases (concerning God and good angels, the web — or line — of our life, sleep and fortune, the spurns that patient merit of the unworthy takes, and the lamentable fact that men have, too often, lost their reason) — as one does with phrases one cannot help using because one has made them absolutely one's own; or somewhat, perhaps, as later writers use certain phrases that afford some readers the pleasure of easy recognition, while the rest take them for granted: phrases, say, from Scripture — or from Shakspere! In other cases a single full-flung adjective or a sharply pointed verb fixed itself upon the inward eye and ear. Thus, sharp upon happy prologues to the swelling act of memory follow the swelling beginnings of various and sundry transferences of epithet [1] which need not puzzle *our* reason, any more than our will, to believe. Nor need there be, if our philosophy could find it out, anything more than natural in the transference or the reflection of ideas by which Shakspere's meditations upon the ethics of life become one and inseparable with Browne's broodings upon the rationale of death. Certain it is that if Browne remembered Shakspere at all, he remembered him first and last: in the sage and serious musings of his young manhood, in the more sombre meditations of middle life, and in the mature wisdom of his old age — in the *Religio Medici*, the *Urn Burial*, and the *Christian Morals*. Withal, Browne never imitated Shakspere. He did assimilate him. For not imitation, but assimilation, is the sincerest flattery, the highest tribute that one man of genius can pay another.

    1. See above, pp. 117–118, 120.

Chapter IV

THE SHAKSPERIAN ELEMENT IN MILTON [1]

SCHOLARSHIP has always delighted to render unto Shakspere and Milton individually the tribute which is their natural due. Strangely enough, however, it has neglected the relationships between them. Specifically, no one hitherto, I believe, has undertaken a systematic investigation of the range and quantity of Shaksperian recollection in Milton, much less of the quality thereof. Such an investigation is here attempted.

That there are numerous points of contact between Shakspere and Milton is, to be sure, a matter of common knowledge, and so is the fact that many likenesses between our poets were noted long ago by Thomas Warton, Warburton, Newton, and others. By 1800 many of these "coincidencies of fancy's sweetest children" had been collected and enlarged upon by Todd in his Variorum edition of Milton,[2] and since then such scholars as Verity [3] and Hanford [4] have added much valuable material. Even so, the sum total of probable Shakspere–Milton relationships thus far recognized is far from complete. What is more, no one has systemati-

1. Reprinted, with additions, from *PMLA*, XL (1925), 645–691. Some of the new matter is based upon unpublished notes kindly sent me by Professor S. F. Gingerich and Dr. Wilmon Brewer. I have also drawn freely upon the important materials made available by Professor George Coffin Taylor in his "Shakspere and Milton Again," *Studies in Philology*, XXIII (1926), 189–199. Items not otherwise credited (see below, p. 142, n. 1) are my own.

2. First edition, London, 1801; revised and enlarged, 1809. References below are to the revised edition.

3. In his editions of *Paradise Lost, Samson Agonistes, Comus, Lycidas and Other Poems*, and *A Midsummer-Night's Dream* (Cambridge University Press, 1910, etc.).

4. See especially his article on "The Dramatic Element in *Paradise Lost*," *Studies in Philology*, XIV (1917), 178–195.

cally assembled and tested the evidence. It may well be that the inherent difficulties have served as a deterrent. Thus, Milton's "instinct of eager assimilation" [1] from all the world of great books necessarily makes somewhat difficult, not to say hazardous, the attempt to assign a definite source to any given thought or phrase of his. And even though it be granted that certain of these are evidently colored by Shaksperian reminiscence, it is not always possible to point to the exact passage in Shakspere from which they are derived; for it is characteristic of the working of Milton's creative imagination that he fused — or transfused, into something new and strange — the rich and varied stores of his memory. Yet one must recognize, on the other hand, that surprisingly similar phrases or ideas may be spontaneously and independently generated by any two poets.

To be sure, when one reads in *Paradise Lost* that

Adam . . . wept
Though not of woman born: compassion quelled
His best of man and *gave him up to tears* (XI, 495–497),

one is moved to recall the coming of Birnam Wood to Dunsinane which cowed the better part of man in a son of Adam who was likewise of no woman born; that Adam gave himself up to tears reminds us that Exeter in *Henry V* did exactly this in mourning the loss of a comrade at Agincourt.[2] Moreover, in this case suspicion virtually becomes certainty because many other passages in Milton prove definitely that he knew and cherished *Macbeth* and *Henry V*. Other cases, however, are by no means so obvious. Indeed, many Shaksperian lines cited by Milton's commentators, early and late, are neither close parallels nor even slight reminiscences, but merely illustrations of current Elizabethan idioms.[3]

1. Cf. Moody, Cambridge *Milton*, p. 95.   2. See below, pp. 162, 180.
3. See, for example, Verity's notes on *Paradise Lost*, I, 206–VI, 374, etc., and Todd's on *P. L.*, VIII, 62, *Il Penseroso*, 35, etc.

The student in search of actual evidence of Shaksperian reminiscence in Milton must therefore thread his way warily through the commentators. Again, commentators and editors usually content themselves with line-by-line notes or glosses upon Milton's text. When they quote Shaksperian "parallels" they rarely put two and two together. Yet to eliminate mere conjecture so far as may be, it is necessary to set side by side, not one or two possible reminiscences from, say, *The Merchant of Venice* or *Julius Caesar*, but all probable or possible echoes of any given play in all of Milton's work, so far as they can be discovered. This method, here adopted, makes it possible to test any single case by the whole body of the evidence. The cumulative effect of the evidence thus adduced frequently serves to establish the probability of Milton's indebtedness to Shakspere in cases that, taken by themselves, might well be thought doubtful; whereas the absence of cumulative evidence suggests that other cases, not without interest in themselves, must be set aside as somewhat remote possibilities.[1] This method will also bring out points of contact between our poets which seem hitherto to have escaped the commentators —or, at worst, an occasional fresh "coincidency" which, since it concerns Shakspere and Milton, may be of interest even if it is only a coincidence. Again, this systematic survey will indicate how many of Shakspere's plays Milton remembered and which ones he remembered best.

The method of presentation in the summaries below, further, is intended to indicate something of the nature and quality of Milton's Shaksperian recollection. Of many possible classifications only two seemed finally practicable. Some of the plays remained in Milton's memory not by virtue of their underlying dramatic concepts but solely by the spell of the Shaksperian word or the fascination of their imagery. Such echoes or likenesses — of epi-

---

1. In this connection see, for example, p. 189, n. 2; pp. 205–206, n. 3, below.

thet, phrase, or figure: all essentially *verbal* or *figurative*, and very often both in one — I have brought together, play by play, in group A. Reminiscences or striking likenesses more essentially *dramatic* in nature — echoes of dramatic theme or mood, situation, or characterization — are presented play by play, in so far as they occur, in group B. The underlying assumption here is that the presence of recognizable verbal or figurative echoes of any one play in Milton, establishes fair ground for considering the possibility that such a play *may* also have influenced Milton's dramatic workmanship. Most of the material below I have independently collected, but it goes without saying that I owe many specific items, and much general aid and comfort, to Milton's editors and commentators. All passages observed by them are noted *passim*.[1] New matter — that is, material not specifically credited to earlier students — has, as a rule, been entered at the end of each of the two groups.

In addition to supplying a reasonably broad and systematic basis for the study of the quantitative and qualitative aspects of Shakspere's influence upon Milton, this study will, I hope, be useful in another way. It should help to dispel a venerable misconception which has blinded many students; namely, the belief that the Elizabethan poets, especially the dramatists, influenced Milton only in his youth; that in his maturity they ceased to interest or inspire him; so that, as Thomas Warton[2] has it, "his warmest political predilections were at last totally obliterated by civil and religious enthusiasm" or crowded out of his memory because classical standards and Puritan doctrine claimed him for

---

1. Usually by initials appended to the passages from Milton: B = Bowle; D = Dunster; N = Newton; S = Steevens; W = Thomas Warton; T = Todd (whose Variorum edition of 1809 may be consulted for citations from these writers); Br. = R. C. Browne (*English Poems by John Milton*, Clarendon Press, 1923); G. C. T. = George Coffin Taylor ("Shakspere and Milton Again," see above, p. 139, n. 1); H = Hanford (see above, p. 139, n. 4); M = Masson (*Poetical Works of John Milton*, 1890); V = Verity (see above, p, 139, n. 3).   2. Cf. Todd, VII, 181.

their own. The critics would seem to have been misled by Milton's bitter comment (in the preface to *Samson Agonistes*) upon the "infamy" into which "tragedy . . . with other common Interludes" had fallen in the Restoration theatre, when the sons of Belial held the stage. They fail to remember that in the preface to *Paradise Lost* he justifies his choice of blank verse partly on the ground that "our best English tragedies" had "rejected rime." Only a few years ago a writer in one of our journals [1] declared categorically, after a "very careful examination" of the prose and verse of this very Milton who thus cites the authority or example of the Elizabethan dramatists, that his "connections with [Elizabethan] dramatic literature were very slight." This astonishing conclusion may be a result of the traditional failure of the critics [2] to see a distinction which this study is intended to emphasize; namely, that while Milton, as time went on, lost patience with the stage and theatre, he always retained imaginative sympathy with the profound and challenging beauty of Elizabethan dramatic poetry. He gave the best possible proof of this by remembering it.

    1. Professor Louis Wann, "*Lycidas* and *Barnavelt,*" *Modern Language Notes*, XXXVII (1922), 473, n.
    2. See also, for example, Professor Hales's "Milton's *Macbeth,*"—*Nineteenth Century*, XXX (1891), 919–932,—a valuable paper, which, however, repeats something of the old mistake. "Milton in his younger days . . . read Shakspere with immense appreciation." But the *Samson* preface, according to Hales, is not to be explained by Milton's disgust with the Restoration theatre. Only the Greek drama was "meet and right" in his eyes. "The modern drama seemed a somewhat dubious growth . . . with which as an author he meant to have little to do, however he might peruse it as a reader." The evidence below will indicate that Milton *as an author*, even though he did not write dramas in the manner of the Elizabethans, had much to do with them by virtue of his memory. A notable exception to the usual critical blindness is to be found in the excellent paper already referred to (see p. 139, n. 4) by Professor Hanford. "There is no evidence," says Hanford, "that Milton ever outgrew his early love of Elizabethan drama. . . . What passes out of Milton is but the more sensuous and esthetic essence of Elizabethan poetry. . . . [His] sympathy with the English renaissance in its moral, philosophical, and human phases deepens with advancing years. Classicism moulds and modifies the Elizabethan influences. Puritanism makes them wear a special expression. But neither Classicism nor Puritanism can efface them."

A glance at the many Shaksperian reminiscences in *Paradise Lost*, *Paradise Regained*, and *Samson*, recorded below, will remind readers that not the least glory of these last and greatest of Milton's works lies in their subtle overtones of memory — their echoes of Shakspere (and his fellows)[1] recollected in tranquillity, amid the din of evil tongues in evil days.

I. THE TRAGEDIES

1. *Titus Andronicus.*[2]

The first Shaksperian tragedy which unmistakably left its mark upon Milton's memory is, as one would expect, not *Titus Andronicus* but *Romeo and Juliet*. It has been thought, however, that a line in *L'Allegro* resembles a phrase in the earlier play:

A.

(1) II, iii, 15:
The green leaves quiver with the cooling wind
And make a *chequered shadow* on the ground.

L'Allegro, 95–96:
Many a youth and many a maid
Dancing in the *chequerèd shade.* — (Richardson; cf. T)

2. *Romeo and Juliet.*[3]

In Milton's first Latin elegy occurs his familiar description of "the pomp of the changing theatre" as he saw it in the days of his youth. Some of the stock characters of Roman comedy pass in review, and "awful tragedy" shakes her "bloody sceptre":

Bitterness mingles with sweet tears as I see some hapless boy, torn from his love, leave all his joys untasted, and fall lamentable; or when the fierce avenger of crime recrosses the Styx out of the shades. (Moody's translation, lines 40–43.)

1. A subject to which I shall return in a later study, on "Milton, and Shakspere's Dramatic Contemporaries." (Cf. *PMLA*, XLIII [1928], 569–570.)
2. See also below, p. 170, n. 4.
3. Some commentators see likenesses (over and above those listed here) between the play, I, iv, 19–21, and *P. L.*, IV, 181 (S); II, ii, 28, and *P. L.*, III, 229 (G. C. T.).

"By the youth," writes Thomas Warton,[1] "he perhaps intends Shakspere's Romeo. In the second either Hamlet or Richard the Third. He then draws his illustrations from the ancient tragedians." That the hapless boy was Romeo several later scholars [2] have independently conjectured, and on the face of it no conjecture could be more plausible than that young Milton must have felt the spell of Shakspere's immortal tragedy of youth. There is evidence — fairly substantial, though less far-reaching than in the case of the greater tragedies — to indicate that he did not soon forget it.

A.

(1) II, iii, 1:
The grey eye'd *morn smiles* on the *frowning night*.

Paradise Lost, V, 124:
When fair *morning* first *smiles* on the world. — (T)
Id., IV, 424:
Dark, waste, and wild, under the *frown of night*. — (T) [3]

(2) II, iii, 9–10 (*from the same speech as* [1]):
The earth that's *nature's mother* is her tomb,
What is her *burying grave* that is her *womb*.

P. L., II, 910–911:
This wild abyss,
The *womb of nature* and perhaps *her grave*. — (T)

(3) I, iv, 37:
For I am *proverb'd* with a grandsire phrase.

Samson, 203:
Am I not sung and *proverbed* for a fool? — (D; cf. G. C. T.) [4]

(4) I, iv, 100–101:
The *wind*, who *wooes*
Even now the frozen bosom of the north. . . .

On the Nativity, 37–38:
She [Nature] *wooes* the *gentle air*.[5]

---

1. Cf. Todd, VII, 181.

2. Cf., for example, E. N. S. Thompson, *Essays on Milton*, pp. 14–15.

3. Verity compares with the "black-*brow'd night*" of *A Midsummer-Night's Dream* (III, ii, 387) "the rugged *brow* of *night*" of *Il Penseroso* (58).

4. See below, p. 167, n. 1. Taylor also compares *R. and J.*, V, iii, 35, with *Samson*, 952–953, but the resemblance between these lines rests upon a commonplace which editors find also in Euripides and Massinger.

5. See also *Macbeth*, I, vi, 1–3, 5–6.

(5) III, ii, 1–21:

Gallop apace, you fiery-footed steeds,
Towards Phoebus lodging; such a
     waggoner
As Phaethon would whip you to the
     west
And bring in *cloudy night* immediately.
Spread thy close curtain, love-per-
     forming night,
That runaway's eyes may wink . . .
     Come, *civil* night,
Thou *sober-suited   matron   all   in
     black* . . .
Hood my unmann'd blood, baiting in
     my cheeks,
With *thy black mantle* . . . Come, lov-
     ing black-brow'd night,
Give me my Romeo

Il Penseroso, 122:
Till *civil-suited* Morn appear. — (T)

Id., 31–33:
Come, pensive Nun, devout and pure
     . . .
All in a robe of darkest grain . . .

P. L., II, 962:
Sable-vested Night, eldest of things.

The Passion, 29–30:
Befriend me, *Night*, best Patroness of
     grief,
Over the pole thy *thickest mantle* throw.

P. L., IV, 598–609:
Now came still evening on, and Twi-
     light gray
Had in her *sober livery* all things clad.
Silence   accompanied . . . Hesperus
     that led
The starry host, rode brightest, till the
     Moon
Rising *in clouded majesty*, at length
Apparent queen, unveiled her peerless
     light
And o'er the dark her *silver mantle*
     threw.[1]

---

1. Of the five passages from Milton here noted, the likeness in language between the first, and Juliet's "sober-suited matron, civil night" is the only one that has been generally recognized. Of the other passages the last two are of especial interest — the lines from *The Passion* because that poem was written within a few years of the *Elegia Prima* (in which Milton, as we have seen, probably alludes to Romeo). The last passage may be more doubtful, but I think it is at least possible — in view of Milton's habit of repeating himself in repeating Shakspere — to recognize in this beautiful evening scene, written late in Milton's life, a memory, however shadowy, of Juliet's "cloudy night" — of the sober-suited matron's mantle turned silver, as it were, in the star-light of memory. (This in spite of the fact that other poets employ the same figure — Todd, for example, citing Phineas Fletcher [*Purple Island*, VI, 54], "night's black livery," and Spenser [*Epithalamion*, 315–332], "Now welcome, Night . . . And in thy sable mantle us enwrap." The phrase "sable night" occurs also in *Lucrece*. See below, p. 203.)

3. Julius Caesar.

A.

(1) II, ii, 18:
Graves have *yawned* and yielded up their dead.

P. L., X, 635:
Sin and Death and *yawning grave.* — (T)

(2) III, 1, 273:
Cry *havoc* and let slip the *dogs of war.*

P. L., X, 616–617 (*on Sin and Death coming to earth*):
See with what heat these *dogs of Hell* advance
To waste and *havoc* yonder World. — (V)

(3) II, i, 230:
Enjoy the honey-heavy *dew of slumber.*

P. L., IV, 614:
The timely *dew of sleep.* — (V) ¹

(4) IV, iii, 226:
The *deep of night* is crept upon our talk.

P. L., IV, 674:
Unbeheld in *deep of night.* — (V) ²

(5) IV, i, 19–26:
    These honors . . .
He shall but bear them *as the ass bears gold* . . .
And having brought our treasure where we will
Then take we down his load and *turn him off*
Like to the empty ass . . .

Samson, 537–539:
A deceitful concubine, who shore me
Like a tame wether, all my precious fleece;
Then *turned me out,* ridiculous, despoiled. — (G. C. T.)

B.

(1) Both Caesar and Samson respond with haughty refusal to the demand that they present themselves publicly — to the Roman Senate and the Philistine lords, respectively:

II, ii, 59–64:
Decius. I come to fetch you to the senate-house . . .
Caesar. Tell them that *I will not come to-day.*
Cannot, is false, and that I dare not, falser;
I will not come.

Samson, 1318, 1332, 1342 (*Samson, bidden to appear before the "illustrious lords" of the Philistines*):
Return the way thou cam'st; *I will not come* . . .
Joined with extreme contempt! *I will not come.* — (G. C. T.)

---

1. Verity compares also *Richard III*, IV, i, 84: "The golden dew of sleep."
2. Cf. also *Merry Wives*, IV, iv, 40: "In deep of night to walk by this Herne's oak."
— (V). See also below, *Lear*, A (4), p. 159.

(2) Compare Cassius's description of Caesar, and Samson's of himself:

I, ii, 135:
He doth bestride the narrow world
Like a Colossus, and we *petty* men
Walk under his huge legs, and peep
about
To find ourselves dishonorable graves.

Samson, 529–531:
Fearless of danger, *like a petty god*,
I walked about, admired of all and
dreaded
On hostile ground, none daring my
affront.

(3) The lofty elegiac close of *Samson* is strikingly like the noble closing tribute to Brutus:

V, v, 56, 68–75:
Brutus only overcame himself . . .
This was the *noblest* Roman of them
all . . .
His life was gentle, and the elements
So mix'd in him that Nature might
stand up
And say to all the world, "This was a
man."

Samson, 1709–1710, 1721–1724:
Samson hath quit himself Like Samson . . .
Nothing is here for tears, nothing to
wail
Or knock the breast; no weakness, no
contempt,
Dispraise, or blame; nothing but well
and fair,
And what may quiet us in a death so
noble.

4. *Hamlet.*

A.

(1) I, i, 44:
Most like; it *harrows* me with *fear* and
wonder.

Comus, 565:
Amazed I stood, *harrowed* with grief
and *fear*. — (S)

(2) I, iv, 52:
Thou, dead corse, again *in complete
steel.*

Comus, 421 (*on chastity*):
She that has that is clad *in complete
steel.* — (T)

(3) I, v, 19–20:
Make . . . each particular *hair* to stand
on end
Like quills upon the *fretful porpentine.*

Samson, 1136–1138:
Though all thy *hairs*
Were bristles . . .
Of chafed wild boars or *ruffled porcu-
pines.* — (N)

(4) I, i, 118–123:
Disasters in *the sun* . . . *The moist star*
Upon whose influence Neptune's em-
pire stands

P. L., I, 592–599:
The sun new-risen
Looks through the horizontal misty
air

Was sick almost to doomsday with
  eclipse . . .
As . . . prologue to the *omen coming
  on.*

(5) III, iv, 45–51:
      O, such a *deed* . . .
Heaven's face doth glow,
Yea, *this solidity and compound mass*
With tristful visage as against the
  doom
Is *thought-sick* at the act.

(6) I, ii, 10–13 (*Claudius, opening
  speech*):
As 'twere with a defeated joy,
With one auspicious and one drooping
  eye,
In equal scale *weighing delight with
  dole.*

(7) II, ii, 485–486:
With *eyes like carbuncles* . . . Pyrrhus
Old grandsire Priam seeks.

(8) II, ii, 508–509:[3]
      The dreadful *thunder*
Doth *rend* the region . . .

(9) I, v, 63–64:
And *in the porches of my ears* did *pour*
The *leperous distilment.*

(10) III, iii, 97–98 (*Claudius praying*):
My *words fly up*, my thoughts remain
  below,

Shorn of his beams, or from behind
  the moon
In *dim eclipse, disastrous* twilight
  sheds
On half the nations, and with *fear of
  change*
Perplexes monarchs. — (T) [1]

P. L., IX, 782–784:
Earth felt *the wound,* and Nature from
  her seat
Sighing through all her works, gave
  signs of woe
That all was lost. — (Davies) [2]

P. L., IV, 892–894:
                        Change
Torment with ease, and soonest *rec-
  ompense*
Dole with delight. — (T)

P. L., IX, 499–500 (*the serpent*):
                        His head
Crested aloft, and *carbuncle his eyes.*
  — (T)

P. L., XII, 181–182:
      Thunder mixed with hail
. . . must *rend* the Egyptian sky.—(V)

Comus, 839–840:
And *through the porch* and inlet of *each
  sense*
Dropt in *ambrosial oils.* — (N)

P. L., XI, 14–15:
To Heaven their *prayers
Flew up,* nor missed the way. — (V)

---

1. Verity compares a somewhat similar figure in *Hamlet,* I, i, 126, and *P. L.,* X, 412–414. See also *King Lear,* I, ii, 112, 130: "*eclipses* in the sun and moon"; "our *disasters.*"

2. For this "sublime passage of the Earth's sympathizing with Adam and Eve when they ate the forbidden fruit," Milton may have been indebted to the lines quoted from Hamlet's remonstrance to his mother upon her crime. (Davies, *Dramatic Miscellanies.*)

3. Passages (7) and (8) are both from the player's ranting speech.

Words without thoughts never *to
heaven* go.

*Sonnet on Mrs. Catherine Thomson, 5–
13 (Her good "works and alms"):*
Stayed not behind, nor in the grave
    were trod;
But . . . *up they flew* . . .
Before the Judge.

(11) I, iii, 78–80:
    To thine own self be true . . .
Thou canst not then be *false* to any
man.

*Samson, 823–824 (Samson to Dalila;
cf. 784):*
Bitter reproach though true
I to myself was false ere thou to me.

(12) III, iv, 51–52 (*the Queen to Hamlet*):
    Ay me! What act
That roars so loud and *thunders* in the
index?

*P. L., X, 813–815 (Adam on the fear of
eternal punishment):*
    Ay me! That fear
Comes *thundering* back with dreadful
    revolution
On my defenceless head.

(13) III, ii, 19–20:
*Suit the action to the word, the word to
the action.*

P. R., III, 9–10:
*Thy actions to thy words accord, thy
words
To thy large heart give utterance due.*

B. The characteristics, thoughts, deeds, and words of certain outstanding *persons* of the play have left their mark upon Milton's
characters:

(1) The Ghost.

(*a*) I, v, 2–4 (*his return to torture*):
    My hour is almost come
When I to sulphurous and *tormenting*
    flames
Must render up myself.

*P. L., II, 89–92 (Moloch, on "the pain
of unextinguishable fire"):*
When the scourge
Inexorably, and the *torturing hour* [1]
Calls us to penance. — (T)

(*b*) I, i, 145–146 (*his invulnerability*):
It is as the *air invulnerable*,
And our vain blows malicious mockery.

P. L., VI, 344–349:
            Spirits . . .
    Cannot but by annihilating die,
Nor in their liquid texture *mortal
    wound
Receive*, no more than can the liquid
    air. — (V) [2]

---

1. Cf. below, *A Midsummer-Night's Dream*, A (6), p. 184.
2. Cf. below, *Macbeth*, B (3) (c), p. 164, and *Tempest*, III, iii, 62–63.

(c) I, i, 158–164 (*Not "abroad" in the Christmas season*):

Some say that ever 'gainst that season comes

Wherein our Saviour's birth is celebrated,

The bird of dawning singeth *all night long;*

And then, they say, *no spirit can walk abroad,*

The nights are wholesome; then no planets strike,

No fairy takes, nor witch hath power to charm.

Comus, 432–437:

Some say, no evil thing that walks by night

In fog, or fire, by lake or moorish fen,

Blue meagre hag, or stubborn *unlaid ghost* [1]

That breaks his magic chains at curfew time,

No goblin or swart *faery* of the mine

Hath hurtful power o'er true virginity.[2]

(2) King Hamlet's picture.

III, iv, 55–59:

See what a *grace* was *seated on this brow,*

Hyperion's curls, the *front* of Jove himself,

A *station* like *the herald Mercury,*

New *lighted* on a heaven-kissing *hill.*

P. L., II, 301–304 (*Beëlzebub in Pandemonium*):

In his rising seemed

A pillar of state. Deep *on his front*

Deliberation sat and public care

And princely counsel . . . — (V)

Id., V, 275–276, 285–286 (*Raphael reaches Eden*):

At once on the eastern *cliff* of Paradise

He *lights* . . . Like *Maia's son he stood*

And shook his plumes. — (N)

P. R., II, 216–218 (*Satan on Christ*):

How would one look from his *majestic brow*

Seated as *on the top* of Virtue's *hill*

Discountenance her, despised . . . [3] —

(D)

(3) Claudius:[4] his prayer, and Satan's, frustrated by persistence in sin.

1. Cf. below, *Cymbeline*, A (2), p. 196.
2. In writing this passage, "Milton had Shakspeare in his head"—Warton (cf. Todd, VI, 313, and Taylor, p. 190).
3. That is, the lure of woman.
4. See also entries A (6) and (10) of this play, p. 149.

III, iv, 64–66:
    What then? What rests?
Try what repentance can. What can it not?
Yet what can it when one cannot repent?

P. L., IV, 79–82:
O then at last relent! *Is there no place Left for repentance,* none for pardon left?
None left but by submission; and that word
Disdain forbids me. — (N)

(4) Polonius, crying out from behind the arras just before he is slain, is alluded to [1] in the *Apology for Smectymnuus* — perhaps to remind Milton's opponents that tedious old fools behind the arras are sometimes in grave danger of sudden annihilation:

III, iv, 22–23:
Polonius [behind]. What ho! help, help, help!
Hamlet [drawing]. How now! A rat? Dead, for a ducat, dead!

Apology (Prose Works, ed. J. A. St. John, III, 140):
This Champion from behind the Arras cries out that those toothless satires were of the Remonstrant's making . . .

(5) Hamlet.— The influence of three of his speeches seems especially recognizable in Milton.

(*a*) I, ii, 129–146 (*Themes, — world-weariness, suicide, woman's inconstancy*):
O that this too, too solid flesh would melt . . .
Or that the Everlasting had not fix'd His canon 'gainst self-slaughter. O God! God!
How weary, stale, flat and unprofitable Seems to me all the uses of this world . . .
Let me not think on 't. *Frailty, thy name is woman.*

P. L., X, 1001–1002 (*Eve in despair, after the fall, suggests suicide*):
Let us seek death, or, he not found, supply
With our own hands his office on ourselves.

Id., X, 1025–1028 (*Adam replies that death*):
So snatched will not exempt us from the pain
We are by doom to pay; rather such acts
Of contumacy will provoke the highest
To make death in us live.

---

1. As Furnivall, and others, have observed (see Munro, *Shakspere Allusion Book*, I, 475, and Milton's *Prose Works*, ed. St. John, III, 140, n.).

> *Samson*,   595–596,   783,   1010–1012
> (*Samson, world-weary; the Chorus
> on Woman*):
>   Nature within me seems
> In all her functions weary of herself.
> — (M) [1]
> Nor should'st thou have trusted that
>   to *woman's frailty* . . .
> It is not virtue, wisdom, valour, wit . . .
> That woman's love can win or long
>   inherit.[2]

(*b*) Hanford [3] has shown that the "To be or not to be" soliloquy is closely related to Adam's self-communion after the fall.

> How gladly would I . . . lay me down . . .
> And sleep secure . . . Yet one doubt
> Pursues me still, lest all I cannot die,
> Lest . . . the Spirit . . . cannot together perish
> With this corporeal clod. Then in the grave
> Or in some other dismal place, who knows
> But I shall die a living death . . . (*P. L.*, X, 775–788.)

Undeniably the passage owes much, in language and sentiment, to the Book of Job, but "the weighing of the problem, the shrinking on the brink of the unknown, the sense of mystery which puzzles the will — 'to die, to sleep! To sleep? Perchance to dream!' — all this is Hamlet." It may be worth while to add that other characters in *Paradise Lost* likewise reflect this characteristic "weighing of the problem": that Adam, tossed "in a troublous sea of passion" (like Hamlet's "sea of troubles," or Isaiah's)[4] has comrades in perplexity. Moloch *knows* that he wants war, but cannot shut his eyes to certain alternatives and questions:

> What fear we then? . . . His utmost ire
> Will either quite consume us . . .

1. See below, on *Macbeth*, B (3) (e), p. 166.
2. See below, on *Cymbeline*, B (2), p. 197.
3. See above, p. 139, n. 4, and cf. *Measure for Measure*, pp. 194–195, below.
4. *Hamlet*, III, i, 59; cf. Verity on *P. L.*, X, 718.

Or, if our substance be indeed divine
. . . we are at worst
On this side nothing. (*P. L.*, II, 94–101.)

Belial, like Hamlet for at least one great moment, argues for the ills we have,

Though full of pain, this intellectual being,
Those thoughts that wander through eternity (*Id.*, II, 146–147),

as preferable to annihilation in the unknown, for who knows whether oblivion — that "beastly oblivion" of which Hamlet speaks — would bring peace:

Who knows . . . whether our angry Foe
Can give it, or will ever? (*Id.*, II, 151–153.)

Eve, finally, meditates upon the now and the hereafter with Hamlet-like question and iteration even before she tastes the apple. God, says she,

Forbids us good, forbids us to be wise!
Such prohibitions bind not. *But if Death
Bind us with after-bands*, what profits then
Our inward freedom? (*Id.*, IX, 759–762.)

And after eating she continues the debate before deciding to let Adam share the fruit.

(c) II, ii, 309–322 (*on the dust and divinity of the world, of man, and of woman*):
This goodly frame, the earth, seems to me a sterile promontory . . . this brave o'erhanging firmament . . . a foul and pestilent congregation of vapours. *What a piece of work is man!* How noble in reason! How infinite in faculty! In form and moving how ex-

P. L., VIII, 15:
When I behold *this goodly frame* this world . . . — (T) [1]

Samson, 667:
God of our fathers! *what is Man* . . .

P. L., VII, 505–511:
There wanted yet *the master-work, the end*

---

1. "This universal frame, thus wondrous fair" (*P. L.*, V, 154–155). Undoubtedly both Shakspere and Milton drew upon the eighth Psalm, but Milton is none the less indebted to Shakspere.

press and admirable! In action how like an angel! In apprehension how like a god! The beauty of the world! *The paragon of animals!* And yet, to me, what is *this quintessence of dust?* Man *delights* not me, — no, nor *woman* neither. . . .

Of all yet done — a creature who not prone
And brute as other creatures, but endued
With sanctity of reason, might erect
His stature, and upright, with front serene
Govern the rest, self-knowing, and from thence
Magnanimous to correspond with Heaven.

Id., VII, 524–525:
Man,
Dust of the ground . . .

P. R., II, 153, 191–192 (*Belial, in council suggests that Christ be tempted with woman*):
[*Belial*] Set *women* in his eye . . .
[*Satan*] These . . . *Delight* not all.

All readers of Milton are familiar with the opening echo here noted, but the probability that he recalled Hamlet's speech as an organic whole has escaped notice. The last phrase, "Man delights not me . . ." would seem to have left its mark, however slightly and strangely, upon *Paradise Regained*, and the rest reappears in *Samson* and *Paradise Lost* in the weighing of man in the balance — man as the quintessence of dust, and man as the paragon of animals, the master-work, the end.

5. Othello.[1]

A.

(1) II, iii, 57–60:
Three . . . noble swelling spirits . . .
Have I to-night flustered with *flowing cups.*[2]

P. L., V, 443–445:
Meanwhile . . . Eve . . . their *flowing cups*
With pleasant liquor crowned. — (V)

---

1. See also below, on *Macbeth*, B (3) (d), pp. 164–165, n. 2, and *Cymbeline*, B (3), pp. 197–198.

2. Verity notes also *Henry V*, IV, iii, 55: "Be in their *flowing cups* freshly remembered."

(2) II, iii, 212:
Though he had twinn'd with me, both
    at a birth . . .

(3) III, i, 52:
To take the safest *occasion* by the
    front . . .

(4) III, iii, 355–357:
And O you mortal *engines*, whose *rude
    throats*
The immortal *Jove's dread thunder*
    counterfeit,
Farewell!

P. L., VII, 453–455:
The earth . . . *teemed* [1] *at a birth*
Innumerable living creatures. — (V)

P. R., III, 172–173:
Zeal and duty are not slow,
But on *occasion's forelock* [2] watchful
    wait. — (D)

P. L., VI, 585–587 (*Cannon, invented
    in hell, directed against the heavenly
    hosts*):
    All Heaven appeared
From those *deep-throated engines*
    belched. — (N) [3]

Id., VI, 490–491 (*Satan boasts*):
    They shall fear we have disarmed
    The *Thunderer* of his only *dreaded bolt*.

B.

(1) Hanford [4] finds in the situation of Adam and Eve in relation to Satan "an essential repetition of that of Othello, Desdemona, and Iago," and observes that Satan resembles Iago in his
malignity, his motive-hunting, and his half-pity for his victims.
(I may note incidentally that Walter Savage Landor in one of the
Imaginary Conversations — between Southey and Landor, on the
comparative merits of Shakspere and Milton — touches upon the
same point: "*Landor.* — Othello was loftier than the citadel of
Troy; and what a Paradise fell before him!" Professor Bradley
also alludes to the general likeness here referred to. [5]) Hanford calls
attention especially to the similarity between Satan's great soliloquy and Iago's, upon first beholding their unconscious victims:

1. Cf. *Macbeth*, IV, iii, 176: "Each minute *teems* a new" grief.
2. Fortune's forelock, however, is mentioned also in the *Distichs of Cato*, and by the
Greek and Latin poets.
3. Cf. below, *Henry V*, A (4), p. 180.
4. See above, p. 139, n. 4.
5. Though he remarks that "to compare Iago with the Satan of *Paradise Lost* seems
almost absurd, so immensely does Shakespeare's man exceed Milton's fiend in evil."
(*Shakespearean Tragedy*, p. 207.)

Oth., II, i, 201–202:
 O you are well tun'd now!
But I'll set down the pegs that make
  this music . . .

P. L., IV, 505–535:
Sight hateful, sight tormenting! . . .
 these two
Imparadised in one another's arms . . .
Yet, happy pair, enjoy till I return
Short pleasures; for long woes are to
 succeed.

I believe there is another curious recollection of Iago in *Paradise Regained*, in the scene in which the tempter tries upon Christ an argument similar to that which Iago had urged home to Roderigo:

Oth., I, iii, 322, 344, 353:
Virtue! a fig . . . Put money in thy purse; . . . fill thy purse with money.

P. R., II, 427–431:
Get riches first, get wealth . . .
They whom I favour thrive in wealth
 amain
While *virtue*, valour, wisdom, sit in
 want.

(2) Many are the sayings of the wise,
  In ancient and in modern books enrolled,
  Extolling patience as the truest fortitude . . . (*Samson*, 652–654.)

This venerable commonplace — the bestowal upon sufferers of proverbial comfort (or "sentences" of "studied argument"), which attempts to patch grief with proverbs — Shakspere dramatized both early and late.[1] Samson's refusal to listen to Manoa's attempt to comfort him, whether or not it owes anything directly to Shakspere, may be worth comparing with Brabantio's negative response to the Duke's sentences:

Oth. I, iii, 199–208; 216–219:
Duke. Let me . . . lay a sentence . . .
When remedies are past, the griefs are
 ended . . .
Patience her injury a mockery makes,
The robb'd that smiles steals some-
 thing from the thief . . .

Bra. These sentences . . . are equi-
 vocal:
But words are words; I never yet did
 hear

Samson, 504–505, 588:
Man. Repent the sin; but, if the
 punishment
Thou canst avoid, self-preservation
 bids . . .
His might continues in thee not for
 naught . . .

Id., 590, 648:
All otherwise to me my thoughts por-
 tend . . .
Hopeless are all my evils, all remediless.

1. Cf. *Comedy of Errors*, II, i, 15–41; *Much Ado*, V, i, 17, etc.

That the bruis'd heart was pierced through the ear.	*Id.*, 652–654 (quoted p. 157); 660–662: *Chor.* With the afflicted in his pangs … Little prevails, or rather seems a tune Harsh and of dissonant mood.

6. *King Lear.*

I believe, for several reasons, that Professor Firth was right in suggesting that the almost disproportionately large "space devoted in" Milton's "*History of Britain* to the story of Lear and Cordelia,[1] is probably a tribute to Shakespeare."[2] Milton's entry, for example, concerning his proposed drama on the subject of *Macbeth*,[3] gives strong support to Firth's suggestion that no small part of "Milton's interest in the legendary and anecdotal side of history" was that of a literary artist in search of material.[4] Furthermore, Milton's frequent and varied echoes of *King Lear*, as indicated below, prove that this tragedy engraved itself indelibly upon his memory.

A.[5]

(1) I, i, 84–85 (*Cordelia*):
          Our joy,
Although the last, not least.
	P. L., III, 276–278:
	                    Dear
	To me are all my works, nor Man *the least*.
	Though last created.[6] — (N)

(2) III, iii, 12–13; III, iv, 16:
These injuries … will be revenged
    home …
But I will punish *home*.
	P. L., VI, 621–622:
	The terms we sent were full of …
	    force urged *home*. — (V)

---

1. That is, 2½ in a total of 20 pages devoted to the sketch of British legendary history, from Albion, son of Neptune, to the coming of Caesar (cf. Milton's *Prose Works*, ed. St. John, V, 164–185).

2. C. H. Firth, "Milton as an Historian," *Proceedings of the British Academy*, 1907–1908, p. 232.

3. See below, p. 161.

4. Firth mentions also Milton's remark (in the *History, Prose Works*, V, 344) to the effect that the amatory adventures of King Edgar were "fitter for a novel than a history."

5. See also pp. 119, n. 3, 181, n. 1.

6. Cf. *Julius Caesar*, III, i, 189: "Though *last, not least*, in love."

(3) I, iv, 248–249:
His *notion* weakens, his discernings
Are lethargized.

P. L., VII, 176–179:
    The acts of God . . .
So told as earthly *notion* can receive.
    — (V) [1]

(4) IV, vii, 34–35:
In the most terrible and nimble stroke
Of quick, *cross* lightning . . .
(Cf. *Julius Caesar*, I, iii, 46–51:
       I . . .
Have bared my bosom to the thunder-
    stone
. . . when the *cross blue* lightning
    seemed to open
The breast of heaven.)

Arcades, 51–52:
And heal the harms of thwarting
    thunder *blue*
Or what the *cross* dire-looking planet
    smites. — (T)

(5) III, i, 4–9 (*Lear*):
Contending with the fretful elements
. . . tears his white hair
Which the *impetuous* blasts, with eye-
    less *rage*
Catch in their fury and make nothing
    of.

P. L., I, 174–175:
      The thunder
Winged with red lightning and *impetuous rage*. — (G. C. T.)

B.

(1) IV, i, 69–74 (*Gloucester to Poor
Tom, on giving him his purse; the
heavenly "ordinance" requiring
that the rich give of their superfluity
to the poor*):
Heavens, deal so still!
Let the *superfluous* and *lust-dieted
man*,
That slaves your ordinance, that will
    not see
Because he does not feel, feel your
    power quickly;
So distribution should undo *excess*,
And each man have enough.

Comus, 768–773 (*The Lady, refuting
Comus's argument against temperance*):

If every just man that now pines with
    want
Had but a moderate and beseeming
    share
Of that which *lewdly pampered Luxury*
Now heaps upon some few with vast
    excess,
Nature's full blessings would be well
    dispensed
In *unsuperfluous* even proportion.—(T)

(2) Professor Taylor has shown [2] that certain descriptive details of the storm in *Lear* reappear in *Paradise Lost*. In dramatic

---

1. Cf. *Macbeth*, III, i, 83: "To half a soul and to a *notion* crazed."
2. "Shakspere and Milton Again," p. 191.

purpose, this storm, as I have previously observed, is virtually identical with the tempest in *Paradise Regained*. In the centre of one stands Lear, "bare-headed"; in the other, Christ, "ill shrouded," endures, unappalled, the malice of Satan. In each case the violent uproar in nature is a symbol of spiritual malignity. Details — which are not of prime importance in this case — are different in some respects, alike in others. All storms have their clouds and winds, lightning and thunder, but not all their "oak-cleaving" thunderbolts; nor are all storms of such intensity as to threaten to annihilate the cosmos:

III, ii, 1–7, 60:
Blow, winds, and crack your cheeks! Rage! Blow!
You *cataracts* and hurricanoes, *spout* . . .
You sulphurous and thought-executing fires,
Vaunt-couriers of *oak-cleaving* thunderbolts,
Singe my white head! And thou, all-shaking *thunder*,
Strike flat the thick rotundity o' the world!
Crack nature's moulds . . .

Kent. — Alack, *bare-headed!*

(Compare also, for verbal likenesses with *Paradise Regained*, and *Paradise Lost*. the following lines from *The Tempest* and *Cymbeline*:

Tempest, V, i, 41–48:
I have bedimm'd
The noontide sun, call'd forth the *mutinous winds*,
And 'twixt the green sea and the azur'd vault
Set roaring war; to *the dread rattling thunder*
Have I given *fire*, and *rifted Jove's stout oak*

P. L., II, 174–178.
                        What if . . . this firmament
Of Hell should *spout* her *cataracts* of fire,
Impendent horrors, threatening hideous fall
One day *upon our heads?* — (G. C. T.)

P. R., IV, 408–421:
                        Either tropic now
'Gan *thunder*, and both ends of heaven
. . .
Fierce rain with lightning mixed, water with *fire*
In ruin reconciled; *nor slept the winds*
Within their stony caves, but rushed abroad
From the four hinges of the world, and fell
On the vexed wilderness, whose *tallest pines*
Though rooted deep as high, and *sturdiest oaks*
Bowed their stiff necks, loaden with stormy blasts,
Or *torn up sheer*. *Ill* wast thou *shrouded* then
O patient Son of God!

<table>
<tr>
<td>

With his own bolt . . . and by the spurs
    pluck'd up
The *pine* and cedar.[1]

Cymbeline, IV, ii, 174–176:
    The rud'st wind
That by the *top* doth take the *moun-
tain pine*[2]
And make him *stoop* to the vale.)

</td>
<td>

P. L. I., 612–614:
    When *heaven's fire*
Hath scathed the *forest oaks* or *moun-
tain pines,*
With *singed top* . . .

</td>
</tr>
</table>

7. *Macbeth.*

The closing entry in the list of ninety-nine subjects which Milton jotted down in the course of his reading between 1639 and 1642, while he was pluming his wings for a greater flight than any he had yet attempted, runs as follows:

Kenneth, who having privily poison'd Malcolm Duffe that his own son might succeed, is slain by Fenella. Scotch Hist., pp. 157, 158.

Mackbeth. Beginning at the arrivall of Malcolm at Macduffe. The matter of Duncan may be express't by the appearing of his ghost.[3]

Professor Hales [4] has suggested that Milton may have thought of writing an independent drama on the theme of Macbeth for two reasons — first, because his "profound respect for historic fact" may have been outraged by Shakspere's free and easy treatment of history in this play, and second, because Milton, being inclined to deal with the problem of evil "in the spirit of the dogmatist," would have wished to emphasize the "wilfulness of Macbeth's ruin" more than did Shakspere. The entry, however, suggests another consideration — perhaps as important as any — upon which Hales touches only in passing. Milton was thinking "of immortality" when he was jotting down these several plans for the great poem he meant to write, and his was not the nature to

---

1. I am indebted to Professor S. F. Gingerich for this reference.
2. See also *Merchant of Venice,* IV, i, 75–77; Variorum *Cymbeline,* ed. Furness, pp. 308, 290–291 and notes; and, below, *Macbeth* A, (1), p. 162.
3. So printed by Todd, V, 503, from the Trinity College MS.
4. See above, p. 143, n. 2.

emulate anything but excellence itself. The very fact, then, of his proposing to treat this theme, suggests that Shakspere's *Macbeth* must have impressed him profoundly. His writings prove that it did, though happily no new *Macbeth* is among them.

A.

(1) I, iii, 75–78:
Say . . . why
Upon this *blasted heath* you stop our way
With such prophetic greeting.

P. L., I, 614–615 (*The mountain pines*):
Their stately growth, though bare,
Stands on the *blasted heath.* — (D)

(2) III, ii, 53:
Night's black agents to their preys do rouse.[1]

Comus, 432:
No *evil thing that walks by night.* — (W)

(3) V, viii, 30–31; 17–18:
Though . . . thou oppos'd, *being of no woman born* . . .
Accursed be the tongue that tells me so,
For it hath cow'd *my better part of man.*

P. L., XI, 495–497:
Adam . . . wept
Though not of woman born, compassion quelled
His best of man.[2] — (Whalley)

(4) III, iv, 128–129:
How say'st thou, that Macduff denies his person
At our *great bidding?*

P. L., XI, 314:
Therefore to His *great bidding* I submit.
— (T)

(5) II, i, 50–51:
        Wicked dreams abuse
The curtain'd sleep.

Comus, 554:
    The litter of *close-curtained sleep.*
    — (T)

(6) III, ii, 40–43:
        Ere the bat hath flown
His cloistered *flight*, ere to black Hecate's summons
The shard-borne beetle with his *drowsy* hums
Hath rung Night's yawning peal . . .

Comus, 552–554:
Till an unusual stop of sudden silence
Gave respite to the *drowsy-flighted* steeds
That draw the litter of close-curtained sleep.[3]

---

1. See item (6) for an echo from Macbeth's speech immediately preceding this.
2. See below, *Henry V*, A (1), p. 180.
3. Warton (cf. Todd, VI, 331) thinks there can be no doubt that in painting his drowsy-flighted steeds, Milton "had his eye upon 'the jades'" who, in the *II Henry VI* (IV, i, 3–6), "drag the tragic melancholy night," and with "their drowsy, slow, and flagging

(7)¹ III, i, 42–44:
    To make *society*
The *sweeter* welcome, we will keep our-
    self
Till supper time *alone*.

P. L., IX, 249–250:
For *solitude* sometimes is best *society*,
And short retirement urges *sweet* re-
    turn.

B.

(1) Hales notes that *Macbeth* and *Paradise Lost* both treat of the origin of evil and the ruin of man; and Hanford points to the similarity between the relations of Adam and Eve and those of Macbeth and his lady, growing out of "Milton's adoption of romantic love as an essential motive."

(2) The weird sisters.

(*a*) Like the witches in *Macbeth*, Comus and his rout have many guileful spells

> To inveigle and invite the unwary sense
> Of them that pass unweeting by the way (*Comus*, 538–539),

and Thyrsis has heard them, night by night, howling

> Like stabled wolves or tigers at their prey,
> Doing abhorred rites to Hecate. (*Id.*, 534–535.)

(*b*) III, v, 23–24 (*Hecate to the witches*):
Upon *the corner of the moon*
There hangs a vaporous drop pro-
    found.

Comus, 1013–1017 (*Thyrsis's song*):
I can ... soar as soon
To *the corners of the moon*. — (V)

(*c*) IV, i, 138–139; III, v, 20–21; IV, i,
    30–31; V, i, 55:
Infected be *the air on which they ride*,
And damn'd all those that trust them.

P. L., II, 540–541 (*Satan's crew*):
    Ride the air
In whirlwind. — (V)

---

wings Clip dead men's graves." No one has ventured to put forward the claims of the great passage from *Macbeth* here suggested as an at least equally probable source of Milton's adjective. If there was a Shaksperian source, this, indeed, would seem the more probable, in proportion to its immense superiority to the *Henry VI* passage, and Milton's far more intimate relationships with *Macbeth*. Incidentally the *Macbeth* passage supports the Cambridge MS. reading, "drowsy-flighted," as against the "drowsy-frighted" of all other earlier editions of *Comus*. Cf. also *King John*, III, iii, 38, on the midnight bell, sounding "into the drowsy ear of night."

    1. See also above, p. 145, n. 5.

I am *for the air;* this night I'll spend
Unto a dismal and a fatal end.

Finger of *birth-strangled babe*
Ditch-delivered by a drab.

Here's *the smell of the blood* still.

Id., II, 662–665:
The night-hag . . . *riding through the
air* she comes,
Lured with *the smell of infant blood,* to
dance
With Lapland witches, while the labor-
ing moon
Eclipses at their charms. — (V)

(3) Macbeth.

(*a*) Professor Hales points out that, just as Malcolm's preferment
to the principality of Cumberland is the signal for the unleashing
of Macbeth's evil ambition (I, iv, 48–50), so does the appointment
of the Son as Vice-regent of Heaven mark the beginning of Satan's
rebellion (*P. L.,* V, 609, 679).

(*b*) II, ii, 36:
Macbeth does *murder sleep.*

P. L., IV, 883 (*Satan comes to Eden*):
To *violate sleep.* — (N)

(*c*)[1] His supposed physical invulnerability is like that of the
spirits in *Paradise Lost:*

V, viii, 8–12.
          Thou losest labour.
As easy mayst thou the *intrenchant air*
With thy keen sword impress as make
    me bleed.
Let fall thy blade on vulnerable crests;
I bear a charmed life.

P. L., VI, 344–348.
          Spirits . . .
Cannot but by annihilating die,
Nor in their liquid texture mortal
    wound
Receive, no more than can *the fluid air.*
    — (N; cf. G. C. T.)

(*d*) Mental and spiritual torment besets Macbeth, Lady Macbeth,
and Samson.

V, iii, 40–45; i, 82; III, 55–56;
Canst thou not minister to a *mind
    diseased,*
Pluck from the memory a *rooted sor-
    row,*
Raze out *the written troubles of the
    brain,*

Samson, 611–627 [*Samson describes his
    torment of the "inmost mind" after
    his fall as a*]
Dire inflammation which no cooling
    herb ·
Or medicinal liquor can assuage. —
    (T)[2]

---

1. Cf. above, *Hamlet,* B (1) (b), p. 150.
2. Editors find similar expressions in Æschylus, Sidney, and Spenser, but nowhere

And with some sweet oblivious *antidote*
Cleanse the stuff'd bosom of that perilous
stuff
Which weighs upon the heart?

Doctrine and Discipline of Divorce,
Preface (*Prose Works*, ed. St. John,
III, 184):

This present truth . . . undertakes the
cure of an *inveterate disease* crept into
the best part of human society; and to
do this with no smarting corrosive but
a smooth and pleasing lesson which,
received, hath [1] the virtue to soften
rooted and knotty *sorrows*.[2]

*More needs she the divine than the phy-
sician.*

Reason of Church Government, Ch. 3
(*Prose Works*, II, 497). [*The minister's
function is to*]

Recover . . . man, both soul and body,
to an everlasting health . . . Two . . .
evil[s] he has to cope with, ignorance
and malice . . . Against the latter . . .
he . . . beginning at the prime causes
and *roots* of the *disease*, sends in these
two divine ingredients of most *cleans-
ing* power to *the soul*, admonition and
reproof; besides which two there is *no
drug or antidote* that can reach *to purge
the mind.*

What *purgative drug*
Would scour these English hence?

---

else is the likeness in thought and word so unmistakable as in Shakspere and Milton. See
also *Othello*, III, iii, 330–333:

> Not poppy nor mandragora . . .
> Shall ever medicine thee to that sweet sleep
> Which thou ow'dst yesterday.

With Milton's "medicinal liquor" compare Shakspere's "medicinal gum," *Othello*, V, ii,
351 (N).

1. Some editors read "both."
2. Todd quotes the part of this passage beginning with "a smooth and pleasing lesson,"
but no one hitherto seems to have noticed the equally close parallel in *The Reason of Church
Government*. (See text immediately below.)

(e) Final despair, Macbeth and Samson.

V, vii, 49–50:
I gin to be *aweary* of the sun
And wish the estate of the world were
     now undone. —

Samson, 595–598:
     Nature within me seems
In all her functions *weary* of herself,
My race of glory run and race of shame,
And I shall shortly be with them that
     that rest.[1]

8. *Timon of Athens.*

A.

(1) IV, iii, 3–5:
Twinn'd brothers of one womb,
Whose procreation, residence, and
     birth,
Scarce is *dividant.*

P. L., XII, 83–85:
     True liberty
. . . Always with right reason dwells
Twinn'd and from her hath no *dividual*
     being. — (D)

(2) V, ii, 203–205:
     With other *incident throes*
That *nature's fragile vessel* does sustain
In life's uncertain voyage.

Samson, 656:
All *chances incident* to *man's frail life.*
     — (G. C. T.)

(3) I, i, 26–37:
Painter. A picture, sir . . . is 't good?
Poet.   I will say of it
It *tutors nature.*

P. R., II, 295:
Nature's own work it seemed, *nature
taught art.* — (M; cf. G. C. T.)[2]

9. *Antony and Cleopatra.*

A.

(1) II, v, 43:
     If thou say Antony lives . . .
I'll set thee in *a shower of gold,* and hail
Rich pearls upon thee.

P. L., II, 3–4:
The *gorgeous East*[3] with richest hand
Showers on her kings *barbaric pearl and
gold.* — (V)

(2) II, ii, 217–223:
A *strange invisible perfume hits the
     sense*
Of the adjacent wharfs. The city cast
Her people out upon her; and Antony,

Comus, 555–560:
At last a soft and solemn breathing
     sound
Rose *like a steam of rich distilled per-
fumes*

---

1. See above, on *Hamlet,* B (5) *(a),* p. 152.
2. Masson and Taylor cite also *Winter's Tale,* IV, iv, 90–91 — "Art . . . adds to nature," but Dunster's references (see Todd) to Spenser and Tasso confirm one's suspicion that this phrase is a commonplace.
3. This phrase appears in *Love's Labour's Lost,* A (3); see below, p. 182.

Enthron'd i' the market-place, did sit
  alone
Whistling to *the air*, which, but for
  vacancy,
Had gone to gaze on Cleopatra too
And made a gap in nature.

And *stole upon the air*, that even *silence*
Was took ere she was ware, and wished
  she might
Deny her nature and be never more,
Still to be so *displaced.* — (G. C. T.)

(3) I, v, 72:
My *man of men.*

P. R., I, 122:
This *man of men.* — (G. C. T.)

(4) IV, xv, 51–52:
The *miserable change* now at my end
Lament nor sorrow at.

Samson, 340–341:
O *miserable change!* Is this the man,
That invincible Samson? — (G. C. T.)

(5) V, ii, 215–217:
          Scald rhymers [will]
Ballad us out o' tune. The quick come-
  dians
Extemporally will stage us . . .

Samson, 203–204:
Am I not sung and proverbed for a
  fool
In every street?[1]

B.

(1) Hanford notes the similarity of the response made by Antony and Adam, respectively, when Cleopatra and Eve, having betrayed their lords, seek to calm them with "soft words." I may add that Samson's response to Dalila's peace overtures [2] is identical with the others:

IV, xii, 30:
Ah, thou spell! Avaunt!

P. L., X, 867:
Out of my sight, thou Serpent!

Samson, 725, 748:
My wife! my traitress! . . . Out, out,
  Hyaena!

(2) The vicissitudes of life familiarize both Cleopatra and Eve with the thought of seeking easy methods to end it:

---

1. Todd here cites *Job*, XXX, 9: "And now I am their song, yea . . . their byword," but it seems to me just as likely that Milton had in mind the scurrilous Elizabethan street-ballads "sung to filthy tunes" mentioned also by Falstaff (*I Henry IV*, II, ii, 48). See also above, *Romeo and Juliet*, A (3), p. 145.
2. See also below, on *Cymbeline*, B (2), p. 197.

V, ii, 358–359:
    Her physician tells me
She hath pursu'd conclusions infinite
Of *easy ways to die.*

P. L., X, 1003–1006:
Why stand we longer shivering under
    fears
That . . . have the power
Of *many ways to die* the shortest choos-
    ing,
Destruction with destruction to de-
    stroy? — (G. C. T.)

(3) The blind Samson's challenge to single combat, addressed to the giant Harapha (an incident which Milton did not find in his Scriptural source), resembles in its dramatic point that which the baffled Antony sends to Octavius. Both challenges are scornfully declined:[1]

IV, i, 4–6:
    Let the old ruffian know
I have many other ways to die; mean-
    time
Laugh at his challenge.

Samson, 1226:
To fight with thee no man of arms will
    deign.

10. *Coriolanus.*

A.

(1) III, i, 239–240:
    Romans . . . they are not,
Though *calv'd* i' the porch o' the Cap-
    itol.

P. L., VII, 463:
The grassy clods now *calved.* — (V)

(2) V, ii, 73:
The glorious *gods* sit in hourly *synod.*

P. L., VI, 156–157:
    The *gods* in *synod*[2] met
Their deities to assert. — (V)

(3) III, ii, 105–106:
You have *put* me now to *such a part*
    which never
I shall discharge to the life.

P. L., IX, 665–667:
The Tempter . . . with shew of zeal
    and love . . .
New parts put on.[3] — (V)

---

1. See above, on *Julius Caesar,* B (1), p. 147.

2. A word "specially used by Shakspere of an asembly of the gods. . . . So Milton" (Verity). See also *P. L.,* II, 391, etc.

3. A figure drawn from the theatre. Verity compares also *P. R.,* II, 239–240.

(4) IV, v, 66–68: [*The face of Corio-lanus*]
Bears a command in 't; *though thy tackle's torn*
Thou show'st a noble *vessel*.

P. L., II, 1041–1044:
Satan
. . . like a weather-beaten *vessel* holds
Gladly the port, *though* shrouds and *tackle torn.* — (G. C. T.)

(5) II, ii, 87–89:
It is held
That *valour* is the *chiefest virtue*, and *Most dignifies the haver.*

P. L., XI, 691–694:
To overcome in battle, and subdue
Nations . . . *shall be held* the *highest pitch*
Of human glory. — (G. C. T.)

II. THE HISTORIES

11. I Henry VI.[1]

A.

(1) IV, ii, 42–44:
He fables not; I hear the enemy.

Comus, 800–801:
She fables not; I feel that I do fear
Her words. — (W)

12. II Henry VI.[2]

A.

(1) IV, ii, 195:
Spare none but such as go in *clouted shoon.*

Comus, 634–635:
The dull swain
Treads on it daily with his *clouted shoon.* — (N) [3]

(2) I, i, 75:
Brave peers of England, *pillars of the state.*

P. L., II, 299–302:
Beezlebub . . . rose . . .
A pillar of state. — (N) [4]

13. III Henry VI.

A.

(1) II, iii, 9:
Our hap is loss, our *hope* but sad *despair.*

P. L., II, 142–143:
Thus repulsed, our final *hope*
Is flat *despair.* — (Malone)

---

1. See below, p. 170, n. 4.   2. See also p. 162, n. 3.

3. Warton adds the passage from *Cymbeline*, IV, ii, 213–214: "I . . . put My *clouted brogues* from off my feet."

4. I reproduce *this* parallel for what it may be worth. Todd finds this phrase also in Gascoigne.

14. Richard III.

Milton remarks, in a well-known passage of his *Eikono-klastes:* [1]

> The poets . . . have been . . . so mindful of decorum as to put never more pious words in the mouth of any person than of a tyrant. I shall not instance an abstruse author . . . but one whom we well know was the closet companion of these his solitudes, William Shakspeare, who introduces the person of Richard the Third speaking in as high a strain of piety and mortification as is uttered in . . . this book [the *Eikon Basilike*]:
>
> > I do not know that Englishman alive
> > With whom my soul is any jot at odds
> > More than the infant that is born to-night.
> > I thank my God for my humility. [II, 1, 69–72.]
>
> Other stuff of this sort may be read throughout the whole tragedy . . .

Obviously [2] Milton is here attacking not Shakspere but Charles I. His close and frequent recollections of *Richard III* prove that this play impressed him strongly.

A.

(1) I, i, 9:
Grim-visag'd war hath smooth'd his wrinkled front.

P. L., VI, 236:
The ridges of *grim war*. — (T)

(2) IV, iii, 54:
Then *fiery expedition* be my wing.

Samson, 1283–1285:
With *winged expedition* . . . he *executes* [3]
His errand on the wicked. — (T)

(3) I, ii, 228–229:
Was ever woman in this humour *woo'd?*
Was ever woman in this humour *won?*

P. L., VIII, 503 (*Eve, conscious of her worth*):
That would be *wooed*, and not unsought be *won*. — (T) [4]

---

1. *Prose Works*, ed. St. John, I, 326–327.
2. Though the contrary has sometimes been supposed. For discussion, see Masson, *Life of Milton*, III, 515.
3. Cf. *Richard II*, I, iii, 79: "Be *swift* like lightning in the *execution*."
4. Shakspere, as Verity notes, was especially fond of this proverbial phrase. It reappears in *I Henry VI*, V, iii, 77; *Titus Andronicus*, II, i, 82–83, and Sonnet 41.

(4) II, iii, 28:
The queen's sons and brothers, *haught and proud* . . .

Psalm LXXX, 31–35:
Thou . . . drov'st out nations, *proud and haut.* — (T)

(5) I, iii, 264:
Our *aery* [eyry] *buildeth* in the *cedar's top.*

P. L., VII, 423–424:
The eagle and the stork
On cliffs and *cedar-tops* their *eyries build.* — (V)

(6) V, iii, 311:
Our strong arms be our conscience, *swords* our *law.*

P. L., XI, 671–672:
    So violence
Proceeded, and oppression, and *sword-law.* — (T)

(7) V, iii, 175:
God and good angels fight on Richmond's side.

P. L., II, 1033:
God and good angels guard. — (T)

(8) I, iv, 58–59:
With that, methought, *a legion of foul fiends*
Environed me, and *howled* in mine ears.

P. R., IV, 422–423:
Infernal ghosts and hellish furies round
Environed thee; some *howled*, some yelled, some shrieked. — (D)

(9) I, iv, 37–39:
    Still the envious flood
Stopp'd in my soul, and would not let it forth
To find the *empty, vast, and wandering air.*[1]

P. L., II, 404–409 [*Satan, bound for earth, tempts*]
    With *wandering* feet
The dark, unbottomed, infinite abyss
    . . .
Upborne with indefatigable wings
Over the vast Abrupt, ere he arrive . . .

(10)[2] III, vii, 94:
So *sweet* is zealous *contemplation.*

Comus, 376–377:
    Sweet retired solitude,
. . . With her best nurse, *Contemplation.*

B.[3]

(1) Hanford points out that Satan resembles Richard III in that both of them, unable to partake of the delights they see about them, with irresistible determination adopt evil as their good:

1. This passage, like item (8), is from Clarence's description of his dream.
2. Taylor compares also V, iii, 185 ("Then fly. What, from myself?") with *P. L.*, IV, 20–22, 75 — a likeness in thought to which I had previously referred in another connection. (See below, p. 173, n. 1, and cf. *PMLA*, XL, 669, n. 57.)
3. See also below, p. 180, n. 1.

I, i, 18–31:
I, that am curtail'd of this fair proportion . . .
To entertain these fair, well-spoken days,
I am determined to prove a villain
And hate the idle pleasures of these days.

P. L., IX, 119–121; IV, 110:
        The more I see
Pleasures about me, so much more I feel
Torment within me . . .
Evil, be thou my Good.

(2) I am inclined to think that the resemblance between Richard III and Milton's *dramatis personae* goes further.[1] Thus, I think it likely that the opening soliloquy of Comus — in which he descants upon the beastly "deformities" with which he has surrounded himself, and, more especially, upon the power of those dazzling spells and glozing words of his which win the easy-hearted to their doom — owes something to Milton's memories of Richard's opening soliloquy and of the one which follows soon after. In all three of these soliloquies the speaker sets forth his evil purpose not only with the utmost frankness, but with the keenest enjoyment of his power for mischief and of his sense of intellectual superiority over his prospective victims:

I, i, 30–41; ii, 228–238:
I am determined to prove a villain . . .
Plots have I laid, inductions dangerous . . .
And if King Edward be as true and just
As I am subtle, false, and treacherous,
This day should Clarence closely be mew'd up . . .
Dive, thoughts, down to my soul; here Clarence comes . . .

Comus, 150–169:
        Now to my charms,
And to my wily trains: I shall ere long
Be well stocked with as fair a herd as grazed
About my mother Circe. Thus I hurl
My dazzling spells into the spongy air,
Of power to cheat the eye with blear illusion
And give it false presentments . . .

---

1. Blackstone's conjecture, however (cf. Todd, II, 423), that Milton might have got "the hint" for his allegory of Sin and Death (*P. L.*, II, 648) from *Richard III*, I, iii, 293,—"sin, death, and hell have set their marks on him,"— is not to be taken seriously. The source, as Verity notes, is Scriptural — *James*, I, 15.

Was ever woman in this humour
woo'd?
Was ever woman in this humour
won? . . .
To take her in her heart's extremest
hate . . .
The bleeding witness of my hatred
by . . .
And I no friends to back my suit
withal
*But the plain devil and dissembling
looks,*
And yet to win her, all the world to
nothing!

I, under fair pretence of friendly ends,
And well-placed words of glozing cour-
tesy,
Baited with reasons not unplausible,
Wind me into the easy-hearted man
And hug him into snares . . .
But here she comes; I fairly step aside,
And hearken, if I may her business
hear.

15. King John.

A.

(1) III, i, 77–80:
To solemnize this day the glorious *sun*
Stays in his course, and *plays* the *al-*
chemist,
Turning with splendour of his *precious*
eye
The meagre cloddy earth to *glittering*
gold.

P. L., III, 606–611:
What wonder then if fields and regions
here
Breathe forth elixir pure, and rivers
run
Potable gold, when, with one virtuous
touch
The arch-chimic Sun . . . Produces
Here in the dark so many *precious*
things. — (N)

(2) V, vii, 46 (*King John, dying*):
Within me is a hell.

P. L., IV, 18–21 (*Satan in Eden*):
Horror and doubt . . . from the bottom
stir
The hell within him. — (T) [1]

B.

(1) Adam's reflections upon death, already referred to above,[2] remind one also of Constance's great apostrophe in this play. Both characters refuse all comfort but the last:

1. Cf. *P. L.*, IV, 75–80; I, 254 ("Which way I fly is Hell, myself am Hell," and "the mind is its own place"), and see below, *A Midsummer-Night's Dream*, A (7), p. 184. The *thought* is the common property of all the poets from Dante to Marlowe.
2. Page 152, *Hamlet*, B (5) (a).

III, iv, 25–36:
Death, death! O *amiable lovely death!*
. . .
Come, grin on me, . . . Misery's love . . .
O, *come* to me!

P. L., X, 854–856:
    Why *comes* not *Death*
With one thrice-acceptable stroke
To end me?

16. Richard II.

A.

(1) V, i, 5–6:
Here let us *rest, if* this rebellious earth
Have any resting.

P. L., I, 183–185:
    Let us . . .
There *rest, if* any *rest* can harbor
    there. — (B)

(2) III, ii, 24–25 (*Richard on touching
    English earth*):
This earth shall have a feeling, and these
    stones
Prove armed soldiers.

Comus, 796–797 (*the Lady, on her
    cause*):
Dumb things would be moved *to sym-
    pathize,*
And *the brute Earth* would lend her
    nerves and shake. — (S)

(3) III, iii, 62–66:
    King Richard doth . . . appear
As doth *the blushing discontented sun*
From out the fiery portal of the east,
When he perceives *the envious clouds*
    are bent
To dim his glory . . .

P. L., I, 592–596:
    Nor appeared [Satan]
Less than Archangel ruined, and the
    excess
Of glory obscured: as when *the sun
    new-risen*
Looks through *the horizontal misty air*
Shorn of his beams. . . . (D)

(4) I, iv, 33 (*Bolingbroke and the com-
    mons*):
[They] had the tribute of his *supple
    knee.*

P. L., V, 787–788:
Will ye submit your necks, and choose
    to bend
The *supple knee?* — (T)

(5) I, iii, 129–130:
    The *eagle-winged pride*
Of sky-aspiring and ambitious
    thoughts.

P. L., VI, 762:
    At his right hand *Victory*
Sat *eagle-winged.* — (T)

(6) II, iii, 65:
Evermore *thanks,* the exchequer of the
    poor.

P. R., III, 127–129:
    Thanks,
The slightest, easiest, readiest recom-
    pense
From them who could return him
    nothing more.

(7) II, i, 252–255 (*on the treasure wasted by Richard*):
Wars hath not wasted it, for warr'd he hath not
But *basely* yielded . . .
More hath he spent in *peace* than they *in war*.

P. L., XI, 784:

Peace to *corrupt* no less than *war* to *waste*.

B.

(1) Milton echoes the patriotic theme of the play, as set forth in John of Gaunt's speech:

II, i, 40, 46:
This scept'red *isle*,
This *precious stone* set in the silver sea.

Comus, 21–23:
All the sea-girt *Isles*
That, like to *rich and various gems*, *inlay*
The unadorned bosom of the deep. — (W)

(2) Adam and Eve start upon their exile from Paradise very much in the mood — and language — of Mowbray, upon facing exile from England:

I, iii, 206–207:
Now no way can I stray
Save back to England, *all the world's my way.*

P. L., XII, 645–647:
Some natural tears they dropped, but wiped them soon;
The world was all before them, where to choose
Their place of rest. — (Johnson)

Again, the Archangel's comforting exhortation to Eve, who is lamenting the prospect of exile, resembles in effect Gaunt's fatherly counsel as Bolingbroke goes into exile from his English paradise:

I, iii, 275–276:
All places that the eye of heaven visits
Are to a wise man ports and happy havens . . .

P. L., XI, 290–292:
Thy going is not lonely; with thee goes
Thy husband; him to follow thou are bound; —
Where he abides, think there thy native soil. — (V) [1]

---

1. The thought, as editors note, is sufficiently familiar. It appears in *Euphues*, and elsewhere.

17. I Henry IV.

A.[1]

(1) III, i, 221–222 (*the dawn*):
The hour before the heavenly-har-
ness'd team
Begins his *golden progress* in the east.

P. L., XI, 173–175:
          The *morn* . . . begins
Her *rosy progress* smiling. — (N)

(2) I, i, 9–10:
Hostile paces . . . like the meteors of
a *troubled heaven.*

P. L., II, 533–534:
          War appears
Waged in the *troubled sky.* — (N) [2]

(3) IV, iii, 68–73:
The more and less . . . followed him
Even *at the heels* in golden multitudes.

P. R., II, 419:
What followers, what retinue canst
thou gain,
Or *at thy heels* the dizzy multitude? —
(G. C. T.)

(4) I, ii, 235–238:
  Like bright metal on a sullen ground,
My reformation, glitt'ring o'er my
fault,
Shall show more goodly and attract
more eyes
Than that which hath no *foil to set it
off.*

Lycidas, 78–79:
Fame is no plant that grows on mortal
soil,
Nor in the *glistering foil*
Set off to the world . . . — (W)

(5) I, iii, 59–62:
And that it was great pity, so it was,
This villanous salt-petre should be
digg'd
Out of the *bowels of* the *harmless earth.*

P. L., I, 685–690: [*Men, following
Mammon's example,*]
Ransacked the Centre, and with im-
pious hands
Rifled the *bowels of* their mother *Earth*
For treasures better hid . . . (G. C. T.)

And *digged out* ribs of gold.

B.

(1) Dalila, in defence of her treachery, asserts her wifely
claims upon Samson — as against those of war and danger with-

---

1. See also *H. IV,* V, iv, 85–86: "Thou art . . . *food for* . . . *worms,* brave Percy," and
P. L., X, 983–986: "Our own begotten. . . . *Food for* so foul a monster" [death] — but cf.
Job, XXIV, 20.
2. Todd quotes two somewhat similar — but not especially significant — sets of parallelism in figure — *H. IV,* V, iv, 65, and *P. L.,* VI, 313; *H. IV,* III, i, 15, and *P. L.,* I, 728.

out — in terms which resemble those of Lady Hotspur to her Harry:[1]

II, iii, 40–67:
O, my good lord, why are you thus
    alone?
For what offence have I this fortnight
    been
A banish'd woman from my Harry's bed?
Tell me, sweet lord, what is 't that
    takes from thee
Thy stomach, pleasure, and thy golden
    sleep? . . .
Why hast thou . . . given my treasures
    and my rights of thee
To thick-ey'd musing and curst mel-
    ancholy? . . .
Some heavy business hath my lord in
    hand,
And I must know it, else he loves me
    not.

Samson, 800–809:
"Why, then, revealed?" . . . I knew
    that liberty
Would draw thee forth to perilous en-
    terprises,
While I at home sat full of cares and
    fears,
Wailing thy absence in my widowed bed;
Here should I still enjoy thee, day and
    night,
Mine and love's prisoner,[2] not the
    Philistines',
Whole to myself, unhazarded abroad,
Fearless at home of partners in my
    love.

(2) It seems to me that Milton, in depicting the relations between Jehovah and the rebellious angels did not altogether forget those between Henry IV and his rebellious lords as represented here and in Part II of this play. At all events, the two poets hold identical views as to the difficulty of reconciliation between mighty opposites, and concerning the penalties of war.

(*a*) V, ii, 4–23 (*Worcester, like Satan, persists in rebellion because reconciliation seems to him impossible*):
It is not possible, it cannot be . . .
He will suspect us still, and find a time
To punish this offence . . .
For treason is but trusted like the fox
    . . .
We . . . shall pay for all.

P. L., IV, 98–99:
For never can true reconcilement grow
Where wounds of deadly hate have
    pierced so deep.

---

1. And, to a lesser extent, those of Portia to Brutus — "You 've ungently, Brutus, stole from my bed." (*Julius Caesar*, II, i, 237–238.)

2. Todd says nothing as to the passage as a whole, but compares this line with Juliet's to Romeo — whom, at parting, she would "pluck back again" like "a wanton's bird . . . So loving-jealous of his liberty." (*Romeo and Juliet*, II, ii, 177–182.)

(*b*) Belial — like Morton and Lord Bardolph in *II Henry IV* — urges his comrades to take their punishment calmly since they had taken the chance of war with a full knowledge of the penalties.

II Henry IV, I, i, 166–168; 180–184:
You cast the event of war . . .
And summ'd the account of chance
    before you said,
"Let us make head." . . .

We all that are engaged to this loss
Knew that we ventur'd on such dan-
    gerous seas
That if we wrought our life 't was ten
    to one
And yet we ventur'd, for the gain pro-
    pos'd
Chok'd the respect of likely peril
    fear'd . . .

P. L., II, 204–208:
I laugh when those who at the spear
    are bold
And ventrous, if that fail them, shrink,
    and fear
What yet they know must follow — to
    endure
Exile, or ignominy, or bonds, or pain,
The sentence of their conqueror.

(3) Milton gives Satan one trait which in the play belongs not to the chief rebel but to the king himself — a cringing humility [1] assumed for the purposes of the moment: in hopes of dispossessing the incumbent of the throne.

I Henry IV, III, ii, 50–52:
And then I stole all courtesy from
    heaven
And dress'd myself in such humility
That I did pluck allegiance from men's
    hearts . . .

P. L., IV, 958–961 (*Gabriel to Satan*):
    Who more than thou
Once fawned and cringed and servilely
    adored
Heaven's awful Monarch? wherefore,
    but in hope
To dispossess him, and thyself to
    reign?

18. II Henry IV.

A.

(1) IV, ii, 20–22 (*the Archbishop*):
The very opener and intelligencer
Between the grace, *the sanctities of
    Heaven*
And our dull workings.

P. L., III, 60 (*Jehovah*):
About him all *the sanctities of Heaven*
Stood thick as stars. — (V)

---

1. See also *Richard II*, I, iv, 24–36, and the *Eikonoklastes* passage, above, p. 170.

(2) IV, v, 184–186:
        God knows, my son
By what *by-paths* and *indirect* crook'd
        ways
I met this crown.

P. L., XI, 629–631:
O pity and shame that they who to live
        well
Entered so fair should *turn aside* to
        tread
Paths indirect, or in the midway faint!
— (V)

(3) III, i, 5–8:
        O Sleep, O *gentle Sleep*,
Nature's soft nurse, how have I
        frighted thee
That thou no more wilt weigh my
        eyelids down
And *steep my senses in forgetfulness.*

P. L., VIII, 287–289:
        There *gentle sleep* [1]
First found me, and with soft oppres-
        sion *seized*
My drowsed sense.

B.[2]

(1) Masson and other commentators have suggested that Milton's "double-mouthed" Fame, as described in *Samson Agonistes*, is first cousin to Shakspere's Rumour, "painted full of tongues." And Rumour "with a thousand tongues" speaks also in Milton's *Quintum Novembris*. Though Milton's Fame may owe something to Ovid, Virgil, and Chaucer, the family resemblance between it and Shakspere's loud-mouthed bearer of false or contradictory reports seems unmistakable:

Induction, 1–16 (*Enter Rumour, painted full of tongues*):
Rum. Open your ears; for which of you will stop
The vent of hearing when *loud Rumour speaks* . . .
The *acts* commenced on this ball of earth.
Upon my tongues continual slanders ride,
The which in every language I pronounce,
Stuffing the ears of men with false reports.

Samson, 970–974:
Fame, if not double-faced, is *double-mouthed*,
And with *contrary blast proclaims* most deeds;
On both his wings, one black, the other white,
Bears greatest names in in his wild aerie flight. — (M, Keightley, Br.)

In Quintum Novembris, 191–193:
Millenisque loquax auditaque visaque *linguis*

1. The phrase appears also in *Richard II* (I, iii, 133).
2. See above, *I H. IV*, B (2) (b), p. 178.

... Rumour is *a pipe*
Blown by surmises, jealousies, conjec-
    tures ...

Cuilibet effundit temeraria; veraque
    mendax
Nunc minuit, modo confictis sermoni-
    bus auget. — (Cf. M)

(2) There can be little doubt but that Milton shared and remembered Shakspere's views of the burdens and responsibilities of true kings, as expressed in *Henry IV* and *Henry V*.[1]

III, i, 31; IV, v, 23:
Uneasy lies the head that wears a
    crown.

P. R., II, 458–459:
    A crown,
Golden in shew, is but a wreath of
    thorns,

O polish'd perturbation, *golden care* ...
*That keep'st the ports of slumber open
    wide* ...

Brings dangers, troubles, *cares*, and
    sleepless nights
To him who wears the regal diadem.

19. Henry V.

A.

(1) IV, vi, 30–32:
But I had not *so much of man* in me,
And all my mother came into mine
    eyes
And gave me up to tears.

P. L., XI, 496–497:
        Compassion quelled
His *best of man, and gave him up to
    tears*. — (Whalley) [2]

(2) II, Prologue 8:
For now *sits Expectation* in the air ...

P. L., VI, 306–307:
        Expectation stood
In horror. — (N) [3]

(3) IV, iii, 25:
Nor care I who doth *feed upon my cost*.

P. R., II, 421:
Longer than thou *canst feed them on
    thy cost*. — (D)

(4) III, Prologue, 33:
The *devilish cannon*.

P. L., VI, 553; IV, 17:
His *devilish enginry* ...
A *devilish engine* ... (V; cf. G. C. T.)

---

1. Though, as Hanford has shown (*PMLA*, XXXVI, 310–311), Shakspere was by no means the sole formative influence that shaped Milton's ideal of kingship.—On *Henry V*, see below. Compare also *Richard III*, I, iv, 78–83,—"Princes have but their titles for their glories. . ."

2. See above, *Macbeth*, A (3), p. 162.

3. Todd, however, finds the phrase ("Expectation ... took stand") in Fletcher's *Bonduca*, III, i. Verity cites *Troilus and Cressida*, Prol., 20–22: "Now Expectation, tickling skittish spirits ... Sets all on hazard."

(5) Opening Prologue, 15–18:
O, pardon! since a crooked figure may
Attest in little place a million;
And let us, *ciphers to this great ac-
   compt,*
On your imaginary forces work.

A Free Commonwealth (Prose Works,
   ed. St. John, II, 138):
For what can [the King] more than
another man? who, *even in the expression of a late court poet,* sits only *like a
great cipher* set to no purpose before a
long row of other significant figures.[1]

B.

(1) In *Paradise Lost* as well as in *Paradise Regained* there are passages strikingly like those in which Henry V speaks of the burdens which rest upon kings,[2] and of the idol Ceremony:

IV, i, 247–259:
Upon the King! let us our lives, our
   souls,
Our debts, our careful wives,
Our children, and our sins lay on the
   King!
We must bear all. . . . What infinite
   heart's-ease
Must kings neglect, that private men
   enjoy!
And what have kings, that privates
   have not too,
Save ceremony, save general cere-
   mony?
And what art thou, *thou idol Cere-
mony?*
What kind of god art thou, that suf-
   fer'st more
Of mortal griefs than do thy worship-
   pers?

P. R., II, 462–465:
On his shoulders each man's burden lies;
For therein stands the office of a king
His honour, virtue, merit, and chief
   praise,
That *for the public all this weight he
   bears.* — (Keightley)

P. L., V, 354–357:
   The tedious pomp that waits
On princes, when their rich retinue
   long
Of horses led and grooms besmeared
   with gold
Dazzles the crowd and sets them all
   agape.

20. *Henry VIII.*

A.

(1) III, ii, 352–357:
This is the state of man; to-day he puts
   forth
The tender leaves of hopes, to-morrow
   blossoms, . . .

Samson, 1574–1577:
What windy joy . . . had I conceived
   . . .
Abortive as *the first-born bloom of
   spring*

---

1. I owe this reference to Dr. Wilmon Brewer. (See also above, p. 119, n. 3.)
2. See above, on *II Henry IV*, B (2), p. 180.

The third day comes a frost, a killing
   frost,
And . . . *nips* his root.

Nipt with the lagging rear of winter's
   frost! — (Warburton) [1]

(2) II, i, 77–78:
Make of your prayers one sweet sacri-
   fice
And *lift my soul to heaven.*

P. L., IV, 687–688:
   Their songs
Divide the night, and *lift our thoughts
   to Heaven.* — (T) [2]

III. THE COMEDIES

21. *Love's Labour's Lost.*

A.

(1) I, i, 171:
This *child of fancy,* that Armado hight.

L'Allegro, 133:
Sweetest Shakspere, *Fancy's child.* —
   (T) [3]

(2) IV, iii, 340–343:
Is not love . . . as sweet and *musical
As* bright *Apollo's lute?*

Comus, 476–478:
How charming is divine Philosophy
Not harsh and crabbed . . .
But *musical as* is *Apollo's lute.* — (B)

(3) IV, iii, 222–223:
Like a rude and savage man *of Ind,*
At the first opening of *the gorgeous east.*

P. L., II, 2–4: [*Satan's throne*]
Outshone the wealth of Ormus and
   of Ind
Or where *the gorgeous East* with richest
   hand . . . — (T) [4]

(4) V, ii, 904:
Daisies pied and violets blue.

L'Allegro, 75:
Meadows trim with *daisies pied.* —
   (W and M) [5]

---

    1. Newton compares *Love's Labour's Lost,* I, i, 100–101:

        "Biron is like an envious sneaping frost
        That bites the first-born infants of the spring."

    2. This likeness is perhaps not especially significant. Todd also quotes Drummond, "And lift a reverent eye and thought to heaven."

    3. If this is, as Todd says, an "obvious parallel," there is a deal of unconscious irony in it.

    4. Editors compare Spenser, *Faerie Queene,* III, iv, 23, on "the wealth of th' East and pompe of Persian kings," but these lines are not nearly so close to Milton's as are Shakspere's.— See above, *Antony and Cleopatra,* A (1), p. 166.

    5. "Almost certainly a recollection of Shakespeare" (Masson).

(5) II, i, 246–247 (*Boyet's description of the King, smitten by the Princess's charms*):

His face's own margent did quote *such amazes*
That all eyes saw his eyes enchanted *with gazes*.

On the Nativity, 69–70:

The stars with *deep amaze*
Stand fixed *with* steadfast *gaze*.[1]

22. *Two Gentlemen of Verona*.

A.

(1) I, i, 45–46:
       The most forward bud
Is eaten by *the canker* ere it blow.

Lycidas, 45:
As killing as *the canker* to the rose. — (W) [2]

(2) V, iv, 51–53:
       Better have none
Than plural faith, which is too much by one.
Thou *counterfeit* to thy *true friend!*

Samson, 189–191:
How *counterfeit* a coin they are who *"friends"*
Bear in their superscription (of the most
I would be understood). — (D)

23. *A Midsummer-Night's Dream*.[3]

A.

(1) II, I, 249–251:
I know *a bank* . . .
Quite *over-canopi'd with luscious wood-bine*. . . .

Comus, 543–545:
       A bank
With ivy *canopied*, and interwove
With flaunting honeysuckle. — (W) [4]

(2) II, i, 69:
The farthest *steep of India*.

Comus, 139:
The nice morn, on the *Indian steep*. — (V)

---

1. This curious likeness in rhyme-words, if it is nothing more, has escaped the commentators.

2. Cf. *Twelfth Night*, II, iv, 114 "concealment, like a worm i' the bud." Warton and Todd hold that "frequent repetition of this image" by Shakspere "suggested it to Milton."

3. "A play," says Verity, "constantly imitated by Milton." Appendix I, on "Milton and *A Midsummer-Night's Dream*," in Verity's edition (Cambridge University Press, 1923) of the play, is an important contribution to our subject.

4. Compare also *M. N. D.*, II, i, 15 and *Lycidas*, 146; and the whole flower passage in *Lycidas* (140–150) with Oberon's flowers.

(3) II, i, 28–29, 141:
And now they never meet *in grove or
green*
By *fountain clear* or *spangled* starlight
sheen . . .
And see our *moonlight revels.*

P. L., I, 781–785:
          Faery elves
Whose *midnight revels, by a forest-side*
Or *fountain* some belated peasant sees,
Or dreams he sees, while overhead the
          Moon
Sits arbitress. — (V)

Comus, 1003:
Far above in *spangled sheen.* — (W. A.
Wright) [1]

(4) II, i, 25:
To *trace* the *forests* wild.

Comus, 423:
Trace huge *forests* and unharboured
heaths. — (Holt White) [1]

(5) III, ii, 380–384:
          Yonder shines *Aurora's har-
binger;*
At whose approach, *ghosts* wandering
here and there
Troop home to churchyards: *damned
spirits* all
That in crossways and floods have
burial,
Already to their *wormy beds* are *gone.*

Song on May Morning, 1:
The bright morning star, *day's har-
binger.* — (V)

On the Nativity, 232–234:
          The flocking *shadows* pale
          Troop to the infernal jail;
Each fettered *ghost* slips to his several
          grave. — (V)

Death of a Fair Infant, 31:
Thy beauties lie in *wormy bed.* — (W)

(6) V, i, 37:
To ease the anguish of a *torturing hour.*

P. L., II, 90–92:
          The scourge
Inexorably and the *torturing hour*
Calls us to penance. — (Thyer)

(7) II, i, 243:
I'll follow thee, and *make a heaven of
hell.*

P. L., I, 254:
The mind is its own place, and in itself
Can *make a Heaven of Hell,* a Hell of
          Heaven. — (V) [2]

(8) V, i, 398–399:
Through this house give *glimmering
light*
By the dead and drowsy fire.

Il Penseroso, 79–80:
Where *glowing embers* through the
room
Teach *light* to counterfeit *a gloom.* —
(W) [3]

---

1. See *M. N. D.,* Furness, Variorum, p. 51, and cf. Verity.
2. See above, *King John,* A (2), p. 173.
3. "Much the same image" as Shakspere's, says Warton, but he cites also Spenser,

(9) III, ii, 389–393:
I with the Morning's love have oft made sport . . .
Even till *the eastern gate*, all *fiery red*,
Opening on Neptune with fair blessed beams,
Turns into yellow gold his salt green streams.

L'Allegro, 59–61:
Right against *the eastern gate*,
Where the great Sun begins his state,
Robed *in flames* and amber light. — (V)

(10) II, i, 107–108, 128–129:
Hoary-headed frosts
Fall in the *fresh lap* of the crimson rose . . .

The sails conceive
And grow big-bellied with the *wanton wind*.

Lycidas, 136–138:
Ye valleys low, where the mild whispers use
Of shades, and *wanton winds*, and gushing brooks,
On whose *fresh lap* the swart star sparely looks. — (V)

(11) I, i, 74–78:
Thrice-blessed they that master so their blood
To undergo such maiden pilgrimage;
But earthlier happy is *the rose distill'd* [1]
Than that which, *withering* on the *virgin* thorn,
Grows, lives, and dies in single blessedness.

Comus, 737–744:
List, Lady, be not coy, and be not cozened
With that same vaunted name, *Virginity* . . .
If you let slip time, like a neglected *rose*,
It *withers* on the stalk with languished head. — (W; cf. T and M) [2]

(12) I, i, 184–185:
More tuneable than lark *to shepherd's ear*
When wheat is green, *when hawthorn buds appear*.

Lycidas, 45–49:
As killing as the canker to the rose . . .
When first the white-thorn blows,
Such, Lycidas, thy loss *to shepherd's ear*. — (T; cf. M)

(13) II, i, 161–164:
But I might see young Cupid's fiery shaft

Comus, 428–445: [*She that has chastity*] [3]
Where very desolation dwells

Faerie Queen, I, i, 14: "A little glooming light, much like a shade." Malone quotes from *Lucrece* (1378–1379) "Ashy lights, Like dying coals burnt out in tedious nights."

1. See below, *Sonnets*, pp. 203–204.
2. This figure, "is a favorite one with . . . Shakespeare, Spenser, Daniel, Drayton, Fletcher" (Masson). See below, p. 193, n.
3. On the dangers that beset chaste beauty in the night, Verity compares *M. N. D.*, II, i, 217–219, with *Comus*, 393–403.

Quench'd in the *chaste beams* of *the watery moon,*
And *the imperial votaress passed on*
In maiden meditation, fancy-free.
Yet mark'd I where *the bolt of Cupid* fell. . . .

She may pass on with unblenched majesty . . .
Hence . . . the huntress Dian . . .
Fair silver-shafted Queen for ever chaste,
     . . . Set at nought
The frivolous *bolt of Cupid.*

B.[1]

    (1) Puck.

    (*a*) Reminiscences of Puck's mischief-making and of his "capricious good-will" appear in *L'Allegro, Comus,* and *Paradise Lost:*

II, i, 33–41; 16:
    You are that *shrewd and knavish sprite*
Call'd Robin Goodfellow. Are not you he
That *frights* the maidens of the villagery . . .
And sometime make the drink to bear no barm,
Mislead night-wanderers, laughing at their harm?
Those that *Hobgoblin* call you and sweet Puck,
You do their work, and they shall have good luck . . .

Farewell, thou *lob* of *spirits.*

P. L., IX, 638–640:
    Some *evil Spirit* . . .
Misleads the amazed *night-wanderer* from the way. — (T)

Comus, 39:
Threats the forlorn and *wandering passenger.*

L'Allegro, 105–110:
    How *the drudging Goblin sweat*
To earn his cream-bowl duly set . . .
His shadowy flail hath threshed the corn
That ten day-labourers could not end;
Then lies him down, the *lubbar fiend.* — (M) [2]

    (*b*) The Attendant Spirit in Comus, says Moody,[3] "in his closing song reminds us of . . . Puck":

II, i, 175–176:
I'll put a girdle round about the earth in forty minutes.

Comus, 1013–1014:
I can fly or I can run
Quickly to the green earth's end.

---

    1. Verity remarks that the passage in *P. L.,* X, 896–908 (on the "innumerable mischiefs" wrought by "female snares" reads "like a commentary" on the proverbial line, "The course of true love never did run smooth" (*M. N. D.,* I, i, 134). Masson quotes approvingly Todd's comparison of *M. N. D.,* V, i, 12, with Milton's *Elegia Quinta,* 19.

    2. The "drudging goblin," writes Masson, "is Shakespeare's Puck," though in some respects Milton's description of him is closer to Jonson's (in the masque, *Love Restored*).

    3. Page 37.

(*c*) The opening speech of Thyrsis confirms the resemblance:

III, ii, 100:
I go, I go; look how I go,
Swifter than arrow from the Tartar's
   bow.

Comus, 80–81:
Swift as the sparkle of a glancing star
I shoot from heaven.

(2) Verity [1] notes that toward the close of the *Vacation Exercise* the fairies dance upon the hearth —"in token of favor and blessing to children in nativity"— very much as Oberon bids them do for the heirs-to-be of the three couples at the end of the play:

V, i, 408–428:
Now, until the break of day,
Through this house each *fairy stray*.
To the best bride-bed will we,
Which by us shall *blessed* be,
And the issue there create
Ever shall be fortunate . . .
[Stainless] *in nativity* . . .
Every fairy take his gait,
And each several *chamber* bless,
Through this palace with sweet
   peace . . .
Trip away, make no stay.

Vacation Exercise, 59–64:
Good luck befriend thee, son, for *at thy
   birth*
The *fairy ladies danced upon* the
   hearth.
The drowsy Nurse hath sworn she did
   them spy
Come *tripping to the room* where thou
   didst lie,
And, sweetly singing round about thy
   bed,
Strew all their *blessings* on thy sleeping
   head.

(3) Change of seasons, as an affliction visited upon man, follows in *A Midsummer-Night's Dream* upon the disturbance of the fairies' sports by Oberon's jealous brawls; in *Paradise Lost* upon man's tasting the apple.

II, i, 88–116:
   The winds, piping to us in vain,
As in revenge have suck'd up from the
   sea
Contagious fogs . . . *the moon*, the gov-
   erness of floods,
Pale in her anger washes all the air
That rheumatic *diseases* do abound . . .
The seasons alter; hoary-headed frosts

P. L., X, 651–666; 677–695; 736:
   The Sun
Had first his precept so to move, so
   shine
As might affect the Earth with cold
   and heat
Scarce tolerable, and from the north to
   call
Decrepit winter . . . To *the blanc Moon*

---

1. Page 148; cf. G. C. Taylor, p. 190.

Fall in the fresh lap of the crimson
rose,
And on *old Hiems thin and icy* crown
An odorous chaplet of sweet summer
buds
Is as in mockery set. The spring, the
summer,
The childing autumn, *angry winter,*
change
Their wonted liveries, and the mazed
world
By their increase now knows not which
is which . . .
And *this* same progeny of *evil comes*
. . . *From our dissension.*

(Compare also *As You Like It*, II, i, 5–
11:
Here feel we not *the penalty of Adam,*
The seasons' difference, as the icy fang
And churlish chiding of the *winter's*
wind . . .
Even till I *shrink with cold.*[1])

Her office they prescribed . . . To *the*
winds they set
Their corners when with bluster to
confound
Sea, air, and shore . . . to bring in
change
Of seasons to each clime. Else had the
spring
Perpetual smiled on Earth with vernal
flowers . . .
Avoided *pinching cold* . . .
These changes . . . slow, produced
Vapour, and mist, and exhalation hot,
Corrupt and *pestilent* . . .
For this we may thank Adam

24. Merchant of Venice.

A.

(1) V, i, 294–295:
Fair ladies, you *drop manna* in the way
of starved people.

P. L., II, 112–114:
    His tongue
Dropt manna and could make the worse
    appear
The better reason. — (N)

(2) V, i, 60–65:
There's not *the smallest orb* which thou
beholdst
But *in his motion* like an angel *sings* . . .
But whilst *this muddy vesture* of decay
Doth *grossly* close us in, *we cannot hear*
it.

Arcades, 72–73 (*On the music of the*
spheres):
The heavenly tune, which *none can hear*
Of *human mould,* with *gross unpurged*
ear. — (W) [2]

---

1. For discussion, see *As You Like It*, Furness, Variorum, p. 65; cf. G. C. Taylor,
p. 192.

2. "I think this was more immediately . . . suggested by Shakspere" than by Plato
(Warton). Verity compares another passage from Lorenzo's speech—"Look how the

(3) II, vii, 65:
All that *glisters* is not gold.

P. L., VIII, 90–94:
   Great
Or bright infers not excellence. The
Earth . . . so small
Nor *glistering*, may of solid good
contain
More plenty than the Sun that barren
shines. — (V)

(4) IV, i, 196–197:
Earthly power doth then show likest
 God's
When *mercy* seasons *justice*.

P. L., X, 58–60; 77–78:
   I intend
Mercy colleague with *justice*, sending
thee
Man's friend, his Mediator. . . . . I shall
temper . . .
Justice with *mercy*. — (T) [1]

25. The Taming of the Shrew.

A.

(1) I, ii, 204–205:
Have I not heard great ordinance in
 the field
And *heaven's artillery* thunder in the
skies?

P. L., II, 714–715:
 As when two black clouds
With *heaven's artillery* fraught come
 rattling on. — (T) [2]

(2) II, i, 174:
Morning roses newly wash'd with dew.

L'Allegro, 22:
Fresh-blown roses washed in dew. —
(W) [2]

---

floor of heaven Is thick inlaid with patines of bright gold," (V, i, 58–59) — with Milton's
"road of Heaven, star-paved" (*P. L.*, IV, 976).

 1. Compare also *Measure for Measure*, II, ii, 75–78:

> How would you be
> If He which is the top of judgment should
> But judge you as you are? O, think on that
> And mercy then will breathe within your lips.

 2. Milton's use of this familiar figure — which, as commentators observe, appears also
in Crashaw, Vaughan, and Dryden — does not in and by itself prove that he remembered
the play. But the parallelism (2) which immediately follows in the text, supports the conjecture that he did — even though Todd finds similar expressions in Greene, and elsewhere. By the same token the single, unsupported parallelism noted under *The Merry
Wives* is hardly sufficient to prove that Milton remembered this play.

26. *The Merry Wives of Windsor.*[1]

A.

(1) V, v, 55–56:
Rein up *the organs of her fantasy*,
Sleep she as sound as careless infancy.

P. L., IV, 800–802 (*Eve, tempted by Satan*):
Squat like a toad . . .
Assaying by his devilish art to reach
The organs of her fancy. — (T)[2]

27. *As You Like It.*

A.

(1) IV, iii, 109–113:
A green and gilded *snake* . . . unlink'd
    itself
And *with indented glides* did slip away.

P. L., IX, 495–497:
The . . . *serpent* . . .
Addressed his way — not *with indented wave*,
Prone on the ground, as since . . .
    — (N)

(2) I, iii, 110–112:
Alas, what *danger* will it be to us,
Maids as we are, to travel forth so far.
Beauty provoketh thieves sooner than
    gold.

Comus, 393–402:
Beauty . . . had need the guard
Of dragon-watch with unenchanted
    eye . . .
Danger will [not] wink on Opportunity
And let a single helpless *maiden* pass.
    — (W)

(3) III, ii, 10:
The fair, the chaste, and *unexpressive*
she.

On the Nativity, 116–117:
Harping . . . with *unexpressive* notes.
    — (M)[3]

Lycidas, 176:
The *unexpressive* nuptial song. — (W)

(4) II, vii, 137–142:

Duke. This wide and universal theatre
Presents more woeful pageants than
    the scene
Wherein we play in.

Colasterion, ad fin. (*Prose Works*, III, 460):
I had rather, *since the life of man is likened to a scene*, that all *my entrances and exits* might mix with such persons only whose worth erects them and

---

1. See above, p. 147, n. 2.
2. See note 2, p. 189.
3. "Warton fancies that Shakespeare may have coined" the word "unexpressive," "but search may find older instances" (Masson). The *N. E. D.* records no earlier occurrence of the word.

Jaques. All the world's a stage
And all the men and women merely
    players;
They have *their exits and their en-*
    trances.

their actions to a grave and tragic de-
portment, and not to have to do with
clowns and vices.[1]

(5) See above, *A Midsummer-Night's
Dream*, B (3), p. 188.

28. *Twelfth Night.*[2]

A.

(1) II, iv, 21–22:
It gives a very echo to *the seat*
Where *love* is throned.

P. L., 589–591:
Love . . . hath his *seat*
In reason. — (V)

(2) III, i, 89:
My *legs* do better *understand* me than
I understand what you mean.

P. L., VI, 621–625 (*Belial, punning on
the terms of weight sent from the
cannon's mouth*):
    Who receives them right
Had need *from head to foot* well *under-*
    stand. — (T) [3]

29. *Troilus and Cressida.*

A.

(1) III, iii, 239:
Great Hector in his *weeds of peace.*

L'Allegro, 119–120:
    Throngs of Knights and Barons
    bold
In *weeds of peace* high triumphs hold.—
(T)

(2) IV, i, 8:
Witness the *process of your speech.*

P. L., VII, 176–178:
    The acts of God . . . to human
    ears
Cannot without *process of speech* be
    told. — (T)

---

    1. A passage called to my attention by Dr. Wilmon Brewer. The *totus mundus* com-
monplace does not adequately account for the likeness here.
    2. See above, p. 183, n. 2.
    3. Todd and Verity suggest that Milton borrowed this "miserable equivocation"
from Shakspere, and quote also, *Two Gentlemen*, II, v, 28: "My staff understands me."
The pun, however, had had a wide currency. Jonson and others laughed frequently at
the "grave *understanders* of the pit."

(3) IV, iv, 120–121:
The *lustre* in your *eye, heaven in* your
cheek
Pleads yor fair usage.

P. L., VIII, 488:
Grace was in all her steps, *heaven in
her eye.* — (N) [1]

B.

(1) Dalila is "as false as Cressid," and, as Professor Taylor [2] has recently indicated, she virtually — like Cressida — pronounces this verdict against herself, in words that recall Cressida's own:

III, ii, 190–203:
Cressida. Prophet may you be!
If I be *false*, or swerve a hair from
truth,
When time is old and hath forgot itself
. . .
And mighty states characterless are
grated
To dusty nothing, yet let *memory*
From false to false, *among false maids
in love*
Upbraid my falsehood! . . .
Yea, let them say, to stick *the heart of
falsehood,*
"As false as Cressid."

Samson, 955–957; 975–979:
Samson. Bewail thy *falsehood,* and the
pious works
It hath brought forth *to make thee
memorable*
Among illustrious women, faithful
wives . . .
Dalila. My name, perhaps, among the
Circumcised
In Dan, in Judah, and the bordering
Tribes,
To all posterity may stand defamed,
With maledictions mentioned, and *the
blot*
Of falsehood most unconjugal tra-
duced . . .

(2) The giant Harapha surveys Samson limb by limb, in the same spirit and for the same purpose as Achilles "perusing" Hector — to vaunt his own superiority:

IV, v, 231–233; 237–259:
Achilles. Now, Hector, I have fed
mine eyes on thee;
I have with exact view perus'd thee,
Hector,
And *quoted joint by joint* . . . I will the
second time
As I would buy thee, *view thee limb by
limb* . . .

Samson, 1082–1091:
Harapha. Much have I heard
Of thy prodigious might and feats per-
formed,
Incredible to me, in this displeased,
That I was never present . . . where
we might have tried
Each other's force . . .

---

1. Todd, however, quotes from *Philaster*, "Heaven is in your eyes," and, less closely, from Phineas Fletcher.
2. "Shakspere and Milton Again," p. 195.

Tell me, you heavens, in which part of
   his body
Shall I destroy him, whether there or
   there or there . . .
Hector. His insolence draws folly from
   my lips;
But I 'll endeavour *deeds* to match
   these *words.*

And now am come to see of whom such
   noise
Hath walked about, and *each limb to
   survey,*
If thy appearance answer loud report.
Samson. The way to know were not
   to *see,* but *taste.* — (G. C. T.)

30. All's Well that Ends Well.
A.

(1) I, i, 99–100 (*Helena upon her
   "bright particular star"*):
In his bright *radiance* and *collateral*
   light
Must I be comforted.

P. L., X, 85–86 (*Christ rising to judge
   Man*):
From his *radiant* seat he rose
Of high *collateral* glory. — (T)

(2) III, iii, 5–6 (*Bertram accepting his
   commission*):
We 'll strive to bear it for your worthy
   sake
To *the extreme edge of hazard.*

P. R., I, 94–95 (*Satan on the coming of
   Christ*):
Ye see our danger on *the utmost edge of
   hazard.* — (Br.)

(3) I, i, 136–138 (*Parolles to Helena*):
It is not politic in the commonwealth
of *nature to preserve virginity.* Loss of
virginity is rational increase.

Comus, 720–738 (*Comus to the Lady*):
   If all the world
Should in a fit of temperance, feed on
   pulse . . .

We should . . . live like *Nature's* bas-
   tards, not her sons,
*Who would be quite surcharged with her
   own weight* . . .
List, Lady be not coy and be not
   cozened
With that same vaunted name, *Virginity. . . .*[1]

---

1. This theme, of course, had wide currency in the literature of the Renaissance. (It was a favorite with the sonneteers, including Shakspere, and appears prominently in Marlowe's *Hero and Leander,* Jonson's *Volpone,* and elsewhere. See above, p. 185, n. 2.) But, though the theme was a commonplace, Shakspere's treatment of it — for which see also *Romeo and Juliet,* I, i, 222–225 — is not likely to have escaped Milton.

(4) IV, iii, 83–84:
The *web* of our life is of a *mingled yarn,
good and ill together.*

Areopagitica (Prose Works, II, 67):
Good and evil . . . in . . . this world
grow up *together* almost inseparably;
and the knowledge of *good* is . . . *in-
terwoven* with the knowledge of *evil*.[1]

31. Measure for Measure.[2]

A. and B.

(1) III, i, 83–85; 118–128 (*Claudio on
    death*):
    If *I* must *die,*
I will *encounter darkness as a bride,*
And hug it in mine arms . . .

P. L., X, 775–778:
            How gladly would I meet
Mortality, my sentence, and *be earth
Insensible!* how glad would *lay me
    down
As in my mother's lap!* — (G. C. T.)[3]

Ay, but to die, and go we know not
    where
To lie in cold obstruction and to rot;
This sensible warm motion to become
A kneaded clod, and *the delighted spirit
To bathe in fiery floods,* or to reside
In thrilling region of thick-ribbed ice;
To be imprison'd in the viewless *winds
And blown with restless violence round
    about* [5]

Id., II, 146–151:
Sad cure . . . To perish . . .
In the wide womb of uncreated light
Devoid of sense and motion. — (T) [4]

Id., II, 598–601:
The bitter change . . . Of fierce ex-
tremes . . .
From *beds of raging fires to starve in ice
Their* soft ethereal *warmth.* — (N) [6]

---

1. The figure of good and evil woven together as in textual warp and woof is not
Scriptural. So far as I know the likeness here indicated has not hitherto been noted. I do
not deny that it *may* be a coincidence.

2. See also above, p. 189, n. 1.

3. I have reproduced Professor Taylor's italics. The mood and figure here seem to
me somewhat different, but the phrase "be earth Insensible" deserves comparison (together with the passage next quoted from *Paradise Lost*) with Claudio's "sensible warm
motion."

4. "Milton evidently alludes to Shakspere, in the expression as well as the sentiment" (Todd).

5. This antithesis is a familiar one (editors cite examples from the *Book of Job*, Dante,
Surrey, etc.), but in this context the likeness is none the less worth noting.

6. Verity compares this and the preceding line with *P. L.,* II, 178–182:

> We perhaps . . .
> Caught in a fiery tempest, shall be hurled,
> Each on his rock transfixed, the sport and prey
> Of racking whirlwinds.

The Limbo passage quoted in the text seems to me the more apposite.

The pendent world . . . 't is too horrible.

Id., III, 487–489 (*When unworthy seekers of heaven reach Limbo*):

A *violent* cross *wind* from either coast
Blows them transverse, ten thousand leagues awry
Into the devious air.

Id., II, 1051–1052:
This *pendent world*. — (T) [1]

Masson [2] observed that "Claudio's celebrated speech . . . was familiar to Milton," but the astonishingly *organic* quality of these recollections has never, I think, been concretely set forth. Specifically, the likeness between the close of the speech and Milton's description of the violent winds of Limbo, seems to have escaped the commentators. The cumulative effect of the indications here supports the conjecture that Milton remembered Shakspere in this as in other details.

32. *Pericles.*

A.

(1) II, ii, 4–7:

Our daughter,
In honor of whose birth *these triumphs* are,
Sits here, like *beauty's child, whom nature gat*
For men to see, and seeing wonder at.

Comus, 745–747:
Beauty is *Nature's brag*, and *must be shown*
In courts, at feasts, and *high solemnities*,
Where most may wonder at the workmanship. — (T) [3]

---

1. For another parallelism, based upon a common (Biblical) source, cf. *Measure*, II, ii, 122; *P. L.*, VIII, 77–78; and *Psalms*, II, 4.

2. Milton's *Poetical Works*, III, 424.

3. Todd, however, quotes also a passage, equally close to Milton, from Drayton's *Legend of Matilda:*

Nature thee ordayned
As her brav'st Piece . . .
(Wherein her former workmanship she stayned) . . .
Hoard not thy beauty when thou has such store.

33. *Cymbeline.*

A.[1]

(1) II, iii, 21:
Hark hark, *the lark at heaven's gate
  sings.*

P. L., V, 197–198:
  Ye birds
That *singing* up to *Heaven-gate* ascend.
  — (T) [2]

(2) IV, ii, 258–281:
Fear no more the heat o' the sun . . .
Ghost unlaid forbear thee . . .
Quiet consummation have,
And renowned be *thy grave.*

Comus, 434:
  Stubborn *unlaid ghost.* — (T) [3]

*Epitaph on the Marchioness of Win-
  chester,* 47–48:
Gentle lady, may *thy grave*
Peace and quiet ever have. — (W)

B.

(1) In his *History of Britain,*[4] Milton gives passing mention to "Kymbeline or Cunobeline," "the wise conduct of old Cassibelan" (Shakspere's "Cassibelan, famous in Caesar's praises" [5]), and to the romantic fabrications of Geoffrey of Monmouth [6] concerning

---

1. See above, pp. 161, 169, n. 3. Todd compares also the following passages:

Cymbeline, II, iv, 87–88 (*Imogen's
  chamber*):
  The roof o' the chamber
  With golden cherubims is fretted.

P. L., I, 714 (*from the description of Pande-
  monium*):
  Doric pillars overlaid
  With golden architrave.

Knight (Variorum *Cymbeline*, ed. Furness, p. 77) sees in *P. R.*, III, 323–325, a possible reminiscence of *Cymbeline,* I, vi, 19–21, but Todd (V, 188) prints a closer parallel from Fletcher's *Purple Island.*

2. Cf. Sonnet 29, "The lark at break of day arising." Commentators cite somewhat similar passages from Phineas Fletcher and John Lyly, but there can be little doubt that Shakspere's line was immediately in Milton's memory here.

3. See also *P. R.*, IV, 426–430:

  Till morning fair . . . *laid* the winds
  And griesly spectres, which the Fiend had raised,

with which Warton compares *Hamlet,* I, i, 147–149:

  And was about to speak, when the cock crew.
  And then it started like a guilty thing
  Upon a fearful summons.

(See above, *Hamlet,* B (1) (a), p. 150.)

4. *Prose Works,* V, 199–202.

5. *Cymbeline,* III, i, 5–6.

6. "Stuff . . . too palpably untrue to be worth rehearsing in the midst of truth."

the "two sons of Cunobeline, Guiderius and Arviragus." This passage in itself does not prove that Milton also had Shakspere's play in mind, but there can be no doubt that he had been impressed by the dramatic — or epic — possibilities of the Cymbeline material. This is indicated by the fact [1] that the name of Arviragus appears also in the famous lines of the *Epitaphium Damonis*,

Brennumque *Arviragum*que duces, priscumque Belinum . . . (164 ff.),

which allude to Milton's proposed epic upon the legendary history of Britain.

(2) In the disillusionment wrought by the supposed evil-doing of Imogen and the real perfidy of Dalila, Posthumus and Samson (and the Chorus) find relief by unpacking their hearts with words — which score bitterly "woman's frailty" [2] and inconstancy.

II, v, 20-32:
            There 's *no* motion
That tends to *vice in man*, but I affirm
It is the woman's part; be it lying, note
   it,
The woman's; flattering, hers; *deceiving*, hers . . .
All faults that may be nam'd, nay, that hell knows . . .
For even to vice
They are not constant, but are changing
   still
One vice, but of a minute old, for one
Not half so old as that.

Samson, 748-750; 1026-1040:
Out, out, Hyaena!   These are thy
   wonted arts,
And arts *of every woman false* like
   thee —
To break all faith, all vows, *deceive,*
   betray . . .
            Inward gifts
Were left for haste unfinished . . .
Of *constancy* no root infixed . . .
         To *wisest men and best* . . .
Once joined . . . she proves — a thorn
Intestine . . .
A cleaving mischief, *in his way to virtue
Adverse and turbulent.*

(3) One of the most dramatic moments in *Paradise Lost* is that which pictures Satan's emotions when, bent upon consummating the fall of man, he sees Eve — who remains unconscious of his presence and whose beauty and innocence for a moment deter him

1. Noted by Masson (Milton's *Poetical Works*, III, 359).
2. See above, *Hamlet*, B (5) (a), p. 152.

from his evil purpose. In dramatic conception, and perhaps also in language, the passage seems to me to owe something to the very similar one in *Cymbeline* which describes Iachimo's equally malignant descent — equally delayed by stirrings of conscience — upon the sleeping Imogen. Satan, in other words, belongs to a dramatic tradition which includes Iachimo as well as Iago.[1]

II, ii, 12–50:
> Our Tarquin thus
> Did softly press the rushes ere he waken'd
> *The chastity he wounded.* Cytherea!
> How bravely thou becom'st thy bed, fresh lily,
> And whiter than the sheets! *That I might touch!*
> But kiss one kiss! . . . I lodge in fear,
> *Though this a heavenly angel, hell is here.*

P. L., IX, 457–469:
> *Her heavenly form*
> Angelic, but more soft and feminine,
> Her graceful innocence . . . overawed
> His malice, and *with rapine sweet* bereaved
> His fierceness of the fierce intent it brought . . .
> *But the hot hell that always in him burns*
> . . . Tortures him now more, the more he sees.

34. *The Winter's Tale.*

A.[2]

(1) IV, iv, 122–123:
> Pale *primroses*
> That *die unmarried.*

Lycidas, 142:
> The rathe *primrose* that *forsaken dies.*
> — (W) [3]

35. *The Tempest.*

A.[4]

(1) V, i, 16–17:
> Winter's *drops*
> From *eaves* of reeds.

Il Penseroso, 130:
> Minute *drops from* off the *eaves.* — (Malone)

(2) IV, i, 62:
> Thy turfy mountains where live *nibbling sheep.*

L'Allegro, 71–72:
> Russet lawns and fallows gray,
> Where the *nibbling sheep* do stray. — (W)

---

1. See above, *Othello*, B (1), pp. 156–157.

2. The phrase "forsake the court" occurs in *The Winter's Tale*, I, ii, 362, and in the *Nativity Ode*, line 13 ("forsook the courts"); but his is a pastoral commonplace.

3. "It is obvious that the general texture and sentiment of this line is from *The Winter's Tale* . . . especially as [Milton] had first written 'unwedded' for 'forsaken'" (Warton). Cf. Mark Pattison, *Milton*, p. 25.

4. See also above, pp. 160–161, *Lear*, B (2).

(3) I, ii, 376–379:
Come unto these yellow sands,[1]
   And then take hands.
Curtsied when you have, and *kiss'd*
   The wild waves whist.

On the Nativity, 64–65:
The winds with wonder *whist*
Smoothly *the waters kissed*
Whispering new joys to the mild
   Ocean. — (M)

(4) IV, i, 148–150:
       These our actors . . .
Are *melted* into air, *into thin air.*

P. R., I, 497–499:
       Satan . . . disappeared,
Into thin air diffused. — (D)

(5) IV, i, 44–47:
  Before you can say *"come"* and *"go,"*
And breathe twice, and say "so, so,"
Each one, *tripping on his toe,*
Will be here with mop and mow.

L'Allegro, 33–34:
Come and *trip it* as you *go*
On the light, fantastic toe. — (N)

(6) V, i, 33–35:
Ye elves . . . that on the sands with
   printless foot
Do chase the ebbing Neptune.

Comus, 897–899:
Thus I set my *printless feet*
O'er the cowslip's velvet head. — (W)

B.

(1) Thyrsis — in *Comus* — is, as Moody notes,[2] "manifestly akin to Ariel." Both are spirits of air, and each serves as guardian and attendant upon virtue and innocence. They resemble each other in song as in deed.

V, i, 88–94:
Where the bee sucks, there suck I . . .
Merrily, merrily, shall I live now
Under the blossom that hangs on the
   bough.

Comus, 976–981:
To the ocean now I fly . . .
Up in the broad fields of the sky
There I suck the liquid air
All amidst the Gardens fair . . . —
   (Warburton)

Another line of Thyrsis's closing song is reminiscent of Prospero's epilogue.

Epilogue, line 1:
Now my charms are all o'erthrown . . .

Comus, 1012:
Now my task is smoothly done . . .
   — (W)

---

1. See also *A Midsummer-Night's Dream,* II, i, 125–126 — "She . . . sat with me on Neptune's *yellow sands*"; and *Comus,* 117 — "the *tawny sands.*" ("For *tawny* the Cambridge MS. has *yellow.*"— Verity.)
2. Page 37.

(2) *The Tempest's* airy voices reëcho through Paradise (before Adam and Eve lose it) as well as through Comus's enchanted wood.

III, ii, 144–149 (cf. III, iii, 17, *stage direction*):
> This isle is full of noises
> *Sounds and sweet airs*, that give delight and hurt not.
> Sometimes a thousand twangling instruments
> Will hum about mine ears, and sometimes *voices*
> That if I then had wak'd after long sleep,
> Will make me sleep again.

P. L., IV, 680–682:
> How often . . . have we heard
> *Celestial voices* to the midnight air. — (D)

Comus, 208:
> Airy tongues that syllable men's names. — (Br.)

P. L., V, 547–548:
> Cherubic songs by night . . .
> Aërial music.

(3) Warton called attention long ago to the analogous use of magic paraphernalia on the part of Prospero and Comus — that is to say, to the implication that the magic powers of these two depend upon their books and glass, respectively.

III, ii, 96–103:
> Thou mayst brain him,
> *Having first seiz'd his books*, or with a log
> Batter his skull . . . *Remember*
> *First to possess his books*; for without them
> He's but a sot as I am, nor hath not
> One spirit to command . . . *Burn but his books.*

Comus, 650–653:
> With dauntless hardihood
> And brandished blade rush on him:
> *break his glass,*
> And shed the luscious liquor on the ground;
> *But seize his wand.*

(4) Comus's first greeting to the Lady is staged and written in the spirit of the dramatic romances, and probably with specific memories of Ferdinand's [1] first scene with Miranda. Ariel's song, and the Lady's, furnish a lyric setting, and then Comus, like Ferdinand, hails the Lady as a wondrous being, and inquires whether she be mortal or goddess.

1. What appears to be an uncomplimentary allusion on Milton's part to another character of this play — the passage in the *Apology for Smectymnuus* in which Milton

I, ii, 421–427 (*after Ariel's song*):
 Most sure, *the goddess*
On whom these airs attend. . . . My
  prime request
Which I do last pronounce, is, *O you
  wonder!*
If you be maid or no?

Comus, 244–268 (*after the Echo song*):
Can any mortal mixture of earth's
  mould
Breathe such *divine inchanting ravish-
  ment?*
     . . . *Hail, foreign wonder!* [1]
Whom certain these rough shades did
  never breed
Unless the Goddess that in rural shrine
Dwell'st here.

(5) The feast in *Paradise Regained*, prepared by Satan to tempt Christ, in its stage-setting, and in the final disposition made of it, distinctly resembles that prepared by Ariel for the ship-wrecked mariners, according to the stage directions of the First Folio.

IV, I, 35 (THE TEMPEST *banquet is
 arranged by Ariel and his "meaner
 fellows."*)

P. R., II, 236–239: [*In preparing for his
 banquet, Satan*]
  Takes a chosen band
Of spirits likest to himself in guile
To be at hand and at his beck appear
If cause were to unfold some active
  scene.

III, iii, 17–19 (and *Stage direction*, ante,
 for the Banquet scene):
Solemn and strange music . . . Enter
 several *strange shapes*, bringing in
 a banquet; and *dance about it* with
 gentle actions of salutation; and,
 inviting the King etc., to eat, they
 depart.

Id., II, 340–367:
A table richly spread in regal mode . . .
  By the wine . . . in order stood
Tall stripling youths rich-clad . . .
Under the trees *now tripped, now*
  solemn stood
Nymphs of Diana's train . . . [2]

---

scores the "antic and dishonest gestures of *Trinculos*, buffoons and bawds"— has been thought to refer not to *The Tempest* but to the play of *Albumazor*, acted at Cambridge in 1614 (cf. Johnson's *Life of Milton, Works of Samuel Johnson*, London, 1825, VII, 70, n.); but this is an open question. (Cf. also Milton's *Prose Works*, III, 115, n.)

  1. On revising this material for republication, I find that R. C. Browne (I, 287) has anticipated my point here to the extent of commenting upon this line, as follows: "Cf. Ferdinand's address to Miranda."

  2. Satan commends the gay attendants to Christ as "Spirits of air, and woods, and springs . . . who come to pay Thee homage" (P.R., II, 374–376). "These spirits," says Dunster, "remind us of Shakspere's 'Elves of hills, brooks, standing lakes, and groves,'"

And all the while *harmonious airs* were
heard . . .
The Tempter now
His *invitation* earnestly renewed.

Alon. What *harmony* is this? . . .
Gon. Marvellous sweet music!

III, iii, 52 (*As they try to eat,* — *Stage direction.*	Id., II, 401-403 (*Christ refuses to eat*):
Thunder and lightning. Enter *Ariel, like a harpy;* claps his *wings* upon the table; and, with a strange device, the banquet *vanishes.*	With that Both table and provision *vanished* quite,[1] With sound of *harpies' wings* and talons heard.

Newton, it should be said, compares Satan's banquet with Armida's in *Jerusalem Delivered* (X, lxiv), and Todd reminds us that similar temptations appear frequently in the romances. Milton's stage-setting, at all events (the music, dance, and the rest), is closer to Shakspere than to Tasso, and Tasso says nothing of the disappearance of the banquet with the flapping of the harpies' wings at the end. *Jerusalem Delivered* and *The Tempest*, however, may each have contributed something, for both lived in Milton's memory.

IV. THE NON-DRAMATIC POEMS

The commentators have not been able to accumulate many instances of probable contacts between Milton and Shakspere's non-dramatic poems. I cannot add to their findings at present, but something may be gained by assembling them. So far as quantity goes, it may safely be said that these relationships are less important than those between Milton and the plays. I subjoin the instances referred to.

to whom Prospero bids farewell just before he abjures his magic. But Dunster, like virtually all the commentators, remains silent as to the stage-management of the two banquet scenes.

1. On this line, compare R. C. Browne's note (*English Poems by John Milton*, II, 308).

1. Venus and Adonis.

A.

(1) 453–456:
A red morn that ever yet betoken'd
. . .
Gusts and foul *flaws* to herdmen and
to herds.

P. L., X, 698:
Snow and hail, and stormy *gust and
flaw.* — (N)

(2) 956–957:
She vail'd her eyelids, who like *sluices,*
stopt
The *crystal* tide.

P. L., V, 132–133:
Two other precious drops . . .
Each in their *crystal sluice.* — (T)

2. Lucrece.

A.

(1) 117–118:
Till sable night . . . *dim darkness* doth
display.

Comus, 278:
Dim darkness, and this leafy labyrinth. — (W)

(2) See above, pp. 184–185, n. 3.

3. Sonnets.

A.

(1) Sonnet 1:
Thyself thy foe, *to thy sweet self too
cruel.*

Samson, 784:
Ere I to thee, *thou to thyself* wast *cruel.*
— (V)

Comus, 679:
Why should you be so *cruel to your-
self?* — (V)

(2) Sonnet 132:
That full *star that ushers in the even.*

P. L., IV, 355:
The *stars that usher evening.*

(3) Sonnet 4: [1]
Unthrifty loveliness, why dost thou
spend
Upon thyself thy beauty's legacy?
Nature's bequest gives nothing, but
doth *lend,*

Comus, 679–687: [2]
Why should you be so cruel to your-
self,
And to those dainty limbs, which *Nature lent*

---

1. "Steevens cited" this sonnet and the passage from *Comus*, "and the comparison is worth while" (Masson). See also above, p. 185, n. 1, and p. 193, n. 1. Masson compares also Sonnet 128 with Milton's *Elegia Sexta*, 39–48.

2. See immediately above, *Sonnets*, A (1).

And being frank she lends to those are free.
Then, *beauteous niggard*, why dost thou abuse
The bounteous largess given thee to give?
Profitless usurer, why dost thou use
So great a sum of sums, yet canst not live?

For gentle usage and soft delicacy?
But you *invert the covenant of her trust*,
And harshly deal, *like an ill borrower*,
With that which you received *on other terms*,
Scorning the unexempt condition
By which all mortal frailty must subsist,
Refreshment after toil, ease after pain.

(4) See above, p. 196, n. 2.

4. *The Passionate Pilgrim*.

A.

(1) Number 10:
Sweet rose, fair flower, untimely pluck'd, soon faded,
Pluck'd in the bud, and faded in the spring!

Death of a Fair Infant, 1–2:
O fairest flower, no sooner blown but blasted,
Soft silken Primrose fading timelessly![1]

I cannot here attempt a full analysis of the material assembled above, but it may be useful — with special reference to the purposes of this study as indicated at the outset — to point to certain conclusions which would seem to follow.

I. If our materials may be trusted to prove anything, they prove conclusively that Milton did not forget Shakspere in his later years. They show, in the first place, that about ten fairly definite Shaksperian reminiscences or allusions found their way into the most unpromising recesses of the controversial prose pamphlets of Milton's middle period. And a count of the totals reveals that two thirds of the whole body of Milton's Shaksperian

1. Masson (Milton's *Poetical Works*, III, 147) sees here a likeness in rhythm, and adds that "Milton's taste in rhythm had by this time outgrown Sylvester's Du Bartas." Number 10 of *The Passionate Pilgrim*, however, is usually held not to be Shakspere's (cf. Neilson's *Shakespeare*, p. 1196).

reminiscence [1] appears in *Paradise Lost, Paradise Regained*, and *Samson Agonistes*.

II. The evidence justifies the conclusion that the form and substance of Milton's work was significantly influenced by his Shaksperian memories — that they took deep impression upon the heart of his poetic fancy in youth, sustained and enriched his epic flights with an infinite variety of dramatic motifs and devices, and helped to establish in the unequalled masterpiece of his declining years a remarkable balance between Greek and Elizabethan dramatic forms. For the sum total [1] of Shakspere's recognizable influence upon Milton, whether by way of verbal and figurative recollection, or as a more or less immediate model in matters of dramatic technique, is surprisingly large. This conclusion seems to me inescapable, even though all reasonable discount be made for accidental or uncertain elements. [2] The thirty-five plays considered above include all those of major importance, with the possible exception of *Much Ado;* and of the whole Shakspere canon only this play and *The Comedy of Errors* are not represented in some way. [3] If from this list we subtract the eight

1. Out of approximately 250 reminiscent passages in Milton here examined, about 75 are from *Comus* and other early poems; about 165 or 170 from *Paradise Lost, Paradise Regained,* and *Samson Agonistes* (some 120, 20, and 30 respectively); and some 10 from the prose pamphlets.

2. Not all the illustrative material presented above may commend itself to every reader. On the other hand, some things that might be accepted without question have doubtless escaped me. Errors of omission — and perhaps of judgment — are inevitable in a study of this kind.

3. Professor G. C. Taylor, in the valuable paper frequently referred to above, holds (p. 196) that it is "no longer necessary to throw *Much Ado* into the discard as a play not influencing Milton." To support his position he brings forward, however, only the following passages (p. 193):

Much Ado, V, i, 38:
And made a *push at chance* and
    sufferance.

P. R., IV, 469–470:
    But wilt prolong
All to the *push of fate.*

This similarity — in the absence of definitely confirmatory evidence — seems to me too slight to establish a real claim for *Much Ado.* (I may add that Masson, to illustrate line

or ten plays ¹ which seem not to have yielded at least two or more
fairly certain echoes, there remain twenty-five which Milton did
not forget, and these include the greatest of the tragedies, histories,
and comedies.   It would be difficult to say which of the three
types made the strongest impression upon him, were it not for the
fact that the influence of *Hamlet* and *Macbeth* is easily recognizable
as the most important of all.   Next in order among the tragedies
are *Lear* and *Othello*.   First among the histories stands the group
of plays centering about Richard II, Henry IV, and Henry V,
with *Richard III* scarcely less important.   Among the comedies
Milton drew most heavily upon *A Midsummer-Night's Dream* and
The Tempest.   It is evident, finally, that quantitatively as well as
qualitatively the several plays contributed their quota of recollection or influence in various ways.   In the case of *Measure for
Measure*, for instance, one great passage impressed itself indelibly
upon Milton's memory, whereas scarcely an act or a major theme
of *Hamlet* and *Macbeth* escaped him.

III. Further study of the materials presented above may
yield more definite conclusions as to the exact *nature* of Shakspere's influence upon Milton than I can undertake to formulate

7 of *L'Allegro*, "The *night-raven* sings," quotes *Much Ado*, II, iii, 83–84: "I had as lief
have heard the *night-raven*." But this bird was a familiar of all the poets, from Peele and
Spenser to Goldsmith. His singing in *L'Allegro*, therefore, does not materially help the
case for *Much Ado*.) — Some time after finishing this study I find that Mr. Taylor and
I have failed to take account of a likeness which may possibly alter the case:

Much Ado, II, iii, 65:   *Lycidas*, 165:
Sigh no more, ladies, sigh no more.   Weep no more, woeful shepherds, weep no
  (Cf. Arden ed., p. 101.)   more. (Cf. notes by Verity and Browne.)

The passage in *Lycidas*, however, is very close also to the November eclogue (167–180) of
The Shepheards Calender.
   1. That is, *Titus Andronicus*, *The Merry Wives*, *Pericles*, *I* and *III Henry VI*, and
possibly *The Two Gentlemen*, *Twelfth Night*, *The Taming of the Shrew* (but cf. above, p. 189,
n. 2), *Timon*, and *Henry VIII*. (I do not include *II Henry VI* and *The Winter's Tale* in
this list of eliminations because one or two of the few echoes from these plays have been
generally accepted as clear and unmistakable.)

at present. The problem, however, would necessarily present difficulties at any time. At best, perhaps, it admits of an estimate of general probabilities rather than of an exact analysis of facts.

For one thing, the reader will have observed that the two classifications under which I have grouped the material — like any that might have been adopted — overlap to some extent. I believe, however, that they have served to emphasize a distinction worth making. Two thirds of Milton's Shaksperian recollection — to employ the quantitative test once more — is verbal or figurative. The remaining fraction, which is dramatic, though less in bulk is no less interesting in kind.

As regards the verbal and figurative material, one or two obvious remarks must suffice. In studying the evidence it is constantly to be remembered that the two poets drew upon a common stock of poetic diction and imagery, the heritage of the Renaissance. This fact, however, does not seriously diminish the sum total of Milton's verbal indebtedness to Shakspere. His borrowings vary in degree and kind. Some, especially his appropriations of descriptive nouns and adjectives, are as sharp and clean-cut as "complete" steel, as sturdily obvious as clouted shoon treading upon this goodly frame, the earth. Others ("drowsy-flighted") steal upon the ear less obviously. These draw in their train shadowy recollections of a turn of phrase, a cadence, or modulation well-loved though scarce remembered; and these have no less power to haunt and startle and waylay. Shakspere's personifications — grim-visaged war, fiery expedition, and their kin — are Milton's familiars as much as Shakspere's. Again, Shaksperian imagery is constantly recognizable in Milton's description of nature — of flowers, birds, and trees, dawn and night, moon and stars and tempest, and in the visible forms he gives to such abstractions as sleep and war, death and peace.

Of the probable or possible influence of Shakspere upon Milton's dramaturgy I have given numerous instances in the body of this study. These may be said to fall into three categories. In the first place, there are many likenesses in dramatic theme — the *Paradise Lost* theme in *Othello* and *Macbeth*, the compound echoes of the *Hamlet* soliloquies in *Paradise Lost*, and the ideal of kingship as developed in the histories, in *Paradise Lost*, and *Paradise Regained*. Next, Milton is probably indebted to Shakspere for certain details in his stage-settings and backgrounds (the aërial voices and the magic shadow-shapes of attendant spirits in *Comus* and *Paradise Lost*, the *Tempest*-like banquet of *Paradise Regained*); and perhaps also for occasional hints of dramatic incident (Antony's challenge, and Samson's), and dramatic symbolism (the change of seasons in *A Midsummer-Night's Dream*, *As You Like It*, and *Paradise Lost*, the storm in *Lear*, *Paradise Lost*, and *Paradise Regained*). Finally, the true inwardness as well as the outward appearances of Shakspere's characters are reflected in Milton's. The majestic figure of the elder Hamlet rises again in the shape of Beëlzebub addressing his peers in Pandemonium; Hecate and the weird sisters cast their spells over the dark shades in which dwell Comus and Sin and Death; but Puck and Ariel lend their airy might to aid Thyrsis in undoing these charms. For the rest, besides finding Dalila as false as Cressid, we have seen that Eve, in *her* infinite variety, suggests Desdemona and Lady Macbeth and Cleopatra, and that Samson lives and dies with something of the same tragic intensity, disillusionment, and nobility as Macbeth, and Antony, and Julius Caesar. Adam, in rare moments, proclaims himself a worthy progenitor of Hamlet; and Satan, noblest of them all, holds in solution all the black malice of Iachimo, Iago, and Richard III, together with the indomitable strength and the lamentable human weakness of Henry IV, and King Claudius, and Macbeth.

Chapter V

MILTON IN THE THEATRE [1]

IN one sense literary and theatrical history presents few instances of tragic irony more striking than the answer which the seventeenth and eighteenth centuries gave to Milton's prayer for that fame which alone seemed to him worth having. His "devout prayer to that eternal Spirit who can enrich with all utterance and knowledge" was heard indeed, and *Paradise Lost* won recognition as a classic in his very lifetime.[2] But even so, fame proved both double-faced and double-mouthed. Aftertimes did not let Milton die, but one feels that the Puritan poet, had he known, would have objected bitterly to some of the methods they took to exploit his work. For the whirligig of time exacted unjust revenges. Milton, the great borrower, did honor to Shakspere and other Elizabethan dramatists by shadowing forth his living memories of them in his pages. The theatre of later times, in turn, paid Milton the somewhat dubious compliment of claiming him for its own. What Scott says particularly of the would-be imitators of *Paradise Lost* applies generally also to the many writers who essayed to adapt Milton's other work for the theatre: "The poets, in particular, seemed to have gazed on its excellences like the inferior animals on Dryden's immortal hind, and, incapable of fully estimating a merit which in some degree they could not help feeling, many were their absurd experiments to lower it to the standard of their own comprehension." [3] The popularity of these theatrical adaptations of Milton from the early eighteenth through the first

1. Reprinted, with additions, from *Studies in Philology*, XVII (1920), 269 ff.
2. See below, p. 222, n. 1.   3. Scott–Saintsbury, *Dryden*, V, 95.

half of the nineteenth century, is an aspect of the Milton tradition which, I believe, has not been given the attention it deserves.

And yet the study of Milton, set off to the world in the very mortal soil of the theatre, leads one through some curious byways and through transformations that seem strange unless one sees them in focus with the taste of the times. Much more of Milton's work than one would expect at first thought reappeared in musical or dramatic entertainments of one kind or another — not only *Comus* and *Arcades* and *Paradise Lost*, but also *L'Allegro*, *Il Penseroso*, parts of the ode *On the Nativity*, and *Samson*, *Lycidas*, and even the *Epitaph on Shakespeare*. Henry Lawes, Arne, Purcell, Handel, Haydn, and Rubinstein by no means complete the list of distinguished composers who busied themselves with Miltonic themes. Among the adapters, the writers of prologues or of new stage versions, — proposed or actually completed, — one meets not only Dryden but also Samuel Johnson, Garrick, and Colman the elder, with perhaps Pope and Voltaire, and certainly a host of lesser men. As for the great actors and actresses who appeared in dramatizations or musical renderings of Milton—in *Comus* particularly, but in other pieces as well — their name is legion. Quin, Garrick, Theophilus Cibber, Mossop, Henderson, Charles Kemble, Mrs. Cibber, Mrs. Clive, Mrs. Bellamy, Anne Catley, Peg Woffington, Mrs. Siddons — these are but a few of them. To treat fully of the relations between these several musicians, writers, players, and their common theme,[1] would be to draw a broad cross-section of the history of music, literature, and the stage for more than a century and a half after the death of Milton. My purpose here is merely to sketch the story in very broad outlines. It will be particularly worth while to notice *how* Milton was adapted, for it would be difficult to find a more striking index of the taste of the times than that which his adapters give us.

1. On this subject see R. D. Havens, *The Influence of Milton*, pp. 28–29, 430–433.

That they made real changes will appear more clearly if, before examining them, we review briefly certain very familiar expressions of Milton upon the theatre and drama. Certainly, as a youth he took keen delight in the well-trod stage, and more particularly in the work of Jonson and of Shakspere, to whose hallowed relics he had, even before the days of *L'Allegro*,[1] paid the highest tribute in his *Epitaph*.[2] And Masson has justly emphasized the point that the young poet who wrote *Arcades* and *Comus* after Prynne had brought to a head the Puritan opposition to the drama,[3] was certainly not one of those who blindly condemned everything dramatic as evil *per se*.[4] Milton's masques, of course, were written for private presentation by a noble family, and not, any more than *Samson Agonistes*, for the public theatre. On the other hand, there is no evidence for the belief that his admiration for Shakspere was brought to a period by the decline of the drama or by his political partisanship in the days of Charles I. The *Eikonoklastes* allusion to Shakspere as the king's "closet companion" in his solitude, as Masson again has noted, is not indicative of contempt for the poet if read in its context,[5] nor is the steadfast tribute of remembrance recorded in the preceding chapter of this book. Milton, moreover,

1. See lines 132–134.
2. The *Epitaph* dates from 1630; *L'Allegro*, 1633. In the first elegy to Diodati (1625–1626) Milton writes enthusiastically of "the pomp of the changing theatre." (Cambridge *Milton*, p. 324.)
3. By the publication of his *Histriomastix* (1633). *Arcades* may have been written the same year. *Comus* was written in 1634 and printed in 1637.
4. Striking evidence to the same effect is supplied by a passage from one of Milton's (Latin) Commonplace Books, which its editor assigns to the time when Milton was at St. Paul's School, or to his early college days: "Lactantius accounts all dramatic activity vicious. Nor does anyone seem once to have reflected that, though corruption in the theatre ought indeed to be put down, still it is not at all necessary therefore to abolish all use of the dramatic art. Nay, it were too absurd! For what in all philosophy is more serious, reverend, or lofty than a properly constituted tragedy? And what is more useful for displaying in one single view the misfortunes and vicissitudes incident to human life?" (*A Commonplace Book of John Milton*, Camden Society, New Series, 1877, p. 50.)
5. See above, Chapter IV, p. 170; Masson, *Life of Milton*, IV, 137. For the other interpretation of the passage, cf. Davies, *Dramatic Miscellanies*, I, 181.

testified amply to his continuing admiration for the literary drama when, in *The Reason of Church Government* (1641), he discussed the rival advantages of the epic and dramatic forms for the great work he was then planning. And in the preface to *Samson* (1667–1671), he again observed that "Tragedy as it was anciently composed hath been ever held the gravest, moralest, and most profitable of all other poems." [1] His admiration of classical tragedy, however, and his appreciation of some of the greatest of the Elizabethans, did not imply an unqualified approval of all the customs and ways of the public theatre. In the *Samson* preface, indeed, there is sharp criticism of Elizabethan and Restoration tragedy itself, rather than of the conditions and circumstances of dramatic performances. "The small esteem, or rather infamy" into which tragedy, "with other common Interludes," had then fallen, is ascribed to the "poet's error of intermixing comic stuff with tragic sadness and gravity, or introducing trivial and vulgar persons." This is, after all, but a narrower application of Milton's earlier criticism of the stage, and of the corrupt tendencies of the times which it mirrored during the last decades before the closing of the theatres in 1642. A year before that event, in *The Reason of Church Government*, he had proclaimed to the world his intention of writing a true poem, not only for its own sake, but as a curative for the evils of the time:

And what a benefit this would be to our youth and gentry may be soon guessed by what we know of the corruption and bane which they suck in daily from the writings and interludes of libidinous and ignorant poetasters, who, having scarce ever heard of that which is the main consistence of a true poem, the choice of such persons as they ought to introduce, and what is moral and decent to each one, do, for the most part lay up vicious principles in sweet pills to be swallowed down, and make the taste of virtuous documents harsh and sour.

1. See above, p. 211, n. 4.

It is significant that Milton does not concern himself with the practical problems involved in any improvement of the theatres, except by suggesting that the authorities "take into their care . . . the managing of . . . publick sports and festival pastimes . . . to . . . civilize, adorn, and make discreet our minds . . . not only in pulpits but . . . at . . . solemn paneguries, in theatres, porches, or . . . other place[s]." For the rest, having once written *Comus*, and knowing his powers as he did, he attempted no "interlude" of his own to give the changing theatre such true plays as he may have thought it required. Instead, he contented himself with setting forth the universal principles of beauty and virtue in his epics and in *Samson*. Though he enjoyed the theatre in his youth and honored the classical drama in his old age, Milton of his own volition would never have exchanged his fit audience, though few, for the miscellaneous plaudits of the pit. Even less would he have done so to win the applause or the rewards of a corrupt court. Nor is there any real contradiction involved in a great poet's enjoying the theatre and yet, in a sense, shrinking from personal contact with the stage. That Milton had something of this feeling appears, I think, in a passage — to which Dr. Johnson called attention — from his *Apology for Smectymnuus:*

In the colleges [writes Milton], many of the young divines and those in next aptitude to divinity, have been seen . . . often upon the stage, writhing and unboning their clergy limbs to all the antic and dishonest gestures of Trinculoes, buffoons, and bawds; prostituting the shame of that ministry which either they had or were nigh having, to the eyes of courtiers and court ladies with their grooms and mademoiselles. There while they acted and overacted, among other young scholars I was a spectator; they thought themselves gallant men, and I thought them fools. [1]

The reader may judge presently whether Milton might not have resented the use of *Comus*, trimmed out as it was later with

1. Milton's *Prose Works*, ed. St. John, III, 115; Johnson, *Life of Milton*.

an eye to the un-Miltonic taste of the audiences it found, almost as much as he did the appearance of young clergymen upon the stage.

I have already referred to the preface of *Samson Agonistes*. In it Milton states that he has omitted the usual division into acts and scenes, since that refers "chiefly to the stage, *to which this work never was intended*." Masson[1] is not inclined to take this phrase literally. It does not imply, he says, "that Milton would not willingly have consented to the production of his *Samson* on the stage, had it been possible. My belief is that he would have regarded such a production as an example towards the restoration of the stage to its right uses." Milton's own remarks make this conjecture appear somewhat doubtful even though it comes from Masson, and there is another passage in Masson which confirms such doubts: "Who are the Philistine lords and ladies and captains and priests assembled on the day of festival? Who but Charles himself and the Duke of York and the whole pell-mell of the Clarendons, Buckinghams, Buckhursts, Killigrews, Castlemaines, Moll Davises, Nell Gwynns . . . with even Anglesey, Howard, and Dryden included, that formed the court society of England in that most swinish period of her annals."[2] It is difficult to believe that Milton would have consented to the production of any work of his upon the public stage defiled by such as these and for their delectation. Not to labor the point, it may readily be admitted that *Samson*, unlike other works of Milton, was not actually produced in a way that could have offended him. Its "stage history" is less complicated than that of some of the other poems, and may therefore be presented first in order.

By 1722 seven or more editions of *Samson* had appeared,[3] and it had won its way steadily, if not as rapidly as *Paradise Lost*. A

1. *Life*, VI, 665.   2. *Id.*, p. 676.
3. Masson, *Milton's Poetical Works*, II, 4. (*Samson* was printed together with *Paradise Regained*, or as part of Milton's collected works.)

discussion of the following passage from Masson will best serve to indicate its connection with the stage. "It is said," writes Masson,[1] "that Bishop Atterbury, about 1722, had a scheme for bringing it on the stage at Westminster, the division into acts and scenes to be arranged by Pope. It was a fitter compliment when Handel in 1742 made *Samson* the subject of an oratorio and married his great music to Milton's as great words." The first part of this statement is presumably based upon a passage in Thomas Newton's *Life of Milton* (1750). Newton observed that "Bishop Atterbury had an intention of getting Mr. Pope to divide *Samson* into acts and scenes, and of having it acted by the King's Scholars at Westminster; but his commitment to the Tower put an end to that design."[2] More direct evidence on the point is supplied by the following extract from Atterbury's letter to Pope, written June 5, 1722:

I hope you will not utterly forget what passed in the coach about *Samson Agonistes*. I shall not press you as to time, but some time or other I wish you would review and polish that piece. If upon a new perusal of it (which I desire you to make) you think as I do, that it is written in the very spirit of the ancients, it deserves your care, and is capable of being improved into a perfect model and standard of tragic poetry, always allowing for its being a story out of the Bible, which is an objection that, at this time of day, I know is not to be gotten over.[3]

Pope's editors have, with some reason, wondered at the spectacle of Atterbury urging Pope to "polish" Milton, for Atterbury — much more than Pope, certainly — appears to have been a genuine lover of Milton and of Milton's blank verse.[4] Bowles flatly asserts that Pope "did not presume to touch" *Samson*, and disdains to say anything more about the point. There is, of course, nothing on the *Samson* theme in Pope's extant work, nor do we know just "what

1. Masson, *Milton's Poetical Works*, II, p. 94.
2. See Newton's ed. of *Paradise Lost*, I, lxii.
3. *Memoirs and Correspondence of Francis Atterbury*, ed. F. Williams, I, 379.
4. See W. L. Bowles's *Pope*, VIII, 140, and H. C. Beeching's *Francis Atterbury*, p. 227.

passed in the coach" on the subject. Pope's own remarks on the general subject of play-writing indicate that he probably never thought seriously of polishing *Samson* for the stage. He told Spence of several of his early essays toward a tragedy, and added, "After I had got acquainted with the town I resolved never to write anything for the stage; though I was solicited by several of my friends to do so." He mentions Betterton among those who made these requests, but says nothing of Atterbury. His "strong resolutions against anything of that kind" were formed, he says, because it did not take him long to realize how much promiscuous and ignorant criticism all playwrights had to stand.[1] The most, then, that can be said definitely of Pope's connection with *Samson*, is that he knew it well, admired it in his own way,[2] and that at one time he may have thought of tagging Milton's verses, for the stage or otherwise. It is just possible, however, that Pope, though he did nothing further with Atterbury's suggestion, may have passed it on, and may thus have been indirectly responsible for a very un-Miltonic version of *Samson* written in 1731 — Voltaire's opera by that title. Voltaire, during his visit to England in 1726, had won the friendship of Pope, Bolingbroke, Dr. Young, and many other members of their circle, had discussed Milton with them, and had written on Milton at length somewhat later.[3] It is at least an interesting coincidence that he should have chosen to work on the *Samson* theme, and that his opera, which was set to music by Rameau in 1732, like Dryden's operatic version of *Paradise Lost*, was never produced.[4]

1. Spence, *Anecdotes*, pp. 209, 149.
2. He repeatedly echoes it in his own work. See Elwin and Courthope's *Pope*, I, 220, 312; II, 405.
3. See Spence's *Anecdotes*, and Parton's *Life of Voltaire*, I, 209–219.
4. It should be noted here that two earlier versions of *Samson*, both tragedies, had been presented in the Italian theatre at Paris. Riccoboni, — traveller, playwright, theatrical manager, and historian of the stage, — who wrote the first of these pieces in 1717, had visited England, and probably knew something of Milton. His tragedy is closer to

The relation of Pope and Voltaire to *Samson Agonistes* may not have been a very close one. Handel's oratorio, on the other hand, owes its being to Milton. And yet Masson is not altogether accurate in stating that Handel "married his great music to Milton's as great words." "Samson, an Oratorio, as it is performed at the Theatres Royal, 1742,[1] set to Music by Mr. Handel," was, as its title-page notes, "*Altered* from the *Samson Agonistes* of Milton." Newburgh Hamilton, the adapter,[2] retains much of Milton's text, and did not do violence to him in any such way as did the adapters of *Comus* — but alter him, he did. Hamilton felt the necessity of condensing the material, and this he did, on the whole, judiciously.[3] But his device of providing "airs" for the singers by putting Milton into rhyme, often leads to poor results. Thus Milton's great lines,

> O dark, dark, dark, amid the blaze of noon,
> Irrecoverably dark, total eclipse
> Without all hope of day . . . [4]

reappear in the adaptation as follows:

> Total eclipse! No sun, no Moon!
> All dark amidst the Blaze of Noon!
> O glorious Light! No chearing Ray
> To glad my Eyes with welcome Day!

Contemporary accounts emphasize the pathetic effect produced by the blind Handel's playing of this air,[5] but the inferiority of the

Milton than is Voltaire's opera. Riccoboni's play was adapted for the German stage, and Romagnesi, who did the second Italian–French *Samson*, followed him closely. (See Voltaire, *Œuvres Complètes*, Paris, 1877, II, 3, and notes.) Saint-Saëns' *Samson et Dalila* (1869–1877) probably owes nothing to Milton, though it may be indebted to Voltaire.

1. Not actually produced till February 17, 1743. (See R. A. Streatfeild's *Handel*, p. 174.)

2. Hamilton also adapted Dryden's *Alexander's Feast* for Handel.

3. Thus, he drops the part of the Public Officer who brings the second message to Samson from the Philistine lords. This scene is brought in as the conclusion of the dispute between Samson and the boastful giant of Gath.   4. *Samson*, lines 80–82.

5. At a performance in 1753, with Handel at the organ. Cf. *Autobiography and Correspondence of Mrs. Delany*, ed. Lady Llanover, III, 177.

lines is obvious.[1] And we shall see presently that Handel personally seems to have insisted upon this sort of tagging in his text. For the moment we may note that a stanza from the ode *On the Nativity*, —

> Thus when the Sun from 's watery Bed
> All curtain'd with a cloudy Red, . . .[2]

supplies the adapter with another air — certainly a less objectionable source than Hamilton's own invention. It is from that source that Milton is supplemented with an antiphonal chorus between the priests of the Israelites and those of Dagon. The latter indulge also in other melodious reflections that are rather far from Milton. The following air —

> Ye Men of Gaza, hither bring
> The merry Pipe and pleasing String,
> The solemn Hymn and chearful Song, —
> Be Dagon prais'd by ev'ry Tongue —

is exceptionally good of its kind, and certainly much superior to Dalila's appeal to Samson, as Hamilton has it, —

> With plaintive Notes and am'rous Moan
> Thus cooes the Turtle left alone. . . .
> To fleeting Pleasures make your Court,
> No moment lose, for life is short:
> The present Now 's our only Time,
> The missing That our only Crime, —

which is a soft, Lydian air, perhaps, but hardly Miltonic in tone, and certainly not immortal verse. The adapter, moreover, in his desire to condense his material, misses some of his best opportunities. Of Milton's splendid picture of Dalila's arrival, for example, he retains only the following meagre lines:

1. Of course it is clear that here and elsewhere the music would perhaps require — and make amends for — these shortcomings of the text. But it is with the text as such that we are concerned.
2. Cf. stanza 26.

> But who is this, that so bedeck'd and gay
> Comes this way sailing like a stately Ship?
> 'T is Dalila, thy Wife!

And he radically weakens the whole conception of Dalila by omitting her final "serpent-sting" — her gloating upon the glory she has won. Instead, he gives us merely these tame couplets:

Dalila.   Traitor to love, I'll sue no more
For Pardon scorn'd, your Threats give o'er.

Samson.   Traitress to Love, I'll hear no more
The Charmer's Voice, your arts give o'er.

So, also, Milton's grand finale — Manoa's "Nothing is here for tears, nothing to wail" — tapers off weakly in the adaptation. It should be repeated that Hamilton retained a great deal of Milton. Without doubt he worked as earnestly and reverently as he knew how, but one cannot leave his version of *Samson* without the feeling that the marriage of Handel's music and Milton's words was not as felicitous a union as it might have been. The oratorio, however, was very successful. It received eight performances in 1743, and we read that "crowds of people were turned away for want of room each night." [1] It was repeated twice in 1744, twice in 1745, twice in 1750, three times in 1753, and seven times — by royal command — in 1769. [2] And single performances are recorded for the years 1754, 1755, 1772, 1777, 1825, and 1829. [3] Meanwhile, at least twelve editions of Newburgh Hamilton's text appeared before 1840. [4]

Before looking into the history of the remaining musical adaptations of Milton, we may do well to note here that sacred music in

1. Schoelcher, *Life of Handel*, p. 278.
2. *Id.*, pp. 292, 315, 322, 331, and Covent Garden Playbills for 1769, 1777 (British Museum).
3. *Theatrical Review* (London, 1772), II, 216; Schoelcher (see nn. 1 and 2); and Covent Garden Playbills for 1825, 1829 (B. M.).
4. British Museum.

the eighteenth century was not presented in quite the manner to which we are accustomed. *Samson* was produced, not in a church, but at Covent Garden Theatre, the scene of Rich's famous pantomimes and the house in which *The Beggar's Opera* had scored its first triumphant success fifteen years earlier. And the oratorio ("that profanation" — according to Charles Lamb — "of the purposes of the cheerful playhouse") had to compete for public favor against the attractions of the Italian opera and the legitimate drama. Handel, himself the composer of scores of Italian operas, knew exactly what to do, and used all the means at his disposal. He assigned leading parts in his oratorio to two famous actresses whom we shall meet again in the course of this study: to Mrs. Clive — Katherine Clive, the "indomitable Pivy," famous farceur and the best chambermaid of the eighteenth-century stage;[1] and, secondly, to Mrs. Cibber — the great Susannah Maria Cibber, daughter-in-law of the laureate Colley and wife of the unfortunate Theophilus Cibber, the same Mrs. Cibber who amused the town by contending publicly against Mrs. Clive for the part of Polly in *The Beggar's Opera*, and who won all hearts by her playing of Constance, Juliet, and Desdemona with Quin and Garrick.[2] And somewhat later the forces were augmented by the beautiful — and notorious — Anne Catley, the famous Euphrosyne of *Comus*.[3] In short, no effort was spared to make the oratorio (the "*roratorio*," as a somewhat later writer [4] had it) successful — and successful it was. Horace Walpole testifies to that effect. "Handel," he writes, "has set up an oratorio against the opera, and succeeds. He has hired all the goddesses from the

1. "The darling of the public. . . . If ever there were a true comic genius, Mrs. Clive was one." (Victor, *History of the Theatre*, III, 142.) On her part, and Mrs. Cibber's, in *Samson*, see also *Autobiography of Mrs. Delany*, II, 271, n.
2. See the *Life of Susannah Maria Cibber*, London, 1887.
3. Oulton, *History of the Theatres*, II, 67. See below, p. 250.
4. See J. Cradock's Epilogue to *She Stoops to Conquer*.

farces, and the singers of 'Roast Beef' from between the acts at
both theatres . . . and so they sing and make brave hallelujahs,
and the good company encore the recitative, if it happens to have
any cadence like what they call a Tune." [1] All of which seems
decidedly far away from Milton, unless we bear in mind that we
are dealing with Milton in the theatre — in the eighteenth century. Before we turn to *Paradise Lost*, one word more concerning
the oratorios of those days may be in order, and the pharisaical
Lady Warrington of Thackeray's *Virginians* may say it:

"Far be it from me to object to any innocent amusement, much less to
the music of Mr. Handel, dear Mr. Claypool," says mamma. "Music
refines the soul, elevates the understanding, is heard in our churches, and
't is well known was practiced by King David. Your operas I shun as
deleterious; [2] your ballets I would forbid to my children as most immoral,
— but music, my dears! May we enjoy it, like everything else in reason
— may we —"
"There's the music of the dinner-bell," says papa . . . "Come,
girls." [3]

The stage-history of *Paradise Lost*, like that of *Samson*, is the
record of a proposed dramatization which was not actually put on
the boards, and then of several adaptations of the material for oratorios. We have already quoted Scott's judgment upon the imitators of *Paradise Lost*, and yet Scott justly notes that *The State of
Innocence* (printed 1674), Dryden's operatic version of the theme,
is by no means beneath contempt — if read fairly in and for itself,
and without too much comparison with Milton. Dryden himself
modestly deprecates such comparison. "What I have borrowed,"
he writes, "will be so easily discerned from my mean production
that I shall not need to point the reader to the places; and truly I

1. Quoted by Streatfeild, *Handel*, pp. 174–175.
2. "The pleasure the best opera gives us," says Indiana in *The Conscious Lovers*
(II, ii) "is but mere sensation."
3. *The Virginians*, chap. 50.

should be sorry, for my own sake, that anyone should take the pains to compare them together, the original being one of the greatest, most noble, and most sublime poems which either this age or nation has produced." [1] Scott has not only done full justice to the merits of Dryden's poem, but has also pointed out its characteristic echoes of the corrupt times in which it was written.[2] There is little reason, then, for renewed comparison here, particularly since Dryden's opera was never produced. Why it was never produced, however, is a question of some interest. Scott's explanation is, I think, somewhat doubtful. "The costume of our first parents," he says, "had there been no other objection, must have excluded *The State of Innocence* from the stage, and, accordingly, it was never intended for the stage." Dryden himself does not say that he did not originally intend the piece for the stage, as he might conceivably have said — had the facts warranted it — to add force to his apology. He apologizes merely for publishing "an opera which was never acted," and states that the publication was made in self-defence, "many hundred copies of it being dispers'd abroad without my knowledge or consent, so that every one gathering new faults it became at length a libel against me." Scott holds that Dryden never intended his opera for presentation, in spite of several conditions which, if anything, seem to point in the other direction. There is the fact, for example, that Dryden was then beginning to labor under his impossible contract with the King's Men, by which he had bound himself to write three plays a year.[3] Even if he began his tagging of Milton's verses [4] merely

1. Scott–Saintsbury, *Dryden*, V, 112.

2. *Id.*, pp., 95–99.

3. For the document which deals with this contract, see Malone–Boswell's *Shakspeare*, III, 173, n. 1. By 1678 the company complained to the Lord Chamberlain about Dryden's breach of contract.

4. For the story of Dryden's visit to Milton, and Milton's consenting to have his verses tagged, see Masson, *Milton's Poetical Works*, I, 14, and Havens, *The Review* (N. Y., June 14, 1919), p. 110.

as a literary exercise, the idea of using it upon the stage and thus doing something toward fulfilling his contract would probably have presented itself to him before he finished. Scott recognizes indirectly another objection to his theory:

> There is one inconvenience which, as the poem was intended for perusal only, the author might have easily avoided. This arises from the stage directions, which supply the place of the terrific and beautiful descriptions of Milton. What idea, except burlesque, can we form of the expulsion of the fallen angels from heaven, literally represented by their tumbling down upon the stage? Or what feelings of terror can be excited by the idea of an opera hell composed of pasteboard and flaming rosin? If these follies were not actually to be produced . . . it could serve no good purpose to excite the image of them in our imagination.

I think Scott has adequately answered his own question. They probably were more or less intended to be produced. If so, they would not have burlesqued Milton except to the degree of the stage manager's limitations in the matter of equipment and imagination. Dryden's stage directions are identical in character with those generally provided in acting plays or operas,[1] and it would seem that they were intended as suggestions to the stage manager rather than as poetic substitutes for Milton. I imagine that the real difficulty in the way of the actual production did not lie in the costuming — a problem which a Restoration manager might have been trusted to meet as adequately (or inadequately) as any of his successors. I take it, rather, that an opera known to be based upon the work of John Milton, Latin Secretary under the Commonwealth, would not have passed even the comparatively genial censorship of Charles the Second.

Paradise Lost, in fact, did not find its way into the theatre until 1760, though Handel seriously considered making it the subject of an oratorio in 1744, the year after *Samson* had been so successfully

---

1. Compare, for example, the stage directions in Dryden's opera of *King Arthur*, which was produced with Purcell's music.

produced. In that year his lifelong friend, the famous Mrs. Delany,[1] prepared a libretto of *Paradise Lost* for him. Her remarks upon her method of preparing the material are worth quoting if only because they suggest a counsel of perfection with which Handel did not altogether sympathize. On March 10, 1744, Mrs. Delany wrote to a friend, as follows:

> I have made a drama for an oratorio, out of Milton's "Paradise Lost," to give Mr. Handel to compose to; it has cost me a great deal of thought and contrivance . . . though all I have had to do has been collecting and making the connection between the fine parts. I begin with Satan's threatenings to seduce the woman, her being seduced follows, and it ends with the man yielding to the temptation. *I would not have a word or thought of Milton's altered*, and *I hope to prevail with Handel to set it without having any of the lines put into verse*, for that will take from its dignity.[2]

It is interesting to note the implication that Handel seems to have had a decided personal share in the changes forced upon Milton by his adapters — a suggestion which, as we shall find presently, is supported by other evidence.

The oratorio was not brought out in Handel's lifetime. In 1760, one year after his death, there appeared "'Paradise Lost,' an Oratorio in 3 Acts and Verse, as it is Performed at the Theatre Royal in Covent Garden."[3] The title-page of its text, further, ascribes the music of the piece to a "Mr. Smith." There is good reason to believe that this was the same Smith who had been Handel's private secretary, and that at least part of the music was the master's.[4] The authorship of the lines is credited to Benjamin

---

1. The friend, also, of King George III, and of his queen, and the correspondent of Fanny Burney, Dr. Young, Swift, and many other great personages.
2. *Autobiography of Mrs. Delany*, II, 280.
3. The playbills for this season, as Genest notes (see his *Account of the English Stage*, IV, 594), "are all in manuscript, with much tautology and many deficiencies." Those at the British Museum throw no light upon the reception accorded this oratorio, and I do not know of any information as to the performers who took part in it.
4. See n. 2, and compare p. 229 below.

Stillingfleet, who, if he made any use of Mrs. Delany's version, did so without acknowledgment, and without paying much heed to her principles of workmanship. He, too, however, pleads that he meant to follow Milton closely. "All the recitative," he writes, "is word for word taken out of my author, and as to the songs, they are in general so much his, that I have tryed to compose them chiefly from the sentiments which I found in him, and, as often as I was able, to preserve his very words." Like Dryden, and with much more reason, he begs for "allowances in so hazardous a comparison as I expose myself to." It is only fair to Stillingfleet to say that in his recitative he keeps almost as much of Milton as might be expected in the radical condensation he undertook — but the songs, though they may represent Milton's sentiments, certainly do no justice to his poetry. One brief specimen, the closing chorus of Act I in Stillingfleet's version, may serve for illustration. The guardian angels at Paradise gates are addressing Satan:

> Rebel hast thou scap'd thy Chain?
> All thy efforts are but vain!
> Hast forgot the Son of God,
> How he scourg'd thee with His Rod?
> Back, oh! back again to Hell,
> Learn obedient there to dwell!

Paradise Lost, however, by no means exhausted its appeal to the great composers with this effort of Handel's follower. When Joseph Haydn made his triumphant visit to London in 1791, Salomon, the violinist and concert manager, gave him a "poem for music" which had been compiled from *Paradise Lost* by a Mr. Lidley or Liddell. Haydn took this with him to Vienna, and a free translation [1] by Freiherr Van Swieten supplied his text for the *Creation* (1798), the most popular of all oratorios with the single

---

1. Paul Rolli had published an Italian translation, *Paradiso Perduto*, folio, in 1736; duodecimo, 2 vols., 1758.

exception of the *Messiah*.[1] By 1800 Van Swieten's version had been retranslated into English, and Haydn's oratorio was sung at the Haymarket and at Covent Garden. It was repeated the next year and, in 1803, was sung once at Covent Garden and six times at Drury Lane, with incidental "select and appropriate readings" from *Paradise Lost*. The playbills [2] for 1814 show that it was repeated at old Drury that year, again with special recitations of Adam and Eve's morning hymn, and other Milton selections.[3] Perhaps it was felt that even a small taste of Milton would help to improve the flat stupidity of the English libretto. Twice translated and thrice removed from its great original as this text [4] is, even its occasional verbal echoes of Milton are, as a rule, either hopelessly dull or ridiculously inept. Compare, for example, Milton's

> But neither breath of morn . . . nor rising sun,
> Nor glittering star-light . . . without thee is sweet
>
> (*P. L.*, IV, 641–656)

with the following bit from the English version of the *Creation:*

> *Adam.* How grateful is
>   Of fruits the savour sweet!
> *Eve.*   How pleasing is
>   Of fragrant bloom the smell!
> *Both.* But without thee, what is it to me?

In short, after reading this text one agrees heartily with Haydn's biographer, who writes that "it is a matter for wonder how for

1. See J. C. Hadden's *Haydn*, pp. 130–139, and the article on Haydn in Grove's *Encyclopedia of Music*.

2. The material here is derived from the playbills in the British Museum.

3. Stage "recitations" of *Paradise Lost* were given also under somewhat different auspices. I quote from John O'Keeffe's *Recollections*, I, 350, concerning the actors, John Henderson and Thomas Sheridan: "Henderson also gave Recitations . . . with Thomas Sheridan . . . Henderson's chief source of humour was reciting Cowper's *Johnny Gilpin*, and Sheridan's tools were Milton's *Paradise Lost*, and *Alexander's Feast*."

4. "The Creation: A Sacred Oratorio Composed by Dr. Haydn, as Performed at the Concert Room, King's Theatre, Haymarket, Under the Direction of Mr. Salomon." London, 1800.

more than a century English-speaking audiences have listened to the arrant nonsense with which Haydn's music is associated." [1] The German version is good poetry — comparatively speaking — though it is not Milton, and the trouble clearly lies with the "miserable broken English" of the second translator.

Very different in every respect is the text of the *Paradise Lost* oratorio of 1862. The anonymous redactor used Milton directly, and Milton only, and he was able to make use of many of the noblest lyric and descriptive passages of the master.[2] The libretto used by the great Rubinstein in 1878 for his "Geistliche Oper" — *Das Verlorene Paradies* — once more goes to the other extreme. The text is, as the German edition states, "*Frei* nach J. Milton" — and it is no exaggeration to say that it is very free indeed. And yet it is infinitely superior to the two — equally free — English translations of it which appeared soon after, both of which make very poor reading indeed.[3]

"Mr. Handel's music," wrote a contemporary of his,[4] "is never employed to greater advantage than when it is adapted to Milton's words. That great artist has . . . done equal justice to our author's *L'Allegro* and *Il Penseroso*, as if the same spirit possessed both masters, and as if the god of music and of verse were still one and the same." We have seen, in the case of *Samson* and *Paradise Lost*, that Milton's words rather than Handel's music were adapted. *L'Allegro* and *Il Penseroso*, to be sure, were not altered, strictly speaking, but it is curious to note that the text of Handel's ode, *L'Allegro, Il Penseroso*, and *Il Moderato* (1740),[5] if it did not

1. J. C. Hadden, p. 131.   2. The music was composed by J. L. Ellerton.
3. These versions were prepared by Josiah Pittman, London, 1880, and Henry Hersee, London, 1882.
4. See Newton's edition of *Paradise Lost* (1750), I, lxii.
5. "Never performed before — at the Royal Theatre, Lincoln's Inn Fields, this day will be performed 'L'Allegro,' &c. . . . Boxes half a guinea, pit 5s., first gallery 3s., upper gallery 2s." (London *Daily Post*, February 27, 1740, quoted by Schoelcher, *Life of Handel*, p. 229).

alter Milton, certainly made rather daring additions to his work. The author of this text was Charles Jennens, a wealthy amateur poet, who also wrote the text of the *Messiah*. His arrangement begins effectively with a kind of *débat* between L'Allegro and Il Penseroso, whose antithetic moods are cleverly set off against each other by a skilful choice of contrasting passages from Milton; and thus two parts of the ode come to a very logical conclusion: one in which nothing is concluded as to the relative superiority of one mood over the other. So far the adapter followed Milton; he had selected and rearranged, but not altered, his material. But Jennens — and probably Handel — were not content to leave matters here. The adapter added a third part, *Il Moderato*, to complete the scheme and to square the circle. He invents an invocation of his own and proceeds good-naturedly to sing the glories of moderation, recommending to the contending parties the happy possibilities of the golden mean:

> Kindly teach how blest are they
> Who Nature's equal Rules obey,
> Who safely steer two rocks between
> And prudent keep the golden mean. . . .

Schoelcher, one of Handel's biographers, has said exactly the right thing concerning this part of the adaptation. "A great poet like Milton," he writes, "would never have imagined this poor Moderato, with his mediocrities." [1] The ode, at all events, was sung three times in London during the season of 1740–1741,[2] and in the following season the composer conducted three very successful performances of it in Dublin. As an indication of Handel's personal approval of the changes in Milton's text, it is interesting to note that in a letter from Dublin, dated December 29, 1741,

1. *Life of Handel*, p. 229.
2. *Id.*, pp. 228, 233, 330–331. Further performances are recorded in 1755, 1772, 1794, 1807, 1808, and 1822. (*Theatrical Review*, London, 1772, and British Museum playbills.)

Handel wrote to Jennens: "I assure you that the words of the *Moderato* are vastly admired." [1] The publishers of the later editions of the Milton–Handel text apparently did not agree with the composer on this point, for they had the good judgment to suppress the *Moderato* in all but the first two editions.[2]

Before leaving *L'Allegro* and *Il Penseroso* we must note that parts of these poems and of *Arcades* were brought into the theatre by other composers, though they are curiously connected with Handel once more. In the Prologue to *The Fairies* (1755), an opera adapted by or for Garrick [3] from *A Midsummer-Night's Dream*, the actor-manager has this to say of the composer:

> Struck with the wonder of his Master's Art
> Whose sacred Dramas shake and melt the Heart,
> Inflam'd, astonish'd at those magic Airs,
> When Samson groans and frantic Saul despairs, . . .
> The Pupil wrote, — his Work is now before you.[4]

The "pupil" was the same Smith whom we have already met in connection with the *Paradise Lost* oratorio of 1760. Either Smith or Garrick, in the advertisement to the 1755 edition of *The Fairies*, states the case of the adapter against his original, whether it be Shakspere or Milton. "Many passages of the first Merit," we read, "and some whole scenes in the *Midsummer-Night's Dream* are necessarily omitted in this Opera to reduce the Performance to a proper length; it was feared that even the best poetry would appear tedious when only supported by Recitative." And he adds — after expressing the hope that his patchwork will not seem "unnaturally" wrought — "where Shakspear has not supplied the

1. Schoelcher, p. 244.

2. The *Moderato* appears only in the editions of 1740 and 1750. It was dropped in the two editions of 1754, and in those of 1779 and 1801.

3. It is not clear how much of this adaptation is to be credited — or debited — to Garrick personally. He certainly spoke and wrote the Prologue. (See Genest, IV, 407, and P. Fitzgerald, *Life of Garrick*, p. 156.)

4. See the 1755 quarto of the opera, or Garrick's *Collected Works*.

Composer with Songs, he has taken them from Milton, Waller, Dryden, Hammond, &c."

The Milton borrowings are not extensive. The first one appears in Act I, Scene i of the Opera. Lysander invites Hermia to meet him in the wood where once before they had done "observance to the month of May," — and that suggests an "air" of twelve lines celebrating the season when

> Young and old come forth to play
> On a sunshine holiday.[1]

In the seventh scene of the same act the Fairy Queen commands her elves to depart — in the words of *Arcades:*

> O'er the smooth enamell'd green
> Where no print of step hath been
> Follow me, as I sing. . . . [2]

In Act III, Scene viii, finally, Theseus's order to wake the huntsmen is the signal for another air based upon *L'Allegro:*

> Hark, hark, how the hounds and horn
> Chearly rouse the slumb'ring morn. . . . [3]

We shall see presently, moreover, that the opening lines of *L'Allegro* were used in a stage entertainment much more important and interesting than *The Fairies* — in none other than the adaptation of Milton's own *Comus* which held the stage for over a hundred years. Our account of *Comus*, however, must wait upon the story of *Lycidas* and the *Epitaph on Shakespeare*, which can be more rapidly disposed of.

The curious use of the *Epitaph* for dramatic purposes is recorded by Genest from a Drury Lane playbill of 1752. This docu-

---

1. The passage in the opera is a free rendering of lines 72–98 of *L'Allegro.*
2. *Arcades*, lines 84–86.
3. Cf. *L'Allegro*, lines 53–56. Line 58 and lines 63–68 were used by Purcell for his fine duet, *Let us Wander, not Unseen.* (Cf. *Six Vocal Duets by Henry Purcell*, ed. A. Moffat.)

ment, dated March 31, informed the public of a benefit for Ross, the actor, and announced *Romeo and Juliet* as the play. The public was further notified that "after the play an Elogium wrote by Dryden, concluding with Milton's Epitaph to the memory of Shakspere will be spoken by Ross, representing the Shade of Shakspere, as figured on his monument in Westminster Abbey." When the gentle Shakspere's ghost made his bow and proceeded to sing his own praise in Milton's words,

> What needs my Shakspere for his honored bones
> The labours of an age in piled stones . . .

the audience must have thought him a mad ghost indeed, or at least a somewhat conceited one. At all events the entertainment surely justified the closing announcement of the playbill: "Nothing under full price will be taken during the performance." [1]

Nor was the stage rendering of *Lycidas* without its element of the incongruous. It was played at Covent Garden on November 4, 1767. "The first new Performance this Season," writes Victor,[2] "was *Lycidas*, an Elegy, set to Music by Mr. Jackson of Exeter,[3] — and well intended by him, as a Condolance on the much-lamented Death of the Duke of York. It was performed the Night after his Funeral — and that Night only." The printed text [4] indicates that the piece enlisted the services of at least eight performers, and also that once more Milton's words and even his sense were sadly marred in the adaptation. Many of his lines are

1. Genest, *op. cit.*, IV, 348. A less extraordinary but somewhat analogous performance was staged at Covent Garden on May 16, 1796. The playbill announces as part of that day's entertainment, "an Ode, selected from Ben Jonson, In Honor of Shakspeare, Composed for Two Choirs, expressly for this evening's Performance, to be sung by Messrs. Incledon, Bowden, Townsend, etc." (Covent Garden playbills, British Museum.)

2. *History of the Theatres*, III, 115.

3. Jackson composed much other music for the stage, and enjoyed considerable popularity. (Cf. O'Keeffe's *Recollections*, I, 374, 375.)

4. "Lycidas: a musical Entertainment. The Words altered from Milton." London, 1767.

kept, but the rise and fall of his cadence is, to a large extent, lost by their rearrangement into the inevitable "airs." The glory has departed. As thus:

> He ask'd the Winds, he ask'd the Waves
> What had befel this gentle Swain,
> And ev'ry Gush of rugged Wings
> That sweeps across the troubled Main, —
> Alas! they knew not of his fate!

After this it may be pardonable to turn for a moment to the music of the original:

> He asked the waves, and asked the felon winds,
> What hard mishap hath doomed this gentle swain?
> And questioned every gust of rugged wings
> That blows from off each beaked promontory.
> They knew not of his story;
> And sage Hippotades their answer brings . . . [1]

The adapter, moreover, shows his independent spirit by suppressing altogether the Pilot of the Galilean Lake, and by giving St. Peter's great denunciation of the evil shepherds whose hungry sheep look up and are not fed — to reverend Camus! Victor did not notice that this version of *Lycidas* differed somewhat from the original, but he had his doubts as to the wisdom of putting it on the stage. "This fine Poem," says he, "was wrote by Milton, in his Bloom of Youth and Genius . . . but any mournful Ditty must be unfitt for a Theatrical Entertainment to follow a Play; where no subject but Mirth or Shew! And no Music but the ballad or facetious Burletta can stand any chance for success." Victor's judgment was sound for more reasons than one, and the first performance of this version of *Lycidas* fitly celebrated its own funeral as well as that of the Duke of York.

No work of Milton enjoyed more favor upon the stage than *Comus*, and perhaps no great poem was ever so buffeted by the

1. *Lycidas*, lines 91–96.

vicissitudes of time and theatrical expediency. In the year 1737 an opera entitled *Sabrina* was written by Paul Rolli for the Haymarket, and the author of the wretched libretto [1] stated that "the basis of the present poem is a mask written by Mr. John Milton." Portions of the temptation scene of *Paradise Lost* and of the Sabrina episode of *Comus* are very poorly utilized in this opera, which seems to have had no more success than it deserved.[2] It may, however, have suggested the production of *Comus* the next year. At all events, from 1738 until the middle of the nineteenth century *Comus* maintained itself upon the stage not only at Drury Lane and Covent Garden, but also in Dublin, Edinburgh, Bath, and the provinces in general. Great professionals vied with noble amateurs in exploiting the popularity of the piece. Few indeed were the players of any consequence who did not have *Comus* in their repertory, and more than a few won fame in it. The versions they used are extant in a score of editions. At least four separate and distinct adaptations were made in the course of time, and of these the first two and the last are particularly worthy of study at close range. Without such observation the popularity of *Comus* with the players and public is not easily explained. With it, the stage-history of the piece becomes a significant commentary upon the taste of the times, and a striking record of the shifty devices by which the managers capitalized the fame of a great poet.

In Genest's record for the year 1738 at Drury Lane Theatre, appears the following entry under date of March fourth:

Never acted, Comus. Comus: Quin; [3] Brothers: Milward and Cibber Jun.; 1st Spirit: Mills; Lady: Mrs. Cibber; Euphrosyne: Mrs. Clive . . . and others.[4]

---

1. Cf. Paul Rolli, *Libretti of Ancient Italian Operas* (London, 1737), vol. VI.
2. Cf. David H. Stevens, *Milton Papers* (Chicago, 1927), pp. 23 ff.
3. Concerning Quin's acting in this part, cf. *Id.*, p. 29.
4. Genest, III, 533.

The first "alteration" of Milton's masque which these players performed Genest describes as a "judicious" one, — a somewhat astonishing verdict from a critic who resented as earnestly as did Genest the comparatively gentler handling which Shakspere received from his eighteenth-century adapters. Genest goes on to say that the adapter, Dr. Dalton, retained

nearly the whole of the original, added or compiled the scenes between the Brothers and Comus' Crew, and *introduced a variety of songs to make it pass off better on the Stage; the B. D.[1] says they are taken from Milton's other works.* The Prologue is modest and sensible —

"Small is our portion, and we wish 't were none."

From such an analysis of this adaptation as our space will permit, the reader may judge as to the truthfulness of the opening assertion of this line, and as to the praiseworthiness of its closing sentiment. In any case, Genest's note requires a supplement.

In fairness to the adapter, allowance must be made for the difficulties inherent in his task. Certain of Dr. Johnson's judgments upon Milton are notoriously out of favor to-day,[2] but his criticism of *Comus* as a drama remains substantially sound, nor can there be any question that it represented the accepted opinion of his time. "A work more truly poetical," Johnson writes, "is rarely found." But — "As a drama it is deficient. The discourse of the Spirit is too long, an objection that may be made to almost all the following speeches; they have not the spriteliness of a dialogue animated by reciprocal contention, but seem rather declamations deliberately composed and formally repeated on a moral question."[3] So far one would scarcely challenge Johnson's findings, or the adapter's

1. That is, the *Biographica Dramatica*. The italics are mine. The ascription of the additional songs to Milton would be an insult to the poet's memory if it were not an obvious absurdity which Genest would have stamped as such had he read the songs. See the discussion below.

2. His estimate of *Lycidas*, for instance, in his *Life of Milton*.

3. *Life of Milton*.

attempt to meet the difficulty. Throughout his version Dalton shortens the speeches, often by a slight interruption or inversion which adds give and take to the dialogue without doing injury to the poetry. To this extent the adapter's work is reasonably "judicious." For the rest it is too often beneath contempt. And yet that is perhaps precisely because he shared another opinion of Dr. Johnson's: "Throughout the whole, the figures are too bold and the language too luxuriant for dialogue: it is a drama in the epic style, inelegantly splendid and tediously instructive." [1] By cutting the original and adding scenes of his own, the adapter [2] lowered the tone of the piece until it rang no longer with the music of its own spheary chime but echoed and reëchoed the riot and ill-managed merriment of the early-eighteenth-century stage. Johnson, it will be remembered, had noted approvingly that Milton's "invitations to pleasure are so general that they excite no distinct images of corrupt enjoyment, and take no dangerous hold on the fancy." The adapter, for his part, spared no pains to show his disapproval of this sort of thing. He cures Milton's tedious instructiveness by making vice as seductive, and virtue as stupid, as possible. Specifically, he does this by adding song after song and dance after dance. Granting that these were set to excellent music, and speaking more particularly only of the songs, one is forced to the conclusion that Milton himself would have regarded some of them as quite superfluous. Others he would have frowned upon — unlike the public — because they are "witty" in the best Restoration sense of the word, and still others he might have condemned as quite shameless in any sense. All subsequent adaptations of *Comus* are based more or less upon this one of Dalton's. A summary of it, therefore, will be in order here.

1. *Life of Milton.*
2. See "Comus, a Mask: now adapted to the Stage, as Alter'd from Milton's Mask." London, 1738.

The adapter stays close to his original in his opening scene, except that he adds "the gentle Philidel," [1] a second spirit, who is "commission'd to direct or share" the charge of Thyrsis. Incidentally, by breaking into his brother spirit's remarks on occasion, Philidel helps to make the exposition move along. The two then separate, Thyrsis to watch over the Brothers, Philidel to guard the Lady through the magic wood. This task he does not perform any too well — but so far no serious exception can be taken to the adapter's work. Nor does one object to his rendering of Comus's first speech, — "The star that bids the shepherd fold," [2] — a long speech which he ingeniously divides into several bits of recitative and song, and assigns, respectively, to Comus, and to "a man" and "a woman." The first real hint of the vulgarization of Milton appears in the adapter's stage direction before the entrance of Comus's rout. Here Milton's "monsters" become merely "a rout of men and women, dress'd like Bacchanals." And this first hint is soon followed by others, not particularly objectionable in themselves, perhaps, but indicative of what is to follow. Comus has invited his followers to begin their revels:

> Come, let us our rites begin;
> 'T is only daylight that makes sin . . . [3]

This theme the adapter elaborates in two songs of his own. A stanza from each will illustrate their merits and defects:

Song by a Man and Woman
From Tyrant Laws and Customs free
We follow sweet Variety;
By Turns we Drink and Dance and Sing,
Love forever on the Wing . . .

Song by a Man
By the gayly circling Glass
We can see how Minutes pass;
By the hollow Cask are told
How the waining Night grows old . . .

1. See below, p. 245.　　2. *Comus*, 93.　　3. *Id.*, 125.

There follows the appearance of the Lady. Her long entrance speech is somewhat shortened by the adapter, and he further cuts up the speech by giving Comus an additional aside. Her Echo Song is kept, and so also is her colloquy with Comus. The adapter then brings his first act to a characteristic close. Comus's crew enters from behind the trees, and we have the following "Song, by a Man":

> Fly swiftly, ye Minutes, till Comus receive
> The nameless soft Transports that Beauty can give, —
> The Bowl's frolic Joys let him teach her to prove
> And she in return yield the raptures of Love.
>
> Without Love and Wine, Wit and Beauty are vain,
> All Grandeur insipid, and Riches a Pain,
> The most splendid Palace grows dark as the Grave:
> Love and Wine give, ye Gods! or take back what ye gave.

> *Chorus*
>
> Away, away, away,
>   To Comus' Court repair;
> There Night outshines the Day,
>   There yields the melting Fair.[1]

Dalton's second act carries on from the point at which he left Milton. The Elder Brother's long speech on chastity, once more, is cut up — the Younger Brother breaking in with several leading questions. Then comes Thyrsis to tell the Brothers of Comus and his crew, and how they can inveigle those who "pass unweeting by the way." At this point the jarring sound of the adapter's timbrel breaks in once more. Dalton gives us a long sequence of shows, songs, and dances, and their wild, tumultuous mirth pro-

---

1. The contrast between this song and Milton's noble scene just preceding is characteristic of this adaptation, for it must be remembered that much of Milton is retained. And such incongruities are not limited to this scene, as the following material will show. A reprint of Dalton's version appeared at one time in "A Collection of the Most Esteemed *Farces* Performed on the English Stage" (Edinburgh, 1782) — and one does not altogether wonder!

claims to the Brothers the presence of those very tempters of whom Thyrsis had told them. "Revelling and by turns carressing each other," they come forward and invite "the god-like youths" to join them — "the happiest of the Race of Men." The Elder Brother, however, tells them that they are only a lot of drunken bacchanals. They venture a soft answer, first, by way of a song which denounces fame as "an empty, airy, glittering bubble," and next, in the shape of a mild reproof from one of the bacchantes: "Oh how unseemly shews in blooming Youth — Such grey Severity!" She continues in this vein (indulging herself, meanwhile, in a curious echo from *Paradise Lost*) and invites the young man to her Bower of Bliss, where he shall

> Taste the Joys that Nature sheds,
> *From Morn to Noon, from Noon to dewy Eve,*[1]
> Each rising Hour by rising Pleasures marked . . .

But the invitation is not accepted, and so the tempters try two more songs — as thus:

> Would you taste the noontide Air?
> To yon fragrant Bower repair . . .
> Where on the Hyacinth and Rose
> The Fair doth all alone repose . . .
> All alone — and in her Arms
> Your Breast may beat to Love's Alarms . . .

> Live and love, enjoy the Fair,
> Banish Sorrow, banish Care . . .

The Brothers and their earthly visitants indulge in a further exchange of views upon virtue and vice and the enjoyment thereof. The rout once more invites the pedant youths, the "beardless cynics," to its Bower of Bliss where yields the melting Fair, but they are not to be won over by this brazen harlotry. And so the second act ends with the rout dancing off, and Thyrsis, as in Mil-

1. Cf. *Paradise Lost*, I, 742–743.

ton, telling the Brothers of the Lady's distress, and of his plans to succor her.[1]

Comus himself opens Dalton's third act with the invocation from *L'Allegro* — "Hence, loathed Melancholy." [2] Then enters an entirely new character — one which became a great favorite with the public and the actresses who portrayed it: "A Nymph, representing Euphrosyne or Mirth," whose business it is to assail the poor Lady with pointed recitative and jolly ballads in the best fashion of the day, all for the purpose of winning her over to Comus.

> No domestic, jealous Jars,
> Buzzing Slanders, wordy Wars,

obtain in *her* kingdom, Euphrosyne assures the Lady —

> Sighs to amorous Sighs returning,
> Pulses beating, Bosoms burning, —
> Bosoms with warm Wishes panting —
> Are the only Tumults here.

The Lady protests in vain against these "odious strains." The only relief she gains is that which comes of a change of torture, for now the sedge-crowned Naiads appear in all their azure sheen — and dance! The "Pastoral Nymph," another invention of the adapter's, next takes up the burden and sings a mournful ditty of her gentle Damon. She mourns him in every hill and every grove — without moving the Lady, so that the sprightly Euphrosyne feels called upon to try again. This time she sings of the joys of the coquette and of her triumphs over mere man, and points out how little such as she need to complete their happiness here below:

> Why should they e'er give me pain
> Who to give me Joy disdain?
> All I ask of mortal Man
> Is to love me — whilst he can!

1. Milton's lines, 631–639, are cut; and the forty-two lines from 617 to 658 are reduced to twenty-three.
2. The first thirty-six lines of *L'Allegro* are brought in at this point.

The sentiment is so admirable, so truly Miltonic, that we may
let it stand for a moment. One is not surprised to read of visiting
French actresses returning to Paris and scoring heavily in these
songs from *Comus* [1] — these songs "which the B. D. says are taken
from Milton's other works"! It is somewhat surprising that Dr.
Johnson let them pass without a word of comment. He must have
known of them, and yet he doubtless meant to do Milton such justice as he could. Indeed, in 1750, he went out of his way to do an
act of charity for Milton's granddaughter, Mrs. Foster, for whose
benefit performance of *Comus* he wrote the Prologue which Garrick delivered.[2] Johnson admonished the public that the poverty
of the poet's granddaughter was a reproach to his memory, but of
the adapter's nimble handling of the poet's fame he said nothing.

Perhaps Johnson was satisfied with the adapter's apologia
which follows the song just quoted, for at that point Dalton apparently felt the need of striking a blow for virtue — and so he
interrupts the merry songs by a "lofty and solemn music from
above, whence the second attendant spirit descends gradually in a
splendid machine." Philidel announces that he comes "from the
Realms of Peace above," and proceeds to sing a song of "awful
Virtue's Hill sublime." There, the song has it, "enthron'd sits the
Immortal Fair," and there "eternal Bliss for transient Pain" is
promised to the virtuous. The Lady thanks the adapter's
"heav'nly songster" — and then, at last, we return to Milton.

1. Mademoiselle Chateauneuf was particularly successful in still another song long
associated with these *Comus* revivals — *Give me Wine, Rosy Wine.* (See Genest, X, 313;
Chetwood, *History of the Stage*, p. 130; also O'Keeffe, I, 139, on successes scored by other
foreign players who appeared in *Comus.*)

2. One hundred and thirty pounds were raised for Mrs. Foster in this way. Johnson
urged public support of this charity not only in his Prologue but also in several letters
published before the event. (See Boswell's *Johnson*, ed. Hill, I, 263). Voltaire's remark,
that Milton's granddaughter was rich within a quarter of an hour after she had been taken
up by the London men of letters, is a characteristic inaccuracy. (Cf. Parton, *Life of
Voltaire*, I, 232.)

Her subtle and eloquent debate with Comus on the subject of chastity must needs have seemed strange after the shows and gewgaws that precede it, nor is it allowed to go very far without interruption. Euphrosyne is not to be denied. "Preach me not your musty Rules," she sings, and then calls for more dancers —

> Ye Fauns and ye Dryads, from Hill, Dale, and Grove,
> Trip, trip it along, conducted by Love . . .
> And in various Measures show Love's various Sport!

They do — and she sings another song, after which Milton's debate is allowed to proceed. The fact that these devices of the adapter rob Comus of all the effect of his subtle and brilliant sophistry, — that the great logician becomes a gross and palpable fraud,— these considerations apparently troubled no one who had anything to do with the production. The adapter, meanwhile, introduces a third spirit to assist in the Sabrina episode. This he follows in the main, though again the weight of his own insertions forces him to save time and to cut Milton unmercifully. Thus, he omits not only the story of Sabrina's parentage and other descriptive bits, but also the shepherd's song of thanks, and considerable parts of the song of Thyrsis at the close.[1] Thyrsis having thus been made to "epiloguize" at forced speed, time is left for epilogue number two, which is done in the best vein of eighteenth-century flippancy. Here Euphrosyne (that is to say the redoubtable Mrs. Cibber, in the original production) is once more in her glory. She pays her respects to the critics, to the mealy fop, the cold prude, the shy coquette, to dull poring pedants, and party fools. And she expresses for the adapter and the company the hope that they have

> . . . Proved at least
> All vice is folly, and makes man a beast.

---

1. And yet, at the very end, he adds a superfluous exchange of what can hardly be described as other than stupid "post-mortems" on the part of the two brothers.

In 1772 Colman the elder prepared a new version of *Comus* for the revival of that year at Covent Garden Theatre. Colman's version, broadly speaking, is merely an abridgment of Dalton's, and *Comus* henceforward appeared as a two-act afterpiece, whereas it had formerly held the chief place in the bill.[1] Colman's preface to the edition of 1772[2] contains certain explanatory and apologetic matter that is worth quoting. He observes that

> pure Poetry, unmixt with passion, however admired in the closet, has scarce ever been able to sustain itself on the stage. In this Abridgment . . . the divine arguments on temperance and chastity, together with many descriptive passages are indeed expunged or contracted.[3] But, divine as they are, the most accomplished declaimers have been embarrassed in the recitation. . . . *Comus*, with all its beauties . . . maintained its place in the Theatre chiefly by the assistance of the musick, but the musick itself . . . almost sunk with the weight of the Drama.

All this suggests pretty well what Colman did in his third-hand reworking of the Masque; namely, that he cut Milton's text much more ruthlessly than his predecessor, but kept most of that gentleman's merry songs and curious inventions. Thus, Colman retained the several tributes to "the melting Fair," the bacchantes' scene with the Brothers, and even the last superfluous colloquy between these two.[4] And in a footnote to his preface, Colman points out that his version has at least one altogether new song of its own. The theme of this song is simple, —

> Mortals, learn your Lives to measure
> Not by Length of Time, but Pleasure, —

and it is introduced to aid Comus's suit to the Lady. In this connection another remark of Colman's deserves attention. "As a

1. Cf. Genest, III, 534.
2. "Comus: a Masque. Altered from Milton. As Performed at the Theatre Royal in Covent Garden. The music composed by Dr. Arne." London, 1772.
3. As noted above, Dalton had retained most of these passages.
4. See above, p. 241, n.

further argument in favour of the Drama in its present form," Colman urges "that the festivity in the character of Comus is heightened." Perhaps the astounding vulgarity with which Milton's delicate conception of Comus is laid low by the adapters, does add to its *festivity!* Certainly the character who in Milton's poem symbolizes the most impassioned, and yet the most subtle, appeal of the sensuous, becomes in their hands a gross sensualist, a mere lascivious magician. The "essentially Miltonic" element in *Comus*, writes Masson, "consists no less in the power and purity of the doctrine than in the exquisite mythological invention and the perfection of the literary finish." [1] These virtues the adapters do not boast, but their "festivity" did serve them long and well with the public.

Thomas Dibdin [2] in 1815, by way of preface to his version of *Comus*, acknowledges his indebtedness to Dalton and Colman, and notes that the piece "has recently been brought forward with great . . . splendor . . . and with still further variations." He refers to the revival of the masque at Covent Garden on April 28, 1815, where *Comus* was played fifteen times altogether that year, by a company of some fifty principals and assisting artists. The playbill announcing the revival suggests that it must have been a lavish spectacle indeed, and it describes in glowing terms — and big letters — some of the chief scenes: "A Wood, a Rivulet by Sunset, a Labyrinth, the Bower of Comus," and (in heavily leaded type) "SABRINA'S SUBMARINE PALACE!" [3] As for Dibdin's version,[4] he himself states truthfully that he steered somewhat be-

---

1. *Life*, I, 622.

2. Prompter at Drury Lane and the author of a number of successful plays.

3. See the British Museum playbills, Covent Garden Theatre. A MS. inventory of the costumes and properties at that playhouse in 1768–1769 (British Museum) mentions among the women's costumes, "Comus's — 90 *l.*," and among the properties, "12 Thyrsis, — Comus; 1 Small Glass and Basket, — Comus."

4. "Comus, a Mask, Altered from Milton. Correctly given from copies used in the Theatres." *London Theatre*, vol. X (London, 1815).

tween Colman and the later Covent Garden spectacle, but adhered "mostly to the latter." The playbill and Dibdin's copy show that by this time *Comus* had been further diluted and dilated by the addition of new songs and shows. A few lines from the pastoral duet just before the close of Dibdin's first act may serve to illustrate the new additions:

Woman.   O thou wert born to please me,
Man.   My life, my only Love,
Woman.   Through all the Woods I'll praise thee,
Man.   My rural Queen of Love.
Woman.   Thus happy, never
Man.   Jealous,
Woman.   Can any harm
Man.   Assail us?
Woman.   Can any harm assail us?
Man.   My rural Queen of Love![1]

Even before this time many other songs had been added on occasion to exploit the talents of new actresses who appeared in successive revivals of the masque.[2] Dibdin, meanwhile, requires no further notice. It will suffice to add that he is as far from Milton as any of his fellow adapters.

The last version of *Comus* [3] that we shall notice here in any detail is the furthest from Milton in more senses than one. It was prepared for the 1842 revival of the piece at Covent Garden — and it is so very far from Milton that it is scarcely an exaggeration to say that if the poet had been at the performance he might have

1. It appears that this song had occasionally been used as early as 1790. See below, p. 255, n. 3.

2. Miss Anne Catley, on October 30, 1776, added "a favorite Scotch air of Dr. Arne's." (See British Museum playbills, and compare p. 250, below.) Mademoiselle Chateauneuf's *Rosy Wine* has already been mentioned. (See above, p. 240, n. 1.) Mrs. Martyr introduced "the favorite song of *The Huntsman's Sweet Halloo*" on May 20, 1783, and Madam Mara sang "*Mad Bess,* in character," during the performance of May 25, 1796. (B. M. playbills, Covent Garden.)

3. See playbill for March 2, 1842. (B. M.)

been seriously puzzled to recognize any part of it as his own, except the Echo Song and a few other airs and bits of recitative. The *dramatis personae* this time numbered well over fifty, and among them appeared such interesting figures as Cupid, two "Syrens," a whole company of "Spirits of the Air," and a "Genius of the Frozen Clime." [1] The adapter states that his "operatic spectacle" was modelled partly on Dalton's version, but he truthfully adds that he omitted most of the earlier interpolations. It must be said for this version that it is comparatively inoffensive — that it omits the songs and shows that were most indicative of bad taste in the earlier adaptations, but also that the text, at least, is quite colorless and, if anything, less like Milton than its predecessors. The latest adapter makes much of the point that the spirit Philidel in Dalton's production was borrowed from Dryden's opera of *King Arthur*. That may have been the case, though Dryden's Philidel,

> An airy shape, the tenderest of my kind,
> The last seduc'd, and least deform'd of Hell . . .
> Desirous to repent and loth to sin, . . .

certainly bears only a nominal resemblance to the Philidel that had come to be familiar in Dalton's version. At all events, the 1842 adapter would have us believe that this earlier association between *Comus* and *King Arthur* led him to substitute for Dalton's work "analogous passages" from Dryden. Although these, as he says, had "the additional recommendation of having been set to music by Purcell," they make a strange, unintelligible patchwork indeed. Thus, in the first act, the Lady appears and sings the Echo Song without any notice having been given as to the danger which threatens her. The Brothers come on but say not a word —

---

1. "Songs, duets, chorusses, etc., in Milton's Comus: a masque in two acts, with additions from the author's poem of L'Allegro, and from Dryden's opera of King Arthur." London, 1842. For a glowing contemporary description of this production see H. S. Wyndham's *Annals of Covent Garden Theatre*, II, 149.

contenting themselves with pursuing Comus and the Lady in dumb show. Meanwhile, bacchanals and bacchantes dance wildly and there is a nonsensical chase of will-o'-the-wisp flames, with accompanying lyrics — all perfectly without rhyme or reason except such as they had in *King Arthur*, in which piece the flames are the trick of an evil spirit who seeks to mislead King Arthur and his knights. The "analogy" manufactured by the adapter lies in the point that Philidel in each case is made to spoil the trick. Again, the second act of this version of *Comus* brings in a "Frost Scene" between Cupid and the Genius of the Frozen Clime — which has certainly nothing to do with the case except in so far as it also appears in Dryden's opera. Sabrina, finally, comes on without any reason being suggested for her doing so. Obviously, the adapter took it for granted that everybody knew the story anyhow! His ingenious explanation, however, for the curious telescoping of *King Arthur* upon *Comus* will bear further investigation.

In this case the playbills tell a somewhat more plausible story. The Covent Garden bill of March 2, 1842 — the day of the first performance — states that the production had been somewhat delayed after its announcement, and that meanwhile Drury Lane had entered the field. "Curiously enough," it adds, "not only *Comus* was advertised as forthcoming at Drury Lane, but, *by a singular coincidence*,[1] Dryden's Opera of *King Arthur*, which had been brought under the consideration of this management by another person." The Drury Lane bills bear out this singular coincidence, for that playhouse had publicly announced a short time before that "Milton's Masque of *Comus*, composed by Arne, and Dryden's *King Arthur*, composed by Purcell, will be the next Musical Revivals of this Theatre."[2] But the Covent Garden management, according to its playbill, did not see fit to "relinquish pre-conceived ideas in consequence of the mere announcement of

1. The italics are mine.　　　2. B. M. playbills.

revivals" by "other establishments." In fact, it looks very much as if the juxtaposition of Milton and Dryden in the Drury Lane announcement suggested to the rival theatre the brilliant idea of combining the two and thus — quite in accord with good old theatrical tradition [1] — stealing a march on old Drury. Covent Garden, at all events, was ready in March, and Drury Lane followed with *King Arthur* on November 16, 1842. It brought out *Comus*, "adapted from the Poet's text . . . the Music except one Air from the original composer, Henry Lawes, by Handel and Arne," on February 24, 1843, with Macready in the title rôle.[2] I have not been able to find a copy of the text, but the chances are that it did not differ very much from that of Colman or Dibdin.

Students of Milton have, of course, long been aware of the popularity of *Comus* on the stage, but I believe it has not been generally understood just how the adapters treated the poet. This belief must serve as my excuse for having treated of the several stage versions of *Comus* perhaps with too much detail and too harshly.[3] To conclude, I have only to give some account of the chief players who appeared in the piece, and then a tabular summary of recorded performances, in so far as I have been able to trace them.[4]

1. On November 7, 1789, Drury Lane produced a play entitled *Marcella*, "without the Author's consent, and got up in such haste to forestall its representation at the other house that it was not much liked." (W. C. Oulton, *History of the Theatres*, II, 54.) For other interesting cases of rivalry between the houses, cf. *The Life of G. A. Bellamy*, II, 98; Genest, IV, 206, 162; and Cibber's *Apology*, ed. Lowe, II, 179–180.

2. See B. M. playbills.

3. Professor David H. Stevens has recently put the case more kindly. "The eighteenth century," he writes, "liked both its morality and its sensory images in full strength. It was in the power of Dalton [see above, pp. 233–241] to create precisely the right blend, and with Quin as interpreter of the Comus rôle he had an admirable means of conveyance. His success, crudely explained by later critics as due to the restoration of Milton 'to himself,' was rather the result of a felicitous combination of appeals suited to the musical and dramatic sense of his audiences." (*Milton Papers* (1927), p. 29.)

4. Perhaps half of the material in the discussion and table below represents a compilation of the references to *Comus* in Genest and other historians of the theatres. This I have supplemented by an examination of the British Museum playbills of Drury Lane and

We have already seen ¹ that *Comus* transformed first appeared
on the boards of Drury Lane in 1738, with a very distinguished
cast. The title rôle was played by James Quin: hero of *Quin's Jests*,
matchless raconteur, gourmand, friend, and actor, and one of Garrick's few great rivals of later days. In his support appeared Mrs.
Cibber, as the Lady, and Mrs. Clive, as Euphrosyne — two justly
famed actresses of whom we have already spoken in connection
with their services rendered to *Samson*. And Theophilus Cibber,
the greatest Pistol of them all, — the interesting but unfortunate
son of an interesting father, the laureate, — played one of the Brothers. He and his wife doubtless did their full duty in their respective parts for the remaining ten performances of the masque
in 1738 — before facing each other in one of the most scandalous
lawsuits of the time, which thoroughly disgraced both of them.²

Quin took the lead also in the production of *Comus* which
took place at the Aungier Street Theatre, Dublin, in 1741. Associated with him were Ryan — famous for his tragic lovers and his
fine gentlemen of comedy — and Mademoiselle Chateauneuf, who

Covent Garden Theatres through the year 1845. Those of Covent Garden begin with the
year 1753, but for the period 1753–1779 the collection is very fragmentary. Thereafter the
sequence is unbroken. Drury Lane is represented by two small volumes of playbills for the
period 1754–1813, with a complete collection thereafter. It was no part of Genest's purpose to list all performances of *Comus*, though he mentions many. I have not had access
to playbills other than those in the British Museum and in general, therefore, could not
supplement Genest's notes on *Comus* performances for the earlier decades of its history.
For this period, then, the number of performances recorded in the table is generally that
given by Genest. But the playbills for the second half of the eighteenth century and the
first half of the nineteenth record scores of performances during many years which Genest
does not touch at all. These are completely accounted for in the summary, which briefly
reviews all the material in the following text. To avoid the multiplication of references,
I have, as a rule, given them in connection with the table; not with the discussion. The
material on the players is based on Fitzgerald's *New History of the Stage*, and on standard
theatrical biography in general, and no detailed references will be required. (See below,
p. 254, n. 3.)

1. Above, pp. 233 ff.
2. Cf. *A Collection of Remarkable Trials*, London, 1739.

later spread the fame of the *Comus* songs to Paris.[1] The production is said to have been staged "with a brilliancy never before known in Dublin," and was "allowed to be the best entertainment presented to the public for many years." [2] Its success led the managers to revive the piece within two years, with "new scenery and decorations" and a fairly strong cast, and it again proved successful.[3] Meanwhile it was repeated several times at Drury Lane in the same year (1743), and the year after found it started on its triumphant career on the boards of Covent Garden. On March third, Quin, Ryan, and Mrs. Clive played their old parts here, the rôle of the Lady this time enlisting the services of another distinguished actress — Mrs. Pritchard, the able successor of Nance Oldfield, and a favorite performer of such diverse parts as Rosalind, Lady Brute, and Lady Macbeth. The same cast repeated the masque at Covent Garden in 1747 for the benefit of one of their colleagues, and it was thereafter frequently given at actors' benefits: a trustworthy indication of its drawing power with the public. And in 1750, as we have seen, it was appropriately chosen for the benefit of Mrs. Foster, Milton's granddaughter, when Johnson and Garrick united their forces in her behalf at Drury Lane.

Another benefit performance of the piece is recorded at Drury in 1751, and the next year brought to that house another talented Irish actor, Mossop, for the part of Comus, and a new Lady, in the person of Mrs. Davies,[4] who is said to have been "excellence itself" in this part.[5] In 1755 *Comus* was revived at Covent Garden,

1. See above, p. 240, n. 1.
2. Fitzgerald, *Life of Mrs. Clive*, p. 29; Genest, X, 313.
3. Another Anglo-Irish actor named Webster is spoken of as particularly successful in *Comus*, in which he played the title rôle and "sang all the principal Bacchanal songs. . . . He also spoke the words well . . ." (O'Keeffe, I, 338.)
4. Wife of Tom Davies, the prompter, playwright, biographer of Garrick, and historian of the stage.
5. Genest, IV, 357, 406.

with "Gentleman Smith," an artist in "genteel comedy" parts, in the lead, while the great Peg Woffington, in spite of her fondness for "breeches parts," did the Lady. Mrs. Cibber, the year after, returned to that part at Drury Lane, together with Mossop, Ross, and Mrs. Clive, and they repeated their performance there in 1758. In that year also Sheridan the elder produced the masque at Dublin, but with somewhat indifferent success.[1]

More benefit performances at Drury came in 1759, while by 1760 Peg Woffington at the other house had given up her part to a newcomer. The new Lady was Mrs. Ward, the great stage beauty who had shortly before created the part of Lady Randolph in Home's tragedy of *Douglas*. That she was successful would seem to appear from the fact that *Comus* was acted eleven times that season. The next season at Covent Garden, however, brought forward an even more famous actress. October 8, 1762 was the date of the first appearance of the vivacious Anne Catley, a latter-day Nell Gwynn, whose beauty and "stage impudence" won her a huge success in the part of Euphrosyne and the Pastoral Nymph. The actress soon became the toast of the gentlemen of London; and the ladies of Dublin — whither she repaired in 1764, with *Comus* in tow — rushed to have their coiffures "Catleyfied," after the fashion, presumably, which the curious observer may still admire in the picture of Miss Catley as Euphrosyne which adorns contemporary editions of *Comus*.[2] Concerning this admirable performer we need merely add that she continued to do full justice to her favorite part at Covent Garden year after year, for some fifteen years altogether. Nor was she without strong support. Gentleman Smith played Comus, and in 1765 there came to join them, in the part of the Lady, the universally admired Mrs. Bellamy, whose wit and beauty, at least, did not require the public sym-

1. Genest, IV, 410.
2. See the *Life of Miss Anne Catley*, London, 1888.

pathy she asked for in her six apologetic volumes concerning her life.

Mrs. Bellamy played the Lady again in 1767, and soon thereafter new actors as well as new actresses came forward in our piece, in London as well as in the provinces. Henderson, of whom Garrick said that "he might be made to figure in any of the puppets of his time," [1] acted two great puppets — Hamlet and Comus — at Bath on December 27, 1774; and a few months later two performers of lesser rank, Cautherley and Mrs. Baddeley, played Comus and the Lady, respectively, for Cautherley's benefit at Drury Lane. Again, in 1776, Spranger Barry's benefit at Covent Garden Theatre enlisted the devoted service of his very gifted wife, a "grand actress" in her day, according to the authorities,[2] in the part of the Lady — a total of half a dozen performances at Covent Garden being scored for *Comus* that year.

Just about this time also, we hear of at least one private performance of the masque by players whose rank approximated that of the first actors at Ludlow Town. Samuel Whyte, the Irish schoolmaster, notes that on September 30, 1776, *Comus* was played at Marlay, the seat of the Right Honorable David Latouche. Whyte wrote the Prologue, and Henry Grattan, the great Irish orator, provided the Epilogue, which was spoken by the Countess of Lanesborough. Before returning to the professional performers, I shall quote some lines from this Epilogue, by way of indicating that the spirit of this production probably did not differ much from those we have hitherto dealt with:

> Hist! hist! I hear a dame of fashion say,
> "Lord, how absurd the Heroine of this play!
> A god of rank and fashion was so good
> To take a lady from a hideous wood,

---

1. Fitzgerald, *New History of the English Stage*, II, 275.
2. *Id.*, pp. 181–185.

And she, quite country, obstinate, and mulish,
Extremely fine — perhaps, but vastly foolish,
Would neither speak, nor laugh, nor dance, nor fling,
Nor condescend, nor wed — nor anything!"
But why choose *Comus?* Comus won't go down!
Milton, good creature, never knew the town. . . .
But, gentle ladies, you'll, I'm sure, approve
Your sex's triumph over guilty love.[1]

Other private performances were doubtless given in the eighteenth and nineteenth centuries, though I have not come upon further record of them until about 1910, when, as Professor G. C. Moore Smith kindly writes me, he "saw an interesting performance of *Comus* at Cambridge . . . with Rupert Brooke as Attendant Spirit."[2]

Notable professional players of earlier times deserve mention before we make an end. One of them, according to Thomas Holcroft,[3] was "the poet Cunningham," who "excelled in *Comus*" as played between 1775 and 1777 by a provincial company which also numbered Holcroft himself and Mrs. Inchbald among its members. In 1777, also, *Comus* came back to Drury Lane, and in the same year it had twenty-one performances at Covent Garden. From 1777 to 1785 Miss Catley, Henderson, and other popular performers[4] appeared in it there many times each season, and on May 15, 1786, the patrons of Drury Lane had the privilege of seeing the greatest tragic actress of the century in the characters of Ophelia and the Lady, which she chose upon the occasion of her own benefit. Mrs. Siddons returned to the character of the Lady a good

1. Samuel Whyte, *Poems* (Dublin, 1792), pp. 60–66.
2. "And one [Professor Moore Smith adds] of *Samson* at Manchester by Mr. W. Poel about the same date, in which the Chorus (absurdly) was one of women." (Various arrangements of *Comus* for school and amateur performance have been printed in recent times. See E. Ferguson's, 1900; Lucy Chater's, 1911; etc.)
3. *Memoirs*, I, 255.
4. Among them Gentleman Smith, Farren, Incledon, Mattocks, Bowden, Mrs. Martyr, and a mysterious "young Gentleman" who was made much of in the playbills of 1782.

many years later, for we may anticipate our record here to note that she acted the two leads in *Richard III* and *Comus* at Covent Garden in 1812, for the benefit of her brother, Charles Kemble, with whom Comus was a favorite part for many years. Meanwhile, scarcely a year went by during the last two decades of the eighteenth century without new triumphs for the piece at one house or the other — particularly at Covent Garden, where it had long since become a tradition and a standby. But Drury Lane did not neglect it. Thus, on the last day of the season of 1798, Palmer appeared there in the two parts of Comus and Father Philip (in Monk Lewis's *Castle Spectre*) — a curious combination of the sublime and the ridiculous, one might say, were it not for the fact that the eighteenth-century *Comus* did not suffer from an excess of sublimity! Again, in 1803, the masque was played there for the benefit of the tragedian Cooke, and in 1805, Elliston — "joyousest of once embodied spirits," according to Charles Lamb — added its title rôle to his repertory.

During the next forty years there were three breaks in this continuous performance. So far as I know, *Comus* did not appear on the boards during the years 1805 to 1812, 1821 to 1828, and 1834 to 1842. But during the other years it retained its popularity, and new players made their mark in the old parts. Bath saw it again at least once more in 1817, with Conway in the lead, and that actor, together with Incledon, Abbott, and Charles Kemble — aided and abetted by the splendid devices of their stage managers — kept it on the boards of Covent Garden year after year. Old Drury, now become New Drury, revived it in 1833, and Madame Vestris, the manager of Covent Garden in 1842, did it the honor of singing its most popular songs, — reënforced by Dryden and Purcell, — when she cleverly anticipated the plans of the other house that year.[1] Macready, as we have seen, spoke the last word for Drury Lane the year after.

1. See above, pp. 244–247.

The following summary [1] of *Comus's* stage career bears ample
testimony to the popularity of Milton in the theatre.

Date	Theatre	Number of Performances [2]
1738	Drury Lane	9 or more [3]
1739	Drury Lane	4 or more [4]
1740	Drury Lane	7 (N)
1741	Drury Lane	9 (N)
1741	Aungier St., Dublin	3 (G)
1742	Drury Lane	5 (N)
1743	Drury Lane	4 (G) and (N)
1743	Aungier St., Dublin	"Several" (G)
1744	Covent Garden	2 (G) and (N)
1745	Drury Lane	4 (G) and (N)
1745	Covent Garden	6 (G) and (N)
1746	Drury Lane	2 (N)
1747	Drury Lane	2 (G) and (N)
1747	Covent Garden	2 (G) and (N)
1748	Covent Garden	4 (G) and (N)
1749	Drury Lane	3 (G) and (N)
1750	Drury Lane	1 or more (G)
1751	Drury Lane	1 or more (G)
1752	Drury Lane	1 or more (G)
1755	Covent Garden	1 or more (G)
1756	Drury Lane	1 or more (G)
1758	Drury Lane	1 or more (G)
1758	Aungier St., Dublin	1 (G)
1759	Drury Lane	1 or more (G)
1760	Covent Garden	11 (G)
1761	Covent Garden	1 or more (G)
1762	Covent Garden	Many; number not given (G)
1764	Smock Alley, Dublin	Same (G)
1765	Covent Garden	3 or more [5]
1767	Covent Garden	2 or more [5]

1. Necessarily incomplete, since by no means all the records are available.

2. See above, pp. 247–248, n. 4.

3. Allardyce Nicoll (*Early Eighteenth Century Drama*, p. 317) lists nine performances.
Genest (III, 533) says "acted about 11 times." Items marked (G) in my list are drawn
from Genest, and may be found by turning to the respective years in his text. As a rule he
does not give the number of performances. Nicoll's list runs through 1749. Items drawn
from him are marked (N). Items not otherwise marked are from the British Museum playbills.

4. Nicoll lists four performances; Genest (III, 604) says the piece was acted "8 times
successively."

5. From *Covent Garden Newspaper Clippings*, British Museum.

Date	Theatre	Number of Performances
1772		13 (Stevens) [1]
1773	Covent Garden	1 or more (G)
1774	Bath	1 or more (G)
1775	Drury Lane	1 or more (G)
1776	Covent Garden	6
1776	Private performance, Marlay (Ireland)	1 [2]
1777	Drury Lane	1 or more (G)
1777	Covent Garden	21
1778	Covent Garden	3
1779	Covent Garden	3
1780	Covent Garden	10
1781	Covent Garden	1
1782	Covent Garden	3
1783	Covent Garden	2
1784	Covent Garden	4
1785	Covent Garden	6
1786	Drury Lane	1 or more (G)
1787	Covent Garden	2
1788	Covent Garden	3
1790	Drury Lane	1 or more [3]
1791	Covent Garden	2
1792	Covent Garden	2
1793	Covent Garden	1
1795	Covent Garden	1
1796	Covent Garden	1
1797	Covent Garden	1
1798	Drury Lane	1 or more (G)
1799	Covent Garden	2
1800	Covent Garden	1
1803	Drury Lane	1 or more (G)
1803	Covent Garden	1
1805	Drury Lane	1 or more (G)
1812	Covent Garden	1
1815	Covent Garden	15
1816	Covent Garden	2
1817	Covent Garden	2

1. *Milton Papers*, p. 31. 2. See above, p. 251.

3. Frederick Reynolds, in telling of his opera, *The Crusade*, which was played at Covent Garden in 1790, says it owed much to the "irresistible humor" of Quick and Edwin, burlesquing "O! thou wert born to please me," then "being sung at Drury Lane . . . with the greatest effect, in Milton's *Mask of Comus*." (*Life and Times of Frederick Reynolds*, II, 59 and n.)

Date	Theatre	Number of Performances
1817	Bath	1 or more (G)
1819	Covent Garden	2
1821	Covent Garden	(see note) [1]
1828	Covent Garden	(see note) [1]
1829	Covent Garden	2
1833	Covent Garden	7
1833	Drury Lane	2
1834	Covent Garden	4
1842	Covent Garden	18
1843	Drury Lane	11
ca. 1910	Cambridge [2]	1

1. The "Sweet Echo" song only, was sung here April 14, 1821, and May 30, 1828.
2. See above, p. 252.

EPILOGUE

ON SHAKSPERE'S EPILOGUES [1]

IN a letter addressed to me under date of February 26, 1927,[2] Sir Arthur Quiller-Couch has kindly set forth his explanation of Silvia's silence at the end of *The Two Gentlemen of Verona*, and of similar silences in other plays. He writes as follows:

> My own very prosaic explanation of many strange silences on the part of Shakespeare's heroines towards the conclusion of a play is simply that the boy actor was no longer on the stage. He had slipped away to the Green Room to change his clothes and prepare to speak an epilogue.

On the face of it this conjecture is decidedly attractive, not only because it comes from a gifted and genial critic but also because it is intrinsically simple, straightforward, and to the point. It takes account of stage necessities, a procedure which is always wholesome when it comes to checking up abstract speculations upon the subject of dramatic technique. It is, moreover, distinctly in line with the conjecture independently offered by other scholars who explain the disappearance of Lear's fool on the ground that the boy actor who played the part may have been needed to double in the part of Cordelia.[3]

Nevertheless, I doubt whether the conjecture squares with such evidence as we have of Shakspere's use of the epilogue, or whether it makes adequate allowance for his general ability to say or do what he wants to with the means at his command. The reasons underlying my doubts I may summarize as follows:

1. Compare Chapter I, p. 17, n. 2.
2. Some time after I had completed this study.
3. See above, p. 38, n. 4.

1. Only eleven of the plays as they have come down to us are provided with epilogues, or with closing songs which probably served as such. These plays are the second part of *Henry IV*, *Henry V*, *Henry VIII*, *Love's Labour's Lost*, *A Midsummer-Night's Dream*, *Twelfth Night*, *All's Well*, *Troilus and Cressida*, *The Tempest*, *Pericles*, and, most important of all, *As You Like It*. It will be noticed at once that the plays which offer the gravest difficulties — that is to say, those which end with the most notable silences by the ladies chiefly concerned: *The Two Gentlemen*, *Measure for Measure*, and *The Winter's Tale* — have no epilogues. It is possible, of course, that some epilogues have been lost. If so, it would manifestly be hazardous to draw any inferences as to Shakspere's practice, from them — from the unknown. And it is well to remember Rosalind's remarks as to the need of an epilogue. She has one to speak, and therefore puts in a good word for those who write and speak epilogues: "Good plays prove the better by the help of good epilogues." But she is aware of the fact that there are two sides to the question: "If it be true that good wine needs no bush, 't is true that a good play needs no epilogue." [1] At any rate, — to return to

1. Compare also *A Midsummer-Night's Dream*, V, i, 362 ff.: "No epilogue, I pray you; for your play needs no excuse. Never excuse; for when the players are all dead, there need none to be blamed . . . Come . . . let your epilogue alone." It may be urged that this is meant only for the contributors to the very tragical mirth of young Pyramus and Thisbe. The fact seems to be, however, that Shakspere had small fondness for the awkward prologues and heavy epilogues — the naïve "without-book" prologues "vilely penned" "in eight and six," "faintly spoke after the prompter"; the "begging" or "insinuating" or merely stupidly apologetic epilogues intended to curry favor with the groundlings — which passed current on the Elizabethan stage, especially in the earlier days. (For allusions to the subject see *Love's Labour's Lost*, V, ii, 305; *A Midsummer-Night's Dream*, III, i, 25, 35, — V, i, 119–123; *Romeo and Juliet*, I, iv, 7; *As You Like It*, Epilogue, 8–10; *II Henry IV*, Epilogue 8–11, etc.) Most of the Elizabethans did not seem to have the knack of writing *happy* prologues to the swelling act. Shakspere — if one may venture a guess on the basis of Hamlet's remark, "Ere I could make a prologue to my brains, they had begun the play" — may have been temperamentally disinclined to prologuizing; just as he was doubtless as impatient with extempore clowning, jigging, and similar sops to the groundlings at the end as in the middle of the play. The custom of sprightly epiloguizing, at all events, did not really come into its own until Restoration times.

the three plays just mentioned,— there is no evidence to show that Silvia, Hermione, and Isabella were required off-stage to prepare to speak an epilogue. Some other explanation of their "curious silences" toward the end would therefore seem to be in order. Helena too, in *All's Well*, remains silent toward the end. In this case, it may be observed, we have an epilogue, but this, like the one to *The Tempest*, is spoken by the King.

2. In the case of the plays that have an epilogue it seems, in every instance but one, to have been spoken by someone other than the boy actor who played the heroine. The exception is *As You Like It*, and here Rosalind expressly tells us that "It is not the fashion to see the lady the epilogue."

3. Rosalind's epilogue to *As You Like It* is instructive for other reasons. In this case the lady does speak the epilogue — the boy actor may have had to slip away to prepare for his final appearance. Yet it is very evident that in this emergency Shakspere found no difficulty in filling in the interval with appropriate business, without doing violence to consistency of characterization (Rosalind, surely, can be accused of no curious silence toward the end of the play) or to any other aspect of his essential dramatic purpose.

If these considerations are valid, it would seem to follow that better reasons or evidence than any yet adduced must be forthcoming to establish conjectures which explain disappearances or silences of important characters on the ground that Shakspere could not — or would not bother to — harmonize his stage requirements with his dramatic purpose. Meanwhile such conjectures remain hazardous.

APPENDIX

Appendix

ILLUSTRATIONS OF SHAKSPERE'S "VULGAR ERRORS" [1]

I. Witches

(1) Browne's testimony in the Duny-Cullender witchcraft trial of 1664:
   "The Fits were natural but heighten'd by the Devil co-operating with
   the Malice of the Witches, at whose Instance he did the Villanies." [2]

(2) "I have ever believed and do now know that there are witches. They that
   doubt of these, do not only deny them, but spirits, and are . . . a sort . . .
   of . . . atheists." [3]

(3) With *Macbeth*, I, i, 9 ("I come, Graymalkin") compare Browne's remark
   concerning the witches' familiars — "the dogs and cats that usually
   speak unto witches." [4]

(4) The devil "endeavours to propagate the unbelief [i. e., denial] of witches." [5]

(5) The devil, "expelled from oracles," acts "his deceits in witches, magi-
   cians, diviners." [6]

(6) The devil "often appeared" in the shape of "rough and hairy goats . . .
   if there be any truth in the confession of witches." [7]

II. The Devil [8]

(1) "The heart of man is the place the devils dwell in." [9]

(2) "I hold that the devil does really possess some men." . . . [10]

---

1. See above, p. 100.
2. F. Hutchinson, *Historical Essay concerning Witchcraft* (1718), pp. 118–120; cf. W
("Supplementary Memoir"), I, lv.
3. *R. M.*, I, xxx—W, II, 366. (Cf. Addison, *Spectator*, No. 110.)
4. *V. E.*, III, i—W, I, 230. Cf. Reginald Scot, *Discoverie of Witchcraft.*
5. *V. E.*, I, x—W, I, 84.
6. *V. E.*, VII, xii—W, II, 245.
7. *V. E.*, V, xxiii—W, II, 90.
8. For general reference, see *V. E.*, I, x and xi—W, I, 75–93; cf. above, p. 100, and
on this page under "Witches," items (1), (4), (5), and (6).
9. *R. M.*, I, li—W, II, 402.
10. *R. M.*, I, xxx—W, II, 367.

(3) "He also made man believe that he can raise the dead," and "hath the key of life and death." [1]

(4) He "doth sometime delude us in the conceits of stars and meteors." [2]

(5) He has insinuated "into men's minds there is no devil at all . . . And to this effect . . . maketh men believe that apparitions and such as confirm his existence are either deceptions of sight or melancholy depravements of fancy." [3]

(6) He has "inveigled no small part of the world into a credulity of artificial magic . . . whence . . . they stand in awe of charms, spells, and conjurations . . . the delusion of dreams and the discovery of things to come in sleep." [4]

(7) With Banquo's query (*Macbeth*, I, iii, 108) — "What, can the devil speak true?" — compare Browne's remark: "Truth . . . hath place within the walls of hell, and the devils themselves are daily forced to practice it . . . They do not only speak and practice truth but . . . in some sense do really desire its enlargement." [5]

(8) With Macbeth's belated recognition of "the equivocation of the fiend" ("these juggling fiends . . . That palter with us in a double sense," — V, v, 43–viii, 19–20) compare Browne's statement that the devil "betrays" his "indivinity" in "juggling" oracles, "whereof having once begot in our minds an assured dependence, he makes us rely on powers which he but precariously obeys." [6] "His favours are deceitful and double-headed; he doth apparent good, for real and convincing evil after it." [7]

---

1. *V. E.*, I, x—W, I, 80. Cf. *Macbeth*, IV, ii, 123: "The blood-bolter'd Banquo smile upon me."

2. *V. E.*, I, xi—W, I, 86.

3. *V. E.*, I, x—W, I, 83–84. Cf. *Macbeth*, III, iv, 62–63 ("This is the air-drawn dagger which, you said, Led you to Duncan"), and III, ii, 8–9 ("Why do you keep alone, Of sorriest fancies your companions making?").

4. *V. E.*, I, x—W, I, 82, 80. Cf. *Macbeth*, IV, i, 50–124: "I conjure you, by that which you profess . . ." and II, i, 20: "I dreamt last night of the three weird sisters."

5. *V. E.*, I, xi—W, I, 92.

6. *V. E.*, I, x—W, I, 81, 83. (See next note.)

7. *V. E.*, VII, xii—W, II, 246; cf. *Macbeth*, I, iii, 123–126:

> Oftentimes, to win us to our harm,
> The instruments of darkness tell us truths,
> Win us with honest trifles, to betray 's
> In deepest consequence.

III. Ghosts

(1) See above, pp. 99–100.

(2) Browne laments "the error of Christians, who holding the dead do rest in the Lord, do yet believe they are the lure of the devil; that he who is in bonds himself commandeth the fetters of the dead . . . or that there is any thing but delusion in the practice of necromancy and popular raising of ghosts." [1]

IV. "Unnatural Natural History"

(1) It cannot be
But I am pigeon-liver'd and lack gall
To make oppression bitter (*Hamlet*, II, ii, 604–605).

"That a Pigeon hath no gall" [2] (*V. E.*, III, iii—W, I, 235 ff.).

(2) *King.* How fares our cousin Hamlet?
Haml. Excellent, i' faith, — of the chameleon's dish; I eat the air, promise-cramm'd (*Hamlet*, III, ii, 97–99).

"That the Chameleon lives only upon air" (*V. E.*, III, xxi—W, I, 321 ff.).

(3) The elephant hath joints, but none for courtesy. His legs are for necessity, not for flexure (*Troilus and Cressida*, II, iii, 113–115).

"That an Elephant hath no joints" (*V. E.*, III, i—W, I, 219 ff.; cf. 225, n. 4).

(4) The toad, ugly and venomous, Wears yet a precious jewel in his head (*As You Like It*, II, i, 13–14).
Some say the lark and loathed toad change eyes (*Romeo and Juliet*, III, v, 31).

"Of Frogs, Toads, and Toadstone." . . . Concerning the . . . stone in the toad's head (*V. E.*, III, xiii—W, I, 284–287, nn., with which compare also *Macbeth*, IV, i, 6–8).

(5) I am no viper, yet I feed On mother's flesh which did me breed (*Pericles*, I, i, 64–65).

"That young Vipers force their way through the bowels of their Dam" (*V. E.*, III, xvi—W, I, 297 ff.).

(6) A clip-wing'd griffin (*I Henry IV*, III, i, 152).

"Of Griffins" (*V. E.*, III, xi—W, I, 273 ff.).

---

1. *V. E.*, I, x—W, I, 80.

2. Here and in most of the references that follow, I quote only the headings of the chapters in which Browne discusses the "vulgar errors" utilized, as indicated, by Shakspere.

(7) The bird of wonder ... the maiden phoenix (*Henry VIII*, V, v, 41).

"Of the Phoenix" (*V. E.*, III, xii—W, I, 296 ff.).

(8) The kind, life-rend'ring pelican (*Hamlet*, IV, v, 146).
Those pelican daughters (*Lear*, III, iv, 77, *etc.*).

"Of the pelican" . . . feeding her young ones with the blood distilled from her (*V. E.*, V, i—W, II, 1).

(9) Turn their halcyon beaks With every gale (*Lear*, II, ii, 84–85).

"That a Kingfisher, hanged by the bill, showeth where the wind lay" (*V. E.*, III, x—W, I, 270 ff.).

(10) I will play the swan And die in music (*Othello*, V, ii, 247–248).

"Of the musical note of Swans before their death" (*V. E.*, III, xxvii—W, I, 357 ff.).

(11) The raven himself is hoarse
That croaks the fatal entrance of Duncan . . .
It was the owl that shriek'd, the fatal bellman (*Macbeth*, I, vi, 39–40; II, ii, 3).

That owls and ravens are ominous appearers . . . presignifying unlucky events (*V. E.*, V, xxiii—W, II, 79–80).

(12) Would they were basilisks to strike thee dead (*Richard III*, I, ii, 151).
The death-darting eye of cockatrice (*Romeo and Juliet*, III, ii, 47, *etc.*).

"Of the Basilisk" . . . commonly called the cockatrice. . . Men still affirm it killeth at a distance (*V. E.*, III, vii—W, I, 250, 254).

(13) I have maintain'd that salamander of yours with fire any time this two and thirty years (*I Henry IV*, III, iii, 52–54).

"That a salamander lives in the fire" (*V. E.*, III, xvi—W, I, 291 ff.).

(14) For night-tapers crop their waxen thighs,
And light them at the fiery glow-worm's eyes (*A Midsummer-Night's Dream*, III, i, 172–173).

Wondrous things are promised from the glow-worm ... It were a notable piece of art to translate the light from the Bononian stone into another body ... (*V. E.*, III, xxvii—W, I, 368, 370).

(15) Tread softly, that the blind mole may not
Hear a foot fall (*Tempest*, IV, i, 194–195).

"That Moles are blind" (*V. E.*, III, xviii—W, I, 312 ff.).

(16) Shrieks like mandrakes' torn out of the earth (*Romeo and Juliet*, IV, iii, 47).

Thou whoreson mandrake, thou art fitter to be worn in my cup than to wait at my heels (*II Henry IV*, I, ii, 16–18).

When 'a was naked, he was, for all the world, like a forked radish (*Id.*, III, ii, 333–334).

"Of Mandrakes"[1] . . . Many false conceptions there are . . . — [One] affirmeth the roots of mandrakes do make a noise or give a shriek, upon eradication. [Another] conceiveth the root thereof resembleth the shape of a man [because of] the bifurcation . . . into two parts, which some are content to call thighs . . . As fair a resemblance is often found in carrots, parsnips . . . and many others (*V. E.*, II, vi—W, I, 192, 197 and n., 192–193).

(17) Telling me the sovereignst thing on earth
Was parmaceti, for an inward bruise (*I Henry IV*, I, iii, 57–58).

"Of the Spermaceti Whale." Country people . . . made use [of spermaceti oil] for cuts, aches, and hard tumours. It may prove of good medical use. (*V. E.*, III, xxvi — W, I, 353, 355–356).

(18) [*Othello's handkerchief*]
Dy'd in mummy which the skillful
Conserv'd of maidens' hearts (*Othello*, III, iv, 74–75).

Witches mummy, maw, and gulf . . .
For the ingredients of our cauldron (*Macbeth*, IV, i, 23–34).

Mummy is become merchandise,[2] Mizraim cures wounds, and Pharaoh is sold for balsams (*U. B.*, Ch. 5—W, III, 46).

(19) *Macduff.* What's the disease he means?
Malcolm. 'T is called the evil: A most miraculous work in this good king (*Macbeth*, IV, iii, 146–147).

[Concerning the King's Evil, see "Supplementary Memoir," W, I, lxii, and note.]

(20) Such things become the hatch and brood of time (*II Henry IV*, III, i, 86).

[On "the doctrine of eggs" (*omnia ex ovo*), see *V. E.*, III, xxviii,—W, I, 373–374.]

---

1. Cf. Donne's "Go and Catch a Falling Star," and see above, p. 110.

2. "Alluding to its use as a drug, which appeared in the London Pharmacopoeia as late as 1721" (*Hydriotaphia*, ed. Greenhill, p. 173, n.).

(21) Haply for I am black [1] . . .
(*Othello*, III, iii, 263).

[On "the blackness of the Moors" see *V. E.*, VI, xi—W, II, 196, and "A Digression concerning Blackness" (*Id.*, VI, xii—W, II, 202:)] From these . . . atramentous . . . conditions the Moors might possibly become Negroes.

(22) *Don Pedro.* You were born in a merry hour . . .
Beatrice. . . . There was a star danc'd, and under that was I born. (*Much Ado*, II, i, 347–350.)

"Of many popular . . . Opinions": [2] We shall not, I hope, disparage the resurrection of our Redeemer, if we say the sun doth not dance on Easter-day (*V. E.*, V, xxiii—W, II, 79, 87).

---

1. "What appears to me nearly certain is that [Shakspere] imagined Othello as a black man, and not as a light brown one" — Bradley, *Shakespearean Tragedy*, pp. 198 ff.

2. See also *Hamlet*, I, i, 158–164:

Some say that ever 'gainst that season comes
Wherein our Saviour's birth is celebrated,
The bird of dawning singeth all night long . . .

INDEX

INDEX

Abbott, W., actor, 253.

Adams, J. Q., 70, 131 n. 4, 136 n. 3.

Addison, 263 n. 3.

Æschylus, 164 n. 2.

Albumazor, 200–201 n.

Alcestis, 68.

Alexander's Feast, 217 n. 2, 226 n. 3.

Alhazen, biographer of Timur, 112 n. 1.

Allen, E. A., 33 n. 4.

All's Well that Ends Well, 12, 54 n. 6, 56–59, 67, 121, 193 f., 258 f.; Helena and Bertram, 17, 57 ff., 65, 77, 83 ff., 259; Maudlin, 32, 56 ff., 85.

Antony and Cleopatra, 21, 49 f., 130, 134, 166 ff., 182 n. 4, 208; Enobarbus, 27; Octavius, 23, 168.

Arcadia, The, 75.

Aristophanes, 103.

Aristotle, 102.

Arne, Thomas A., his music for *Comus*, 210, 242 n. 2, 244 n. 2, 246 f.

As You Like It, 52 n. 2, 64 f., 80 ff., 91 n. 2, 104 n. 4, 105, 118 n. 3, 121, 123, 126, 188, 190 f., 208, 265; Adam, 37; Celia and Oliver, 51, 65, 80, 93; Rosalind and Orlando, 4, 21, 33 n. 2, 37 f., 51, 52 n. 2, 53, 81, 249; her Epilogue, 258 f.; Touchstone and Jacques, 33 n. 2, 38, 49 f., 81, 105; the dukes, 21 n. 1, 53, 77, 81, 88.

Atterbury, Francis, proposes "polishing" of *Samson Agonistes*, 215 f.

Augustus, the Emperor (Octavius Caesar), 109.

Audience, the, *see under* Elizabethan.

Aungier Street Theatre, Dublin, 248.

Autobiography and Correspondence of Mrs. Delany, 217 n. 5, 220 n. 1, 224 f.

Autocrat of the Breakfast-Table, The, 110 n. 1.

Back to Methuselah, 5 n. 2, 82.

Bacon, Sir N., 97 n. 1.

Baker, G. P., 72 ff., 79 n. 2.

Barry, Spranger, actor, 251.

Barrymore, Ethel, 36 n. 2.

Beaumont, 91, 112 n. 1, 192 n. 1.

Beeching, H. C., 215 n. 4.

Beggar's Opera, The, 220.

Bellamy, Mrs. G. A., 210, 250 f.

Betterton, Thomas, 216.

Biographica Dramatica, 234, 240.

Blackstone, Sir William, on Shakspere and Milton, 172 n. 1.

B. L. T., *see under* Taylor, B. L.

Boccaccio, 101.

Bolingbroke, Henry St. John, 216.

Bolingbroke, Shakspere's, *see under Henry IV and Richard II*.

Bonduca, 180 n. 3.

Boswell, J. (the younger), 75 n. 1, 222 n. 3.

Bowle, John, 142 n. 1, 174, 182.

Bowles, W. L., 215 n. 4.

Bradley, A. C., 7 n. 2, 8, 9 n. 2, 12 n. 3, 26 n. 1, 31 n. 1, 37, 39–47, 52, 60, 62 n. 1, 63 n. 1, 79, 100 n. 2, 156, 267 n. 2.

Brandl, A., 38 n. 4.

Brewer, W., 139 n. 1, 181 n. 1, 191 n. 1.

Brooke, C. F. Tucker, 112 n. 1.

Brooke, Rupert, in *Comus*, 252.

Browne, E., 107.

Browne, R. C., 142 n. 1, 179, 193, 200, 201 n. 1, 202 n. 1.

Browne, Sir Thomas, 96–138; scientific and literary explorer, 97 f.; his general literary relationships, 101 ff.; supposed scorn of the English poets, 102 f., 108–110; defence of the moderns, 108; fondness for the theatre, 103 ff.; his verses, 109; allusions to Elizabethan poets, 111 ff.; his memory, 107; verbal recollections of Shakspere, 115–121, 137 f.; likenesses in ideas and moods, 122–136; reservations, 114 ff., 122 ff.; analytical summary of the evidence, 136–138; illustrations of Shakspere's "Vulgar Errors," 99 ff., 263 ff.; on witches, 263; the devil, 100, 119, 263 f.; unnatural natural history, 265–268.

Works cited: *Antiquities of Norwich*, 136 n. 5; *Christian Morals*, 101 n. 1,

INDEX

Cassius and Brutus, 23, 54, 148; Portia, 21 n. 3.

Juvenal, 113.

Kaye-Smith, Sheila, 84 n. 3.
Keightley, T., 179, 181.
Kellett, E. E., 4 n. 1.
Kemble, Charles, 210, 253.
King Arthur, 223 n., 245–247.
King John, 15, 116, 118 n. 5, 131, 162–163 n. 3, 173, 184 n. 2, 220.
King Lear, 10, 54 n. 6, 66 f., 85 ff., 119, 123 n. 4, 124, 131, 134, 147 n. 2, 149 n. 1, 158 ff., 206, 208, 266; Lear and Cordelia, 4, 12, 21, 23, 25 f., 34, 37 f., 46, 52, 55, 66, 93; Edgar, 47, 60 f.; Edmund, 60 f.; his silence, 47, 55; Gloucester, 47, 52, 60 ff., 85; the Fool's disappearance, 6, 37 f., 257.
King Leir, 67.
King's Men, the (Killigrew's company), 222.
Kittredge, G. L., 31 n. 1, 44 n.
Knight, C., 196 n. 1.
Knollis, R., 112 n. 1.
Kuhl, E. P., 69 n. 4.

Lactantius, 211 n. 4.
Laertius, 109.
Lamb, Charles, 220, 253.
Landor, Walter Savage, on *Othello* and *Paradise Lost*, 156.
Lanesborough, Countess of, 251.
Lang, Andrew, 86.
Lanier, Sidney, on Shakspere's speech, 3; on Shakspere's silences, 5.
Latouche, David, 251.
Lawes, Henry, his music for *Comus*, 210, 247.
Lawrence, W. J., 32 n. 1, 38 n. 4.
Lawrence, W. W., 67, 70, 74 n. 1, 85 f., 91 n. 3, 92 n. 2.
Lee, Sir S., 100 n. 3.
Legend of Matilda, The, 195 n. 3.
"Letter to Thomas Browne," 116 n. 1.
Life of G. A. Bellamy, The, 247 n. 1.
Lincoln's Inn Fields Theatre, 227 n. 5.
Llanover, Lady, 217 n. 5.
Lewis, Monk, 253.
Lodge, Thomas, 33 n. 2, 37.

Lounsbury, T., 65, 68, 73, 75 n. 1.
Love's Labour's Lost, 64, 68, 71 ff., 125, 166 n. 3, 182 f., 258 n.
Love Restored, 186 n. 2.
Lowe, R. W., 247 n. 1.
Lowell, James Russell, on Ophelia, 23 n.; on Sir Thomas Browne and the "incommunicable" quality of the poetic imagination, 98 f., 122.
Lucrece, The Rape of, echoed by Milton(?), 146 n., 184–185 n. 3, 203.
Lyly, John, 75, 175 n., 196 n. 2.

Macaulay, G. C., 65.
Macbeth, 10, 39, 41–46, 49, 66; Sir Thomas Browne's, 101, 106, 114, 118 n. 3, 120 f., 129, 132 n. 2, 136 n. 4, 138, 263–267; Milton's, 114, 140, 145 n. 5, 150 n. 2, 153 n. 1, 155 n. 1, 156 n. 1, 158, 159 n. 1, 161–166, 180 n. 2, 206, 208; Banquo, 33, 54, 264; his children, 45 f.; his guilt, 41–44, 48 n.; Macbeth and Lady Macbeth, 12, 21, 23–26, 31, 33 f., 42 ff., 54, 66, 164 ff., 208, 249; their children, 44–46, 52 n. 2; Malcolm's, 46, 56 n. 3; Duncan, 12 n. 2, 33, 41 ff., 52 n. 2, 54; his "ghost," 33 n. 3, 161.
Machiavelli, 101.
Macready, W. C., 247, 253.
Macrobius, 109.
Maid's Tragedy, The, 112 n. 1.
Malizpini (Malespini, R.?), 101 n. 2.
Malone, E., 75, 169, 184–185 n. 3, 198, 222 n. 3.
Mantuan, 113.
Marlowe, 76, 79, 111 f., 173 n. 1, 193 n.
Mara, Mme., actress, 244 n. 2.
Marcella, 247 n. 1.
Martyr, Mrs., actress, 244 n. 2, 252 n. 4.
Massinger, 145 n. 4.
Masson, D., 142 n. 1, 153, 166, 170 n. 2, 179 f., 182 n. 5, 185 f., 190 n. 3, 195, 197 n. 1, 199, 203 n. 1, 204 n. 1, 205 n. 3, 211, 214 f., 217, 222 n. 4, 243.
Matthews, Brander, 20 f., 65, 73, 81 n. 3, 82 n. 2, 83, 85 n. 2, 86 f.
Mattocks, W., actor, 252 n. 4.
Measure for Measure, 65, 83 ff., 91 n. 2, 153 n. 3, 189 n. 1, 206, 258; Isabella and the Duke, 6 ff., 16, 18–21, 24, 77, 84,